Skills and Techniques for Human Service Professionals

COUNSELING ENVIRONMENT, HELPING SKILLS, TREATMENT ISSUES

Second Edition

Edward Neukrug

Old Dominion University

SAN DIEGO

Bassim Hamadeh, CEO and Publisher
Amy Smith, Senior Project Editor
Casey Hands, Production Editor
Jess Estrella, Senior Graphic Designer
Stephanie Kohl, Licensing Coordinator
Kristina Neukrug, Copy Editor
Natalie Piccotti, Director of Marketing
Kassie Graves, Vice President of Editorial
Jamie Giganti, Director of Academic Publishing

Excerpts from National Organization for Human Services (NOHS), Ethical Standards for Human Service Professionals. Copyright © 2015 by National Organization for Human Services. Reprinted with permission.

Cover image copyright © 2019 iStockphoto LP/Macrowildlife.

Printed in the United States of America.

3970 Sorrento Valley Blvd., Ste. 500, San Diego, CA 92121

Dedicated To All The Hard Working Human Service Professionals
(and my wife)

ABOUT THE AUTHOR

 Raised in New York City, Dr. Ed Neukrug obtained his B.A. in psychology from SUNY Binghamton in 1973, his M.S. in counseling from Miami University of Ohio in 1974, and his doctorate in counselor education from the University of Cincinnati in 1980. After teaching and directing a graduate program in counseling at Notre Dame College in New Hampshire, he accepted a position at Old Dominion University, in Norfolk, Virginia where he is currently a Professor of Counseling and former Chair of the Department of Educational Leadership and Counseling.

In addition to teaching, Dr. Neukrug has worked as a counselor at a crisis center, a substance abuse counselor, an outpatient therapist at a mental health center, an associate school psychologist, a school counselor, and as a private practice psychologist and licensed professional counselor. Dr. Neukrug has held a variety of positions in local, regional, and national professional associations in counseling and human services. He is currently co-editor of the *Journal of Human Services*.

Dr. Neukrug has written dozens of articles and book chapters and has written or edited ten books. In addition to Skills and Techniques for Human Service Professionals, his books include: Theory, Practice and Trends in Human Services: An Introduction to An Emerging Profession (6th ed.); The World of the Counselor (5th ed.); Experiencing the World of the Counselor: A Workbook for Counselor Educators and Students (4th ed.); Counseling Theory and Practice (2nd ed.); Essentials of Testing and Assessment for Counselors, Social Workers, and Psychologists (3rd ed.); A Brief Orientation to Counseling: Professional Identity, History, and Standards (2nd ed.); Skills and Tools for Today's Counselors and Psychotherapists; and The Dictionary of Counseling and Human Services. He is editor of the two volume Sage Encyclopedia of Theory in Counseling and Psychotherapy.

In addition to his books, Dr. Neukrug has been developing an interactive and animated website entitled Great Therapists of the Twentieth Century. If you get a chance, visit the site which can be found on his web page at www.odu.edu/~eneukrug.

Dr. Neukrug is married to Kristina, a former school counselor who is currently developing counseling-related workbooks and activities for mental health professionals. They have two children, Hannah and Emma. If you are interested in their books and counseling-related activities, visit www.counselingbooksetc.com.

BRIEF CONTENTS

CONTENTS

SECTION II: HELPING SKILLS   33

SECTION III: TREATMENT ISSUES   129

Chapter 8: Case Management   131

PREFACE

Welcome to the second edition of *Skills and Techniques for Human Service Professionals*. Although the basic structure of the text has remained the same, there have been substantial changes in this edition. Similarities between this and the first edition include the book being partitioned into three sections (Section I: The Counseling Environment, Section II: Helping Skills, and Section III: Treatment Issues) with the chapters' foci being fairly similar to the first edition. Thus, if you have used the first edition, this second edition will feel familiar. As in all revisions, of course, references have been updated and new cutting-edge issues have been added. Some chapters have had significant changes, while others have been largely left alone. Also, a large variety of experiential and reflective exercises has been added throughout the text. The following provides an overview of the sections and chapters and some of the changes made within them.

SECTION I: THE COUNSELING ENVIRONMENT

Section I describes characteristics of the effective helper and aspects of an agency's environment that may enable, or disable, the helping relationship.

Chapter 1: Characteristics of the Effective Helper briefly highlights a number of attitudes that human service professionals should avoid then, examines eight characteristics deemed important in building a safe and comfortable atmosphere and helping relationship. They include showing empathy, being genuine, exuding acceptance, being cognitively complex, embracing wellness, being competent, having cultural sensitivity, and developing your "it factor."

Chapter 2: Entering the Agency examines appropriate ways that agencies should respond to initial contacts of clients, whether it is by phone, email, or when a client walks into an agency. This chapter particularly highlights the atmosphere created by the support staff and by the surroundings, whether the helper has embraced the personal characteristics of the helper highlighted in Chapter 1, the comfort level of the helper's office, and the appropriateness of a number of helper nonverbal behaviors, such as attire, eye contact, body positioning and facial expressions, personal space, touch, and voice intonation.

Changes to this Edition: In Chapter 1, some of the characteristics of the effective helper from the last edition have been removed while others have been added. Chapter 2 offers an expanded focus on how to respond by email, phone, or in person to new clients and updates information related to nonverbal behaviors of the helper.

SECTION II: HELPING SKILLS

Section II provides an overview of the various skills and techniques often used by helpers and presents them in logical order, from those most likely to be used at the beginning of a relationship to the more advanced skills and specialized training tools used somewhat later.

Chapter 3: Foundational Skills are those skills, perhaps we should say attitudes, that all helpers should provide early on in the relationship and are the prelude to the more focused helping skills. They include honoring and respecting the client, being curious, delimiting power and developing an equal relationship, non-pathologizing, and demonstrating the 3 C's: commitment, caring, and courteousness.

Chapter 4: Essential Skills are core skills that should be used in any helping relationship and often initiate movement toward goal identification and even goal achievement. They include silence and pause time, listening skills, reflecting feelings and content, paraphrasing, and basic empathy.

Chapter 5: Commonly Used Skills help the client move toward solving problems. Although all of them will not be used in every helping relationship, they are skills we often find exhibited by helpers, and include affirmation giving, encouragement, and support; offering alternatives, information giving, and advice giving; modeling; self-disclosure; collaboration; and advocacy.

Chapter 6: Information Gathering and Solution-Focused Questions distinguishes between these two important types of questions which may be used in the helping relationship. The information gathering skills include open questions, closed questions, tentative questions, and "why" questions, while the solution-focused questions include preferred goals questions, evaluative questions, coping questions, exception-seeking questions, and solution-oriented questions.

Chapter 7: Advanced Skills and Specialized Training are skills and specialized trainings that are selectively used based on the needs of the clients. They include the advanced skills of advanced empathy; confrontation: challenge with support; interpretation; cognitive-behavioral responses; and specialized training in the areas of assessment for lethality: suicidality and homicidality; crisis, disaster, and trauma helping; token economies; positive helping; and coaching.

Change to this Editions: Many of the helping skills discussed in the first edition of the text have been kept in this edition; however, their order of presentation has been somewhat altered. Moreover, new skills have been added in this edition. Also, the chapter titles have been changed to better match the skills found within them. Pay particular attention to the new solution-focused questions in Chapter 6 and many of the newly added advanced skills and specialized training techniques in Chapter 7.

SECTION III: TREATMENT ISSUES

This section of the text examines a number of important treatment issues including case management, cross-cultural counseling concerns, and understanding ethical codes and the ethical decision-making process.

Chapter 8: Case Management examines those skills necessary for the maintenance of the optimal functioning of clients. Thus, we review the process of providing informed consent and professional disclosure statements; conducting assessment for treatment planning; developing, evaluating, and monitoring progress toward client goals; monitoring the use of psychotropic medications; writing process notes, case notes and reports; ensuring the security and confidentiality of records; managing and documenting client contact hours; making referrals; conducting follow-up; and practicing time management.

Chapter 9: Culturally Competent Helping examines the changing demographics in the United States and its impact on being a culturally competent helper. The chapter then offers an overview of eight reasons why counseling is not working for some diverse clients. The chapter next identifies some definitions of culturally competent helping and reviews two models of cross-cultural helping: the RESPECTFUL Model and the Multicultural and Social Justice Competencies. The second half of the chapter examines strategies for working with a number of select populations, including: different ethnic and racial groups; people from diverse religious backgrounds; women; men; lesbian, gay, bisexual, and transgender individuals; the homeless and the poor; older persons; individuals with mental illness; individuals with disabilities; and substance users and abusers.

Chapter 10: Ethical Issues and Ethical Decision-Making examines the purpose of and limitations to ethical guidelines and then goes on to examine four ethical decision-making models (problem-solving, moral, developmental, and social-constructionist). It next presents ethical issues that human service professionals face related to informed consent; competence and scope of knowledge; supervision; confidentiality; privileged communication; dual and multiple relationships; sexual relationships with clients; primary obligation—to the client, agency, or society;

continuing education; multicultural counseling; and values in the helping relationship. Ethical vignettes associated with each of these areas are examined. The chapter concludes with an examination of 88 behaviors of human service professionals, and the reader is asked to decide whether he or she believes they are ethical.

Changes to this Edition: A number of important updates were made to Chapter 8, such as the inclusion of a discussion of the recently released Diagnostic and Statistical Manual-5, updates on and an expanded discussion of psychotropic medications, and updates on laws related to confidentiality. Chapter 9 presents some recent definitions of culturally competent helping, some new models of working with diverse clients, and greatly expanded examples of how to work with a variety of different ethnic and cultural groups. Chapter 10 was revised in keeping with the development of a new ethics code by the National Organization of Human Services in 2015. Also, the section on ethical decision-making models was expanded, a study of human service professionals' understanding of ethical behaviors was offered, and a discussion of the kinds of ethical issues important to human service professionals was added.

ACKNOWLEDGEMENTS

I'd like to give my heartfelt thanks to a number of people for their assistance in the revision of Skills and Techniques for Human Service Professionals. First, Dr. Tammi Milliken and other faculty from Old Dominion University's human service program assisted me by offering me ideas for updating the text. In addition, other human service faculty from around the country also gave me feedback and ideas for this new addition. Specific help with this edition included having Mike Kalkbrenner develop the glossary and Ashley Pittman conduct the copy editing. They were both amazing. Thanks Mike and Ashley for your hard work. In addition, my daughter Hannah Neukrug took on the challenge of proof reading the text and also did some additional copy-editing. She too was amazing. My other daughter, Emma Neukrug handled the author index and was masterful! Thanks so much to all of you! I'd also like to thank Carole Borstein Weisner for her legal assistance. Finally, my loving thanks to my wife, Kristina, for assisting with a wide variety of tasks with this book. I couldn't have done it without her. Love her!

INTRODUCTION

The skills identified in this text are directly related to, and an outgrowth of, the work of the human service professional. This work has historically focused on one or more of 13 roles and functions identified by the Southern Regional Education Board (SREB, 1969) and 12 competencies identified in the development of Skill Standards that were based on a national job analysis of human service practitioners (Taylor, Bradley, & Warren, 1996). The 13 roles and functions include:

1. *Outreach worker* who might go into communities to work with clients.
2. *Broker* who helps clients find and use services.
3. *Advocate* who champions and defends clients' causes and rights.
4. *Evaluator* who assesses client programs and shows that agencies are accountable for services provided.
5. *Teacher/educator* who tutors, mentors, and models new behaviors for clients.
6. *Behavior changer* who uses intervention strategies and counseling skills to facilitate client change.
7. *Mobilizer* who organizes client and community support in order to provide needed services.
8. *Consultant* who seeks and offers knowledge and support to other professionals and meets with clients and community groups to discuss and solve problems.
9. *Community planner* who designs, implements, and organizes new programs to service client needs.
10. *Caregiver* who offers direct support, encouragement, and hope to clients.
11. *Data manager* who develops systems to gather facts and statistics as a mean of evaluating programs.
12. *Administrator* who supervises community service programs.
13. *Assistant to specialist* who works closely with the highly trained professionals as an aide and helper in servicing clients.

The 12 competencies identified in the Skill Standards include:

1. *Participant empowerment*
2. *Communication*
3. *Assessment*
4. *Community and service networking*
5. *Facilitation of services*
6. *Community and living skills and supports*
7. *Education, training, and self-development*
8. *Advocacy*
9. *Vocational, educational, and career support*
10. *Crisis intervention*
11. *Organization participation*
12. *Documentation*

Skills and tasks related to the above competencies are a direct outgrowth of the competencies (Taylor, Bradley, & Warren, 1996; National Alliance for Direct Support Professionals, 2011).

Competency Areas ⟶ Skills ⟶ Tasks
(Job Functions) (Activity Statements)

As one example, for the competency of "Communication," one skill would be to use "effective, sensitive communication skills to build rapport" (Taylor, Bradley, & Warren, 1996, p. 26), and one activity instrumental to accomplishing this skill is the use of active listening skills. Thus, in the book we provide a section on listening skills (see Appendix A for definitions of the twelve competencies areas).

The purpose of this book is to identify many of the skills and techniques necessary for successful implementation of the roles, functions, and competencies of the human service professional as identified by SREB and by the Skill Standards project. In that effort, the text is divided into three sections: Section I is focused on the counseling environment, Section II on helping skills, and Section III on treatment issues.

SECTION I

THE COUNSELING ENVIRONMENT

"Sit down, feel comfortable, and relax. You are safe here." How the client initially perceives the helping environment is key to building a successful helping relationship and allows the client to quickly feel free to discuss issues and concerns. Defined broadly, the helping environment includes both the personal characteristics that helpers, and others in an agency, bring with them to their work, as well as the configuration of the physical environment.

Chapter 1: Characteristics of the Effective Helper briefly examines a number of attitudes that human service professionals should avoid, then examines eight characteristics deemed important to building a safe and comfortable atmosphere. The eight characteristics include showing empathy, being genuine, exuding acceptance, being cognitively complex, embracing wellness, developing competence, developing cultural sensitivity, and developing your "it factor."

Chapter 2: Entering the Agency reviews how the agency responds to phone calls and emails, the atmosphere created by the support staff and surroundings, whether or not the helper has embraced the personal characteristics of the helper highlighted in Chapter 1, the comfort level of the helper's office, and nonverbal behaviors on the part of the helper, such as attire, eye contact, body positioning and facial expressions, personal space, touch, voice intonation, and cross cultural perspectives on nonverbal behaviors.

When an inviting, safe, and comfortable environment is established early, it sets the tone for the rest of the relationship. When provided midway into the relationship, it deepens the bond. When provided near the end of the relationship, it demonstrates commitment upon the part of the helper and signifies that the client is always welcome to come back, should he or she need to, after the relationship has been terminated.

CHAPTER 1

Eight Characteristics of the Effective Helper

LEARNING OBJECTIVES

1. Identify toxic behaviors that can be detrimental to the helping relationship.

2. Explore a number of characteristics critical to an effective helping relationship, including:

   a. Showing empathy

   b. Being genuine

   c. Exuding acceptance

   d. Being cognitively complex

   e. Embracing wellness

   f. Developing competence

   g. Being culturally sensitive

   h. Developing your "it factor"

INTRODUCTION

Ever have a friend, parent, or significant person in your life act critical, dogmatic, or moralistic toward you? Called the toxins of a helping relationship, such qualities are anything but productive and should not be part of the helper's repertoire of responses. However, some qualities have been shown to be particularly helpful in creating the environment conducive to effective helping, and these are the qualities we will mostly focus upon in this chapter. But first, let's briefly discuss some of the toxins.

TOXIC BEHAVIORS TO BUILDING A HELPING RELATIONSHIP

Many, if not most of us, are brought up in environments where we are partially exposed to behaviors that are ineffective in developing a strong sense of self and sometimes are responsible for creating low self-esteem. For instance, consider those whose parents or significant others are often times critical, disapproving, disbelieving, scolding, threatening, discounting, ridiculing, or punishing. Or imagine if significant people in a person's life were argumentative, accusatory, coercive, demeaning, condemning, rejecting, sexist, or racist. Certainly, these qualities don't lend themselves to healthy relationships or healthy development. Unfortunately, all too many of us have found ourselves in relationships with people who embody these qualities. And, sometimes, because we have been exposed to these qualities, we too embody them—even though we generally know better. One of the most important habits that an effective helper can learn is how to *not* let those negative or toxic habits rear their ugly heads (Wubbolding, 2015). In fact, one of the first things you can do is identify toxic behaviors you were exposed to and examine how they have impacted your life (se Reflection Exercise 1.1).

Reflection Exercise 1.1:
Toxic Behaviors Outside and Inside of You

Write down a list of toxic behaviors that you were exposed to in your life. Then, respond to the following questions:

1. How did being exposed to those behaviors make you feel?
2. How effective do you think the expression of those behaviors would be in working with clients?
3. Do you see yourself having any of those behaviors? Which ones?
4. Are there other toxic behaviors that you sometimes exhibit that you need to avoid?
5. How easy do you think it would be to prevent yourself from exhibiting those behaviors noted in items 3 and 4?
6. What do you need to do to ensure that toxic behaviors that you have will not be expressed?

Given a little forethought, we can become fairly cognizant of our toxic behaviors, and with a bit of restraint, prevent them from impacting our helping relationships. In fact, I believe it's generally easier to stop ourselves from being toxic with our clients than with our loved ones. Why is this? With our loved ones we have ongoing, close relationships with people who know how to "push our buttons," and those buttons sometimes lead to responses that include toxic behaviors. Although we should certainly focus on eliminating all toxic behaviors in our lives, it's usually easier to not exhibit them with our clients than with our loved ones. So, perhaps we can see our relationships with our clients as a training ground for learning how not to be toxic with our loved ones. As we move ahead and examine those characteristics known to be important to developing healthy helping relationships, remember that a voice in your head should always be monitoring and preventing you from exhibiting toxic behaviors. One too many times I've seen mental health professionals acting irresponsibly towards a client. I hope that you never become one of them!

EIGHT CHARACTERISTICS OF EFFECTIVE HELPING RELATIONSHIPS

Recent research has increasingly shown that there are a number of common behaviors critical to the work of the helper (Wampold, 2010; Wampold & Budge, 2012). Jointly, these behaviors work to build a *working alliance* between the helper and the client. Such an alliance may be the most significant factor in positive client outcomes. How we connect with our clients, or how we build our working alliance, is complex. However, it seems like some of the more prominent methods of developing an alliance include showing *empathy*, being *genuine*, exuding *acceptance*, being *cognitively complex*, embracing *wellness*, developing *competence*, developing *cultural sensitivity*, and developing your *"it factor"* (see Figure 1.1).

When the above qualities are not shown by the helper, the likelihood of success is very small, if at all. That is because, the helper who continually makes empathic failures cannot hear the client's problems and develop effective plans, and the helper who seems false, judgmental, and dogmatic creates defensiveness. Similarly, the non-accepting and the cognitively rigid helper puts off the client, and the physically, emotionally, or spiritually impaired helper, has a hard time taking care of someone else's needs. Finally, the incompetent and culturally insensitive helper does not have the tools to work effectively with the client, and the helper who does not know his or her own "it factor," flounders in the relationship as he or she tries to discover who he or she is. Given the above, let's take a look at how we can embrace the qualities necessary for building the working alliance and effective helping relationship.

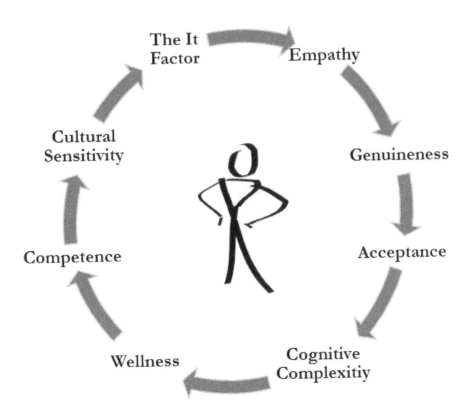

Figure 1: Eights Characteristics of the Effective Helper

Being Empathic

Empathic individuals have a deep understanding of another person's point of view. They can feel, sense, and taste the flavor of another person's experience (Neukrug, Bayne, Dean-Nganga, & Pusateri, 2012). They can get inside another person's shoes and understand what it's like to be that person. Carl Rogers (1957), the most influential psychologist of the 20th century, often noted that the empathic person could sense the private world of the client as if it were his or her own, without losing the "as if" feeling. Empathic individuals accept and understand people in their differences and communicate this sense of acceptance to them. Today, being empathic is viewed as one of the most important qualities related to positive client outcomes (Elliot, Bohart, Watson, & Greenberg, 2011; Laska, Gurman, & Wampold, 2014; Norcross, 2011).

Empathy can be viewed as both a way of being in the world that enhances our personal and professional relationships and as a skill that is taught and used in the helping relationship with our clients. Thus, to some degree, human service professionals should embody this characteristic in all of their relationships and practice listening and understanding others. In regard to the helping relationship, empathy is a skill that can build rapport, can help to elicit information, and can be used to show acceptance on the part of the helper toward the client (Egan, Owen, & Reese, 2014). Therefore, in Chapter 4 we will examine ways of enhancing our empathic ability with clients. To gain a sense of how empathic you are, do Reflection Exercise 1.2.

Reflection Exercise 1.2:
Are You Empathic?

Separate into triads and label each person as "Number 1," "Number 2," or "Number 3." Number 1 begins by talking with Number 2 about an emotionally charged situation he or she has experienced. Number 1 should be as real as possible in relating the situation while Number 2 be as empathic as possible. Number 3 will observe and record the interaction or take notes about it. After about ten minutes, review the notes or recording, and using the five-point scale below, rate Number 2 on each of the six items. Then, find an average for all six items. Next, have a second person be Number 2 and do the same. Finally, have the third person be Number 2. After all three persons have been rated, take the average ratings for the group.

1--------------2--------------3--------------4--------------5
Not At All Like This   **Somewhat Like This**   **Very Much Like This**

1. *Talks minimally:* The empathic person will talk considerably less than the individual who is describing the situation.
2. *Asks few questions:* The empathic person will tend to ask few, if any questions.
3. *Does not offer advice:* The empathic person will give little if any advice.
4. *Does not judge:* The empathic person will not judge the person he or she is listening to.
5. *Does not interpret:* The empathic person will not analyze or interpret the other person's situation.
6. *Does not cut off:* The empathic person will not cut off the other person and will allow himself or herself to be cut off by the person talking.

Continued on Next Page

Reflection Exercise 1.2:
Are You Empathic? (Cont'd)

If after scoring the responses, any individual, or the group, averages 3.0 or more (the ratings were mostly 3s, 4s, and 5s), you are doing well. If, however, your average is lower than 3 (the ratings were mostly 1s, 2s, or 3s), you have work to do. Chapter 4 examines the skill of empathy in more depth and offers the opportunity to fine-tune this important skill.

Genuineness

People can generally tell when a person is genuine or real with them or when someone is acting in a false and deceptive manner. People who are genuine are aware of their feelings and are willing to express them through their thoughts and actions, when appropriate. In contrast, those who are not genuine are deceptive and fake, tend to be out of touch with their feelings, and their feelings are not reflected in what they say or do. Sometimes, such people can sense an internal tug that says, "something's not right inside" or "I know I'm acting weirdly or falsely with this person." Other times, individuals are so out of touch with their genuine side that they go through life ignorant of the fact that they are living dishonestly (see Reflection Exercise 1.3).

Reflection Exercise 1.3:
Keeping Secrets

Keeping secrets is one way we prevent ourselves from being real with others. In the space provided, make a list of secrets you have kept from significant people in your life. Then answer the questions given. Your instructor may have you gather in small groups to discuss what you discovered about your secrets (don't feel obligated to discuss specifics of your secrets but do feel free to talk about your secrets without revealing details).

1. _____.
2. _____.
3. _____.
4. _____.
5. _____.

Questions

1. Was it relatively easy to remember five secrets?
2. Why have you kept these secrets?
3. Have you found it easier to keep these secrets than dialoguing with the person from whom you are holding the secret?
4. What might happen if the secret(s) was (were) revealed?
5. What are the benefits of keeping the secret?
6. What are the drawbacks of keeping the secret?
7. Might the benefits of keeping your secret outweigh the drawbacks?
8. Might the drawbacks of keeping your secret outweigh the benefits?
9. What does keeping the secret do to the depth of the relationship?
10. Would you want someone to keep a secret from you?

Carl Rogers (1961, 1980) believed that genuineness was a crucial element in all relationships, including the helping relationship. He thus suggested that helpers must model realness. However, he pointed out that, at times, it might not be wise to immediately express one's true self. For instance, it might not be wise to express anger at a new client because these feelings often dissipate after one gets to know the individual. Furthermore, expressing anger early on can cause a rupture in the relationship. Often if a helper waits, the anger will dissipate as the helper sees beyond the client's persona and is able to get to know the client in deeper way. This process of being able to monitor one's emotions and wait to see if a feeling persists or to postpone the expression of a feeling to a more appropriate time is sometimes called *emotional intelligence* (Ciarrochi & Mayer, 2007). Like empathy, genuineness has been shown to be one more quality related to positive outcomes in the helping relationship (Laska, Gurman, & Wampold; 2014; Norcross, 2010; Zuroff, Kelly, Leybman, Blatt, & Wampold, 2010).

Some contend that every helping relationship must address the important issue of *transparency* or *realness* (Gelso, 2009; Gelso et al., 2005). For instance, they believe that those helpers who do not reveal themselves during a helping relationship must somehow deal with how their clients will react to the wall they have put up. So, you might want to consider your ability to be real or genuine, as well as your emotional intelligence. Are you in touch with your feelings, and can you monitor them and express them at appropriate times?

Acceptance

Individuals who show acceptance feel comfortable allowing others to express their points of view, and they do not feel as if they need to change others to their way of understanding the world. Such *nonjudgmental* and *nondogmatic* individuals are open to understanding the views of others, open to feedback, and even open to changing their perception of the world after hearing other points of view. Such individuals are relatively free from biases and can accept people in their differences, regardless of dissimilar cultural heritage, values, or beliefs. In contrast, lack of acceptance can prevent one from listening effectively to another person. This is because when individuals are non-accepting, they are subtly, and sometimes not so subtly, expending energy trying to convince others to embrace beliefs that they do not hold. That energy prevents them from hearing others effectively. In a helping relationship, an accepting helper can hear about and understand a client's differences unconditionally, without "strings attached" to the relationship. Carl Rogers (1957) called such acceptance *unconditional positive regard*. Not surprisingly, research shows a relationship between the ability to be accepting and a good listener, and that acceptance leads to positive client outcomes (Laska, et al., 2014) (see Reflection Exercise 1.4).

Cognitive Complexity

During the 1960s, William Perry (1970) studied the cognitive development of college students and found that they tended to be *dualistic*, or black and white thinkers, when they entered college and somewhat more *relativistic*, or complex thinkers, when they graduated college. Although times have changed and college students are certainly different than they used to be, much of his theory probably holds up today. Perhaps with the knowledge gained from Perry's research, recent theorists who promote the *narrative therapy* approach to counseling suggest that people can have *thin descriptions* or *thick descriptions* of their lives (Neukrug, 2011). Somewhat like being dualistic, those with thin descriptions explain their lives simply. Those who have thick descriptions, on the other hand, can understand *multiple realities* people live by. For instance, one person with a thin description of his or her life may respond to the question "Why did you enter the helping professions?" with the following simple, but accurate response: "Well, I entered the human service profession to help people." In contrast, someone with a thick description of his or her life may state: "I entered the helping professions for many reasons. I wanted to help people. I thought I would be good at it. I thought I could make money in the field. I was the middle child and was always a mediator in my family. My mother was nurturing and I got that from her," and so on. These individuals can identify multiple origins that led them to where they are today, and such individuals can generally help others see different points of view within themselves. Or think of the client

Reflection Exercise 1.4:
Accepting Differences

In class, divide into triads. From the list of situations below, assign one person to be "pro" and one person to be "con." Your task is to spend about 5 to 10 minutes discussing the situation in the roles that were given to you (pro or con). Try to go back and forth, presenting your point of view while listening to the other person's point of view. It is important that, regardless of how you actually feel about the role, to take on the role given to you. During the exercise, or at *any point* afterward, do not reveal how you actually feel about the situation. The third person is the "moderator" who should take notes and later give feedback as to how each individual was responding to the role-play. Then, repeat the situation, or do another situation, but this time the moderator takes on the role of pro or con and one of the other individuals is the moderator. Then do it a third time, ensuring that each person has had the opportunity to be a moderator. When you have finished, answer the questions listed under "points to consider."

Situations
1. Abortion
2. Increased taxes
3. Affirmative action
4. Opening an X-rated bookstore in your neighborhood
5. Capital punishment
6. Affordable Care Act ("Obamacare")
7. Increased tuition
8. A database to monitor immigrants
9. Building a wall on our Southern border to prevent "illegal immigrants"
10. Increased gun control

Points to Consider
1. Did you become so emotionally charged about the situation that you had difficulty hearing the other person?
2. Did you think the other person was "wrong?"
3. Did you get tense while discussing the situation?
4. Did the individual with whom you were discussing the situation consider you open or closed to his or her point of view?
5. Did the "moderator" consider you to be open or closed?
6. Did you think you were open or closed?
7. Did you tend to cut off the other person from talking?
8. Were you preoccupied with coming up with a response in order to refute what the other person was saying?
9. Did the other person's point of view make sense to you?
10. Did you consider changing your point of view based on what you heard?

After considering points 1-10, reflect on ways that hindered you from hearing the other person. Discuss this in your small group and in class.

who is having a torrid affair, and says, "I don't know what to do, I love my spouse." A helper who is dualistic may judge and not understand this person, while a relativistic helper can understand the multiple realities and complex lives we all have (see Reflection Exercise 1.5).

Reflection Exercise 1.5:
Creating Multiple Narratives

Part 1: Malcom is in a street gang and has been involved in a series of gang fights and looting. After being arrested, he has been assigned to a social worker who meets with him to try and understand his situation. He describes himself in the following manner:

1. There are no good jobs out there for me.
2. My friends are all in the gang.
3. My dad sucks—in fact I haven't seen him in years.
4. School sucks—no one cares and I've never done well in it.
5. The only thing I like about my life is my friends—my gang.

In small groups, consider the responses that Malcom has made. Then, think about the "truth" of his statements. See how you might devise responses to his statements that could help him re-think his responses; that is, help him see his responses in more complex ways. For instance, to the item "school sucks" you might ask him, "Was there any teacher that ever was nice to you?" "Was there ever a time that you felt happy in school?" And so forth. Your responses to Malcom:

Part 2. Reflect on a part of your life that has been difficult—perhaps a part that you see little hope in changing. Then, consider alternate ways of viewing your situation and alternate narratives that might describe your life during that difficult time. Or, consider how you can focus on other parts of self that were positive during that difficult time in your life. Are you able to develop new narratives, or new ways of viewing and understanding the situation? Describe them here briefly:

Wellness

Can you help others if you yourself need help? Helpers, like all people, struggle with life's concerns, and issues such as burnout, stress, *vicarious traumatization*, *compassion fatigue*, psychological issues, and unfinished personal concerns, can limit the helper's ability at building a working alliance with a client (Cole, Craigen, & Cowan, 2014; Lawson & Myers, 2011; Puig, et al., 2012). There are many roads to becoming a healthier person, and as you might expect, one that is frequently taken in the helping professions is seeking one's own counseling.

Participation in one's own counseling has a number of benefits for the budding helper. First, it obviously can assist the helper in dealing with his or her own personal difficulties. Second, the helper can experience, firsthand, those techniques that might seem most beneficial. Third, having been in counseling enables the helper to understand what it's like to sit in the client's seat. Fourth, personal counseling yields great insight into self which creates greater cognitive complexity and, subsequently, a more effective helper. Finally, personal counseling helps prevent *countertransference*, or the process of projecting one's issues onto the client (Neukrug, 2011).

It appears that mental health professionals understand the importance of being in counseling, as 85% of helpers have attended counseling (Bike, Norcross, & Schatz, 2009; Orlinsky, Schofield, Schroder, & Kazantzis, 2011). However, some helpers resist, perhaps for good reasons (e.g., cost, concerns about confidentiality, stigma, feeling as if family and friends offer enough support, or believing they already have effective coping strategies) (Neukrug, Kalkbrenner, & Griffith, 2017).

Is counseling the only road to emotional health? Assuredly, not. However, it can foster a very special relationship that is not achievable through friendships or other significant relationships. Other activities such as support groups, diet, meditation, prayer, exercise, journaling, reading, and more have all been shown to have positive effects on one's emotional health. However, personal counseling for helpers is one of the best means of positively impacting the helping relationship and building strong therapeutic alliances with clients. So, if you have not been in your own personal counseling, you may want to consider that as one means of taking care of yourself and limiting countertransference with clients. Reflection Exercise 1.6 addresses a number of factors to help you assess your level of wellness.

Competence

Effective human service professionals have a thirst for knowledge and understand that such knowledge is closely related to competence. They exhibit their quest for knowledge through their studies, their desire to join professional associations and read professional journals, and their ability to broaden and deepen their own approach with clients. Effective human service professionals understand that some techniques are more effective than others with certain client populations, and such professionals have a desire to learn what works best with whom (Baker, 2012).

Competent professionals view education as a lifelong process, and they believe that human service professionals have both an ethical and a legal responsibility to be competent (Corey, Corey, Corey, & Callanan, 2015). For instance, the Ethical Standards of Human Service Professionals (National Organization of Human Services, 2015) suggests that helpers (1) know the limit and scope of their abilities, (2) seek appropriate consultation when necessary, (3) be involved in ongoing professional development activities, and (4) continually seek out new and better treatment methods. The legal system reinforces these guidelines by stating that helpers are ineffective when they demonstrate they are less competent than the majority of others in their profession (Kaslow et al., 2007).

Reflection Exercise 1.6:
Assessing Your Wellness

Myers and Sweeney (2008) developed the Indivisible Self Model which examines different aspects of self. Below are abbreviated definitions of their five factors that constitute wellness. For each factor, rate yourself on a scale of 1 to 10 as noted below:

| 1 | 2 | 3 | 4 | 5 | 6 | 7 | 8 | 9 | 10 |

Needs Improvement   Proficient/Competent

Factor 1: Creative Self: Being mentally aware. Allowing oneself to fully express one's thoughts and feelings. Being positive and unique. Being who you truly are. *Score:*

Factor 2: Coping Self: Having good self-esteem while knowing that humans are imperfect. Keeping stress at a reasonable level and being able to find solutions to life's problems. Being realistic about one's problems. *Score:*

Factor 3: Social Self: Feeling comfortable in social situations. Being able to feel a sense of connection with family and friends. Having friends and being able to love others. *Score:*

Factor 4: Essential Self: Knowing and feeling comfortable with different aspects of self, such as our gender identity, cultural identity, placement in our families (e.g., "father," "first daughter"), and spiritual self (however one defines that). Being comfortable with how one makes meaning in life. *Score:*

Factor 5: Physical Self: Eating healthy foods and being physically active. Not participating in restrictive eating or overeating. Being knowledgeable of one's physical limits and positively addressing physical needs. *Score:*

Conclusion: After finishing your ratings, consider those factors in which you have scored lower (perhaps a score below 7). Then, reflect on what you can do to increase your scores. Finally, add up all of your scores, and if you scored below a 35, consider how you can increase your global scores.

How much do you value the acquisition of knowledge and the importance of being competent? Take the questionnaire in Reflection Exercise 1.7 to get a sense of how to rate your competence.

Reflection Exercise 1.7:
How Much Do You Value Competence?

Take this inventory and see how much you embrace competence. If you do not embrace this characteristic, think about why you do not at this point in your career, if you believe you ever will, and how not embracing it can impact your work with clients.

For the 10 items that follow, place the number that best reflects your beliefs.
1. I very much disagree with this statement
2. I disagree with this statement
3. I neither agree nor disagree with this statement
4. I agree with this statement
5. I very much agree with this statement

Items
1. ___I love the learning that takes place in school.
2. ___I often pick up books, journal articles, or other written materials concerning subjects I want to learn more about.
3. ___I wish I did not have to take classes and someone could just give me a degree!
4. ___I view learning as a lifelong process.
5. ___I tend to be cynical in class.
6. ___I have or plan to join a professional association.
7. ___When I have a job in my profession, I plan on becoming active in one or more of my professional associations (e.g., be on a committee, run for office, etc.).
8. ___Research can add little to my knowledge of clients.
9. ___When I write research papers, I do an exhaustive search of the literature.
10. __Consulting with other professionals is generally a waste of time.

Scoring the inventory: For items 1, 2, 4, 6, 7, and 9, give yourself the number of points that you wrote in for that item. For items 3, 5, 8, and 10, reverse score. That is, if you answered "1" give yourself 5 points, "2" give yourself 4 points, "3" give yourself 3 points, "4" give yourself 2 points, and "5" give yourself 1 point. The closer you scored to 50, the more you cherish the quality of competence.

Cultural Sensitivity

The United States is becoming an increasingly diverse country. Soon, fifty percent of the country will be minorities. With this in mind, it's a sad state of affairs that many clients from diverse backgrounds are fearful of seeking out help from social service agencies, are misdiagnosed more frequently than Whites, and have a tendency to discontinue services at a higher rate than Whites (Harris, Edlund, & Larson, 2005; Lo, Cheng & Howell, 2013; Sewell, 2009). This may be due to the fact that there continues to be a considerably higher percentage of Whites who administer and work in social service agencies than are reflected in the country. It may also be that regardless of your cultural and ethnic background, if you're different from your client, you are more likely to have a harder time understanding him or her compared to someone from your own cultural or ethnic background.

With the above knowledge, cultural sensitivity and cultural competence have become paramount. A number of models and theories of how to work with clients who are different from ourselves have been developed, and some of these will be discussed in Chapter 9. For now, suffice it to say that all helpers should be sensitive to their clients and knowledgeable, or willing to gain knowledge of their client. One pragmatic approach, the RESPECTFUL Counseling Model, highlights ten factors that all helpers should consider when working with clients (see Reflection Exercise 1.8).

R: religious/spiritual identity
E: economic class background
S: sexual identity
P: level of psychological development
E: ethnic/racial identity
C: chronological/developmental challenges
T: various forms of trauma and other threats to one's sense of well-being
F: family background and history
U: unique physical characteristics
L: location of residence and language differences

(Lewis, Lewis, Daniels, & D'Andrea, 2011, p. 54)

In addition to the information you will gain in Chapter 9 on cross-cultural counseling, you will hopefully have coursework on social and cultural issues infused throughout your program and you may have a separate course on social and cultural issues.

The "It Factor"

A book such as this will teach you how, and to some degree when, to use a number of basic and critical skills in the helping relationship. And, the knowledge and use of such skills is crucial to positive client outcomes. But, what about our personalities? How do they come into play?

My belief is that each of our unique personalities impacts the helping relationship in profound, and perhaps, mysterious ways. So, rather than trying to repress who we are, I suggest we embrace it. I call this our "it factor." For instance, my "it factor" is the ability to be really good at being kind, caring, and empathic with clients. That's who I am (with clients!). In contrast, I had a colleague who was incredibly effective at using humor in his relationships with clients. And, another colleague of mine was great at using metaphors to help clients see their situations in new ways. I've also known "scientist helpers" who were excellent at being aloof, taking scrupulous notes, and using deductive reasoning when helping their clients. All of these helpers had different "it factors."

All of us need to understand our own "it factor," which is reflective of who we are and how we act in relationships. After identifying our "it," it is incumbent of us to use "it" effectively with our clients. Don't ever forget your core skills, as they will ultimately provide the vehicle for positive client outcomes. But, remember that you also have to be you. However, one word of advice: If your "it factor" is being a grouch, critical, mean, cynical, or nasty, you probably want to find another part of yourself that you can present to your clients. Presenting toxic personality factors is probably not your "it factor"—it's probably some leftover unfinished business that you need to work through (see Experiential Exercise 1.9).

Reflection Exercise 1.8:
Counseling Myths Questionnaire

Using the scale below, write the number to the left of each statement that best represents your view. When finished, the class can discuss their varying responses. Allow different points of view to be expressed and heard. Your instructor may want to obtain an average score for each of the items listed.

1	2	3	4	5
strongly agree	agree	no opinion	disagree	strongly disagree

1. __ Certain clients should be avoided because of their past experiences.
2. __ Cultural myths and stereotypes cannot be avoided when working with diverse clients.
3. __ Cultural myths and cultural stereotypes are often a reality.
4. __ Large behavioral differences exist between clients as a function of culture.
5. __ Helpers have fewer problems when they understand their clients' backgrounds.
6. __ Helpers work best within their own cultural group.
7. __ Clients from the same ethnic background, religion, or culture have similar issues.
8. __ Diverse clients should be referred to helpers from the same cultural group.
9. __ Client and helper cultural differentness are a significant factor in helping relationships.
10. __ Cultural variations exist regarding verbal and nonverbal communication.
11. __ Everyone is culturally different; thus, helpers need a model that will serve all clients.
12. __ All types of social services are available for all persons who desire them.
13. __ All cultures receive fair treatment in the helping relationship.
14. __ Clients from nondominant groups use profanity more than White clients.
15. __ White clients are more likely to respond to helping than non-White clients.
16. __ Generally, clients from low-income backgrounds are very difficult to help.
17. __ Many individuals from diverse cultures have shown they do not trust helpers.
18. __ Family ties are extremely weak for many clients from culturally diverse background.
19. __ Value systems for many clients from nondominant groups are inferior.
20. __ Clients from a low socioeconomic status do not trust middle-class helpers.
21. __ Sociocultural history is the most important ingredient in the helping relationship.
22. __ Clients from nondominant groups tend to lack initiative and assertiveness.
23. __ Clients from diverse cultures tend not to be logical thinkers or good decision makers.
24. __ All helping relationships have a cross-cultural component.
25. __ Religious differences are not as important as cultural differences when helping.
26. __ Age differences are not as important as cultural differences in the helping relationship.
27. __ Gender differences are not as important as cultural differences in helping.
28. __ When helping, sexual-orientation differences are not as important as cultural differences.

Reflection Exercise 1.9:
Your "It Factor"

On your own, write down what you think your "it factor" is, and give some examples of how you might have expressed it in your life. Then, in small groups share your various "it factors" and discuss how they might be used with clients. Discuss the possible pitfalls of using your "it factor" with clients as well as how your "it factor" may deepen your relationships with clients.

BRINGING IT ALL TOGETHER

This chapter examined eight characteristics that seem to empirically or theoretically relate to effectiveness as a helper: showing empathy, being genuine, exuding acceptance, being cognitively complex, embracing wellness, developing competence, being culturally sensitive, and developing your "it factor." Few, if any of us, have embraced all of these characteristics fully. More likely, as we travel the road of our professional lives, we should periodically pause and take a personal inventory that focuses upon how fully we are embracing each of these qualities. Experiential Exercise 1.10 gives you an opportunity to review all the characteristics examined in the chapter.

SUMMARY

This chapter examined the characteristics of the effective helper that are important in building a successful helping relationship. They included showing empathy, being genuine, exuding acceptance, being cognitively complex, embracing wellness, developing competence, being culturally sensitive, and developing your "it factor."

Highlighted first was the importance of being empathic, or the professional's ability to understand another person's experience of the world. Made popular by Carl Rogers, we noted that being empathic was a way of being in the world as well as a skill that can be taught.

Next, we discussed the importance of genuineness and knowing how and when to be real or transparent with clients. Along these lines, we discussed emotional intelligence, or the ability of the helper to manage his or her emotions in reference to knowing when to reveal an aspect of self within the helping relationship. We noted that it has also been suggested that realness is an issue that all helpers must deal with at some point in a helping relationship.

Acceptance, or being non-judgmental, was the third quality discussed, and we noted that this characteristic allows a client to feel understood and safe in the helping relationship. Also called unconditional positive regard by Carl Rogers, this quality ensures that there are no "strings attached" to the relationship.

The quality of cognitive complexity was next highlighted. We pointed out that Perry discussed this characteristic in light of being a dualistic or relativistic thinker and that the postmodernists, such as narrative therapists, suggested that those with thicker descriptions of their lives have deeper and more complex narratives. We suggested that the best helpers see the world from multiple angles and can help a client move from thin, dualistic narratives to thick, or complex narratives.

Experiential Exercise 1.10:
A Self Inventory of the Eight Characteristics

Using the scale below, place the appropriate number next to each characteristic based on the importance you place on it (I consider them all critical). Then, using the same scale, rate yourself on each characteristic. After you have finished, find two or three persons who know you well, ask them to rate you, and place their ratings in the appropriate box. Then make a note of when you last exhibited that quality and what you can do to enhance that characteristic, if need be. This exercise should give you an overview of how well you display each of the eight characteristics.

1   2   3   4   5   6   7   8   9   10
An Extremely Low Rating   **An Extremely High Rating**

	Impor-tance	Self-Rating	Other-Rating	Last Exhibited?	How Can You Improve?
Empathy					
Genuineness					
Acceptance					
Cognitive Complexity					
Wellness					
Competence					
Cultural Sensitivity					
Your "It Factor"					

Wellness, the next characteristic, was viewed as important because it can help prevent countertransference. It was suggested that there are many ways of developing a healthy or wellness focus, including being in one's own counseling, attending support groups, caring for one's diet, meditation, prayer, exercise, journaling, reading, and more. We gave a summary of the Indivisible Self Model and suggested that you examine your own wellness on its five factors: the creative self, the coping self, the social self, the essential self, and the physical self.

Although perhaps obvious, being competent was the next quality we highlighted, and we pointed out the importance of ensuring that one continues to have a thirst for knowledge throughout one's career. We suggested that competence was an ethical issue and a legal concern. With America becoming increasingly diverse, we noted that cultural sensitivity was another characteristic helpers should embrace. This characteristic is particularly important as clients from nondominant groups have historically not been served well by many so-called helpers. We offered one model in particular, the Respectful Model, which highlights a number of areas to examine when working with diverse clients.

Finally, we defined the "It Factor," the last characteristic. This quality is different for each person and has to do with how one brings oneself into the helping relationship. It was suggested that we all need to know how we can use our unique personalities to foster positive helping relationships

KEY WORDS AND TERMS

Acceptance
Characteristics of the effective helper
Cognitively complex
Compassion fatigue
Competence
Countertransference
Cultural sensitivity
Dualistic
Emotional intelligence
Empathy
Genuine
Indivisible Self Model
It factor
Multiple realities
Narrative therapy
Nondogmatic

Nonjudgmental
Realness
Relativistic
RESPECTFUL counseling model
Rogers, Carl
Thick descriptions
Thin descriptions
Toxic behaviors
Transparency
Unconditional acceptance
Unconditional positive regard
Vicarious traumatization
Wellness
William Perry
Working alliance

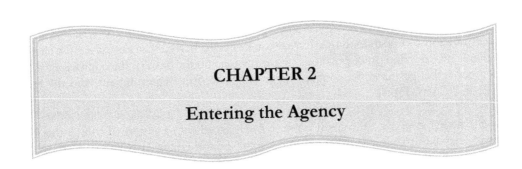

CHAPTER 2

Entering the Agency

LEARNING OBJECTIVES

1. Understand the importance that the client's initial contact with an agency has to building a strong helping relationship.

2. Examine how email and phone contact, agency atmosphere, and office atmosphere impacts the helping relationship.

3. Reinforce the notion that showing empathy, being genuine, exuding acceptance, being cognitively complex, embracing wellness, developing competence, being culturally sensitive, and developing one's "it factor" are all important in building strong helping relationships.

4. Review how nonverbal behaviors can facilitate communication, including attire and dress, eye contact, body positioning and facial expression, personal space, touch, and voice intonation.

5. Understand that cross-cultural differences can mediate the effectiveness of nonverbal behaviors.

INTRODUCTION

> . . . alliance formation, as understood by clients, actually begins before the counselor fully engages the client, as clients may develop predispositions or impressions on the basis of the counselor's attire, the counselor's nonverbal gestures, the counselor's greeting the office environment, and the reception staff . . . (Bedi, 2006, p. 33)

When initially contacting an agency, the client is immediately faced with a variety of stimuli that encourages or inhibits openness and says to the client "come in," "bolt," or something in between (Bedi, 2006; Neukrug, 2016). This chapter will, therefore, highlight some items that go into facilitating a healthy working relationship with a client or cause a client to want to run out of the agency. These include 1) how the agency responds to phone calls and emails; 2) the atmosphere created by the support staff; 3) surroundings the client is faced with when he or she initially walks into the agency; 4) whether the helper has embraced the personal characteristics of the helper highlighted in Chapter 1; 5) the comfort level of the helper's office; and 6) the nonverbal behaviors on the part of the helper (attire, eye contact, body positioning and facial expressions, personal space, touch, and voice intonation). The chapter concludes with a brief discussion of the importance of cross-cultural awareness and sensitivity when considering nonverbal behavior.

CLIENT'S INITIAL CONTACT WITH THE AGENCY

Be nice, be nice, and be nice. I can't say these words enough. All too often, I have seen clients faced with angry, frustrated, cynical, and burnt out support staff and helpers at an agency. Almost assuredly, these qualities were not ones that the support staff or helpers had when first entering this field. So, whether a client is emailing an agency, contacting the agency by phone, or walking into an agency, please remember—be nice.

Email and Phone Contact

Often, clients initially contact an agency by email or by phone. Email responses can vary dramatically from agency to agency; however, there are some tried and true responses to phone calls that should be kept in mind. If you work at an agency which uses email as a source of initial contact, most of the following can be adapted to an email system. If a client initially telephones an agency, a number of general guidelines should be followed. These include:

- Be kind and be courteous.
- Caringly ask who you are talking with and what the client is requesting.
- Patiently explain the process for seeing a helper at your agency.
- Courteously give referrals to the potential client if the agency is not the correct one to address the client's needs.
- Carefully and kindly assess the client to ensure that he or she does not need immediate attention (e.g., assess for suicidality and homicidality). If immediate attention is needed, ensure that your agency has a plan in place (see Chapter 8 for assessment of lethality).
- Assure the client that there will be a helper ready to see him or her when he or she comes into the agency.
- Patiently and kindly make an appointment.
- Gather demographic information, especially phone number, email address, home address, and so forth to follow up in case of "no shows."
- Warmly and courteously tell the client you look forward to seeing him or her at the agency (see Reflection Exercise 2.1).

Reflection Exercise 2.1:
Calling an Agency

Pair up with a student. One of you be a helper answering the phone at an agency while the other play a client contacting the agency wanting help. The client should have a reason for wanting to come to the agency, and the helper should be prepared to respond using the points just noted. When you have finished, discuss the exercise in small groups or as a class.

Walking into an Agency

Imagine a client walking into an agency. She steps into a dingy, cluttered waiting room and walks up to the receptionist who ignores her. She says to the receptionist, "Excuse me," at which point the receptionist looks up and responds in a rather nasty tone of voice, "What do you want?" and then asks her to sit down and says to her: "Wait your turn." She sits down on an uncomfortable chair and ponders the sign on the wall that says, "Turn Off Your Cell Phones." She sits there wondering if anyone will hear what she has come to the agency for.

Now, imagine another agency. A client walks into the waiting room. It is nicely lit, and there is pleasant art on the walls. The chairs look comfortable and when the client goes up to the receptionist, he says to her, "I'm sorry that I'm kind of busy at the moment, but I want to talk with you as soon as I can. Please have a seat and I'll be right with you." She says, "Thank you" and sits down. Although the couch is not new, she can tell that it is clean and feels comfortable. The receptionist then warmly calls her over, and they talk about why the client has come in today.

The two vignettes above are real. I've certainly been in agencies where I've had the unfortunate experience represented in the first vignette, as well as the pleasant experience in the second one. As you can tell, the first time a person enters an agency can leave a lasting impression on the client and can result in the client responding in a negative or positive fashion to the helper.

Unfortunately, I have found that helpers often feel little responsibility for the atmosphere of the waiting room—or sometimes of the agency in general. I believe that the helping relationship does not start in the helper's office, but with the initial contact the client has with the agency—whether by email, by phone, or by walking in. Thus, I encourage all human service professionals to take an active role in creating an agency environment that is conducive to establishing a positive helping relationship. Taking responsibility for the total atmosphere of the agency is part of our ethical obligation of respecting the dignity and welfare of our clients (NOHS, 2015):

> The fundamental values of the human services profession include respecting the dignity and welfare of all people; promoting self-determination; honoring cultural diversity; advocating for social justice; and acting with integrity, honesty, genuineness and objectivity. (Preamble)

and

> Human service professionals participate in efforts to establish and maintain employment conditions which are conducive to high quality client services. Whenever possible, they assist in evaluating the effectiveness of the agency through reliable and valid assessment measures. (Standard 24)

Many items contribute to creating an inviting atmosphere for clients (e.g., soft lighting, comfortable furniture, placement of furniture), and I am confident that you can come up with a number on your own. In class, complete Reflection Exercise 2.2, and your instructor will lead a discussion addressing agency atmosphere. When you have completed Reflection Exercise 2 .2, do Reflection Exercise 2.3.

Reflection Exercise 2.2:
Identifying Comfort Items

If you were a client walking into an agency, list items that you would like to see in that agency that would help you feel comfortable and safe. In class, your instructor will make a larger list from student responses.

1._____

2._____

3. ._____

4. ._____

5. ._____

Reflection Exercise 2.3:
The Agency Atmosphere (Vignettes)

On your own, respond to the following scenarios. Then, in small groups or as a class, discuss your responses.

1. You're a mental health aide at a mental health center. You walk into your agency in the morning and hear the receptionist berating a client. What do you do?

2. You work as a counselor at a group home for individuals with intellectual disabilities. Despite constant pleas to your advisory board to spend a little money to paint the home and buy some new furniture, they refuse. You are embarrassed when other professionals come to the home to consult with you. What do you do?

3. You realize that most of the staff at your agency do not seem to care that the reception area is dirty and overcrowded. What do you do?

Office Atmosphere

Building a trusting relationship begins with the client's initial contact with the agency and continues when the client sits in the helper's office. Providing an office space that is quiet, comfortable, and safe, and where confidentiality can be ensured, is crucial to successful helping relationships. Even if a helper does not have an "official" office, he or she can usually find a place where most of these qualities are provided.

How a helper arranges his or her office can be important in eliciting positive attitudes from clients (Bedi, 2006; Nassar & Devlin 2011).). Most agree that an office should be relatively soundproof, have soft lighting, be uncluttered, have client records electronically or physically secured, be free from such distractions as a phone ringing or knocks on the door, and have comfortable seating. Large pieces of furniture, like a desk, should generally not be between the helper and the client, although this might vary as a function of the helper's counseling style, personality, and the particular situation (e.g., I've worked with volatile clients when I felt it would be "wise" to have a desk between me and them). As the helper "creates" his or her office, each will try to find a balance between how the office reflects his or her taste and having it still be appealing to the vast majority of clients (see Reflection Exercise 2.4).

Experiential Exercise 2.4:
Arranging Your Office

Take out a blank piece of paper and draw your own office. For furniture, use the suggested items below and place as many (or as few) in your office as you would like (duplicates are allowed). If time allows, use magazine pictures to help create the furniture in your office. Feel free to add additional pieces of furniture of your own. Compare your office to the office of other students. What makes your office conducive to creating a positive helping relationship as compared with other students'? Justify your office arrangement based on your counseling style.

Desk	File cabinet	Couch
Chair	Computer	Plant
Bookcase	Coffee table	Radio/CD player
End tables	Printer	Pictures
Large lamp	Small lamp	Rocking chair
Desk chair	Wicker basket	Magazine rack
Other?	Other?	Other?

How the helper arranges furniture is not the only thing that will affect whether a client will be emotionally available during an interview. Often, the kind of literature or other items on display can greatly affect a client's willingness to be open. To highlight this point, complete Reflection Exercise 2.5 and then discuss in class whether you think the items listed should be included in one's office. Of course, no matter how a helper arranges his or her office, some people will be offended by something. In addition, it may be that you will want to attract certain clientele who would feel comfortable with a particular ambiance. For instance, a Christian

23

counselor might include articles of a religious nature in his or her office, while a person dealing with mostly gay and lesbian issues might include related literature.

Reflection Exercise 2.5:
Selecting Items to Place in Your Office

Review the items below and decide whether any of them would be offensive to you if you walked into a helpers' office. Then, think about the most liberal and the most conservative person you know, and imagine how he or she might feel with each of the following:

- Feminist literature
- A bear rug
- Information on transgender issues
- Fundamentalist religious literature
- A cluttered desk
- Information on abortion
- Leather furniture

- A compulsively clean desk
- An AIDS pin
- A desk between helper and client
- Information on human sexuality
- A Christian cross
- An American flag
- A Confederate flag

PERSONAL CHARACTERISTICS OF THE HELPER

As you remember from Chapter 1, toxic helpers, or those that are critical, scolding, judgmental, nasty, cynical, and so forth, are not helpful to clients, and can actually lower the self-esteem of some clients and raise the wrath of others. Although already discussed in Chapter 1, it's important to remember that the manner in which helpers connect with and build a working alliance with their clients is likely related to a number of important characteristics including: showing empathy, being genuine, exuding acceptance, being cognitively complex, embracing wellness, developing competence, being culturally sensitive, and developing one's "it factor." As you read through this chapter, always remember that these eight characteristics are the bedrock to a positive working relationship with clients.

NONVERBAL BEHAVIORS

> Yet when humans communicate, as much as eighty percent of the meaning of their messages is derived from nonverbal language. The implication is disturbing. As far as communication is concerned, human beings spend most of their time studying the wrong thing. (Thompson, 1973, p. 1)

Although the above quote was written years ago, research continues to show that nonverbal behavior is a major aspect of how people communicate with one another (Knapp et al., 2014; Matsumoto, Frank, & Hwang, 2013). In fact, nonverbal behavior seems largely out of a person's conscious control and can be difficult to censor. As compared to verbal behavior, nonverbal behavior is often a more accurate representation of how the client and helper feel. Such things as attire or dress, eye contact, posture, and/or tone of voice that communicate "Don't open up to me" will obviously affect clients very differently from those that communicate "I'm open to hearing what you have to say." Some nonverbal behaviors of which we should be aware include one's attire or dress, eye contact, body positioning and facial expressions, personal space, touch, and voice intonation.

Attire or Dress

How the helper dresses can project an image to the client that the helper wants to listen to and assist the client, or it can shut the client down (Segal et al., 2011). Should jeans be worn at work? What about an expensive suit? Are the helper's clothes revealing? What does jewelry or hair style say about the helper? Are shoes nicely polished or scuffed? Are sneakers okay to wear? Are clothes tucked in neatly or falling out all over the place? Is it okay to have piercings, tattoos, tattered clothes, and so forth?

Human service professionals should be conscious about how their appearance will affect clients. Is there anything in the helper's style of dress that a client would find offensive or startling? They should always keep in mind that how the client perceives them is part of the helpful environment they are trying to create.

Also important in determining how to dress is whether the agency has a covert or overt dress code. If the agency has a written dress code, helpers should certainly observe it. However, rather than agencies having written rules, agency employees have often established a de facto code; that is, certain styles are more or less expected. If most people in the agency wear jackets, ties, and business suits, a helper would appear out of place in jeans, and vice versa. Reflection Exercise 2.6 further explores the role that dress plays in working with clients.

Reflection Exercise 2.6:
What Are You Wearing?

Find four other students in class who you don't know well and join them in a small group. Based on what the other students are wearing, write down your initial impressions of each of them. When each student finishes writing, place your responses to each person in a pile that represents that person you just wrote about. Then, one member should pick up one of the piles and read the responses out loud to the group. Whoever is being read about should sit quietly. When all the response are finished, that person can respond by either agreeing or disagreeing to group members' conclusions. Then, do the same for each other group member. Were initial impressions of group members, which were mostly based on dress, accurate? Why or why not? What implications does this exercise have for what one wears?

Alternative exercise: Instead of gathering in small groups, the instructor can find pictures of people online in various attires, and students can discuss their ideas about how each picture would elicit positive or negative responses by clients.

What Will You Wear At Work?

25

Eye Contact

How a helper looks at a client reveals much about the helper's willingness and desire to work with the individual (Howes, 2012; Knapp, Hall, & Horgan, 2014). Similarly, the type of eye contact the client gives the helper can reveal much about the willingness of the client to work with the helper or potential fears of relating the client may have. Although intense eye contact (e.g., staring) will certainly turn off almost any client, the helper who has difficulty maintaining any eye contact will not have an easy time building a trusting relationship with a client. Thus, finding the "correct" amount of eye contact that tells a client the helper is ready to listen to him or her is the goal of any helping relationship. For many helpers this comes naturally; however, some helpers have difficulty maintaining eye contact with individuals. You may want to explore your ability at maintain eye contact (see Experiential Exercise 2.7).

Experiential Exercise 2.7:
Comfort Level with Eye Contact

People's ability to tolerate eye contact can vary greatly and may be related to cross-cultural differences. To test this out, your instructor will randomly divide the class into groups of four to six students. Then have one person be the helper while others take turns being the client. The helper should be comfortable with eye contact and offer a reasonable amount to each person in the group, one at a time, as the group members share a small issue or problem in their lives. When finished, discuss whether the participants' level of comfort with eye contact varied considerably, and if so, why? Share your responses with the larger group.

How Comfortable Are You With Eye Contact?

Body Positioning and Facial Expressions

One of the most important nonverbal behaviors that clients initially observe is how the helper positions his or her body during the helping relationship (Knapp et al., 2014; Matsumoto & Frank, 2013). Body posture telegraphs whether the helper wants to work with the client. For instance, is the helper leaning forward as if he or she is anxious to listen to the client or sitting in a defensive mode with arms folded? Optimally, the helper should have his or her feet on the ground, body leaning forward slightly, and have arms positioned in an open manner, all of which suggests to the client the helper is ready to listen.

In addition to how the helper positions his or her body, head motions and facial expressions are also important. Is the helper's head movement saying to the client, "Yes, I hear you" and "Keep on talking," or is it indicating to the client that the helper is bored, restless, and/or simply not interested? Do the helper's facial expressions show care and concern, or does the helper have a smirk on his or her face that says, "I don't believe a word you are saying"? In general, positioning of one's body, as well as facial expressions, are vital communication pieces to the helping relationship. To see how important body language can be, complete Reflection Exercise 2.8 and 2.9.

Reflection Exercise 2.8:
Playing with Body Positions

Sit back to back with a partner. One person describes a figure (e.g., a car) while the other person draws it. However, you must not use any words to give away what it is (e.g. tires, steering wheel). For instance, you might say: "Draw a rectangle. Now, place four circles on the bottom of it—two in the front and two in the back." And so forth. Then do the same exercise using a different object, but this time facing one another; the person doing the describing needs to keep his or her arms crossed. Then do it one last time, this time using your arms. Reflect on how much easier these activities are when we are able to use our body.

Reflection Exercise 2.9: Head
Motions and Facial Expressions

Find a fellow student to listen to. As he or she talks, provide as many head motions and facial expressions that you can come up with that say, "keep talking" or, "I'm listening to you." Then reverse roles. Make a list of as many positions as possible and discuss them with the class. Or, on your cell phones, take pictures of various head positions and share them in class.

Personal Space

The amount of space between a helper and client is an immediate message to the client about the helping relationship and can positively or negatively affect the relationship (Knapp et al., 2014; Sommer, 2007). Mediated to some degree by culture, age, gender, and other identity factors, individuals vary greatly in their level of comfort with personal space. Therefore, the helper must choose an amount of personal space that is not too close or too distant—an amount that allows the client to feel close, safe, and comfortable. Although this will generally happen in subtle ways, the helper should take the lead in creating an appropriate distance through respect for the client's needs and through awareness of what might be optimal for the helping relationship. Reflection Exercise 2.10 examines your own comfort level regarding personal space.

Reflection Exercise 2.10:
Your Comfort with Personal Space

Your instructor will have you stand in two lines, five feet apart, with each person facing one another. Then, all students in one of the lines move a comfortable distance across from students in the second line. Based on personal space levels of comfort, some students will move closer while others will likely move further away. Then, after standing for about fifteen seconds, the students in the first line (the line that didn't move) will be asked to move forward or backward based on how comfortable they feel with the level of distance between them and students in the other line. After having stood in your lines, discuss your level of comfort when the person across from you moved closer or further away from you.

Touch

Touch is another aspect of nonverbal behavior important to the client's experience of the helping relationship (Calmes, Piazza, & Laux, 2013). Of course, touching at important moments is quite natural. For instance, when someone is expressing deep pain, it is not unusual to hold the person's hand or to lightly embrace the person while he or she sobs. Or, when a person is coming to or leaving a session, many helpers may find it natural to place a hand on a shoulder or give a hug. However, in today's litigious society, touch has become such a delicate subject that it is important for all helpers to be sensitive to their clients' boundaries, their own boundaries, and the limits of touch as suggested by our professional codes of ethics. Brammer and MacDonald (2003) suggest that physical contact with a client should be based on (1) the helper's assessment of the client's needs, (2) the helper's awareness of his or her own needs, (3) what will be helpful within the context of the helping relationship, and (4) knowledge of agency policies, customs, as well as ethical codes and the law (see Reflection Exercise 2.11).

Reflection Exercise 2.11:
Your Level of Comfort with Touch

Sit across from another student in class and have one role-play a helper and the other a client. As the client discusses a made-up situation, the helper should gently touch the client on the leg or shoulder or hold the client's hand (be as appropriate as possible). When you have role-played this for a few minutes, the client should discuss how comfortable he or she felt with touch. Then reverse roles. Then, all students can discuss, in class, their level of comfort with touch and when it should, or should not, be used.

Voice Intonation

Voice intonation, the final nonverbal aspect of the helping relationship, can also affect the client's experience of the helper (Frank, Maroulis, & Griffin, 2013; Knapp et al., 2014; Sommer, 2007). Helpers must be aware that what they say may not always match how they're saying it. For instance, saying "I like you" in an angry tone gives a mixed message. Thus, helpers must be keenly aware of what they are communicating through their tone of voice. Also, all helpers will make a number of guttural responses to clients during a session. Such responses as "uh huh" can go a long way in telling clients whether they are being attended to. Human communication takes place in many complex ways, more ways than sometimes we would like to admit, and the helper's manner of response can mean more than it seems to mean on the surface (Watzlawick, Beavin, & Jackson, 1967) (see Reflection Exercise 2.12).

Reflection Exercise 2.12:
Tone vs. Words

Sit across from a student in class. Look at the person and say "I like you" in as many ways as you can. Say it with a loving voice, an angry voice, a cynical tone, and so forth. When you finish, discuss how voice intonation and tone can convey more information than words alone, and that sometimes, voice intonation and tone can conflict with the words one is saying. Consider how important voice intonation and voice tone are when working with clients.

A Cross-Cultural Perspective on Nonverbal Behaviors

Traditionally, helpers have been taught to lean forward, have good eye contact, speak in a voice that meets the client's affect, and rarely touch their clients. However, research suggests that cross-cultural differences exist in the ways that clients perceive and respond to nonverbal helper behaviors (Knapp et al., 2014; Matsumoto & Hwang, 2013). Therefore, it is now suggested that helpers be acutely sensitive to client nonverbal differences while being knowledgeable and skilled in culturally appropriate responses.

Culturally skilled helpers are able to send and receive both verbal and nonverbal messages accurately and appropriately. Although some nonverbal behaviors are off bounds in the helping relationship (e.g., seductive looks, inappropriate touch, harshly critical facial expressions), when it comes to nonverbal behavior, culturally competent helpers are not otherwise restricted to certain ways of responding. They must be sensitive to the fact that client responses to such behaviors may be culture bound. When they sense that their helping style is limited and potentially inappropriate due to the client's cultural background, they can anticipate and ameliorate its negative impact.

Effective cross-cultural helpers must understand that some clients will expect to be looked at, while others will be offended by eye contact; that some clients will expect the helper to lean forward, while others will see this as intrusive; that some clients will want a hug when they leave, while others will see this as crossing a boundary and inappropriate. Effective helpers keep in mind that what works for many will not work for all, and they are sensitive to the individual needs and responses of all of their clients.

CONCLUSION

As discussed throughout this chapter, a number of factors go into creating a welcoming atmosphere for clients. These include the tone of emails or support staff as a client contacts and enters an agency; how inviting the agency surroundings are; the comfort level of a helper's office; whether the helper has embraced the eight characteristics of the effective helper enumerated in Chapter 1; how effective the helper is at demonstrating nonverbal behaviors of attire and dress, eye contact, body positioning and facial expressions, personal space, touch, and voice intonation; and the helper's ability at making adaptations for cross-cultural differences. An acronym, I came up with called "FACESLOVE" can help us remember many of the nonverbal cues discussed in the chapter follows:

F: Facial expressions   L: Leaning forward
A: Attire and dress   O: Open (body posture)
C: Cross-cultural   V: Voice
E: Eight characteristics   E: Eye contact
S: Space

Now that you learned about various types of nonverbal behaviors, do Experiential Exercise 2:13 to review your understanding of them.

Experiential Exercise 2:13:
Practice Nonverbal Behaviors

In class, break up into groups of five students. Have one student role-play a "helper" while another student role-play a "client" for three or four minutes. The other three students are to watch the role-play, and using the chart below, write comments about the nonverbal behaviors of the "helper." Be specific. After you finish each role-play, give the "helper" feedback.

	Positive Qualities	Needs Improvement
Attire		
Eye Contact		
Body Positioning		
Facial Expressions		
Personal Space		
Touch		
Voice Intonation		
Cross-cultural Considerations		

SUMMARY

In this chapter we gave an overview of a number of items that can influence the overall atmosphere of the agency. Starting with the client's initial contact with the agency, we noted that a client's first contact with an agency is often through email or phone. We highlighted a number of points to consider if a client calls the agency and suggested that these tips could be adapted to email contact. We then talked about the ethical obligation of treating a client warmly and with respect when they initially walk into an agency. We noted that such items as soft lighting, comfortable furniture, placement of furniture, and a pleasant attitude were critical when a client first contacts and/or walks into an agency.

Moving to the office atmosphere, we discussed the importance of an office being relatively soundproof, having soft lighting, being uncluttered, having client records filed and secured, being free from distractions (e.g., phone ringing or knocks on the door), and having comfortable seating. We briefly pointed out that some items (e.g., fliers denoting a point of view) could inadvertently turn off a client and suggested one carefully consider what items to place in one's office. We reminded you about the eight personal characteristics of the helper that should be embraced: showing empathy, being genuine, exuding acceptance, being cognitively complex, embracing wellness, developing competence, being culturally sensitive, and developing one's "it factor."

A good portion of the chapters discussed the importance of appropriate nonverbal behaviors when working with clients, and we noted that some have suggested that as much as eighty percent of the meaning of communication can be deduced through nonverbal language. Some of the important nonverbal behaviors we discussed included attire and dress to wear at work, eye contact, body positioning and facial expressions, personal space, touch, and voice intonation. We identified the acronym "FACESLOVE" to describe many of the nonverbal behaviors identified in the chapter.

We concluded the chapter by noting that cross-cultural differences could impact the level of comfort that clients have with the nonverbal behaviors examined in the chapter. We emphasized that effective helpers should keep in mind that what works for many is not always helpful and appropriate for all.

KEY WORDS AND TERMS

Agency atmosphere
Attire or dress
Body Positioning
Cross-cultural issues and nonverbal behavior
Eye contact
Facial Expressions
Initial email and phone contact with agency

Nonverbal behaviors
Office atmosphere
Personal characteristics of the helper
Personal Space
Touch
Voice intonation
Walking into agency

IMAGE CREDITS

SECTION II

HELPING SKILLS

The core of the helping relationship and the ability to establish positive outcomes for clients involves the effective use of helping skills. This is the focus of Section II, understandably called "Helping Skills." The skills are presented in order, from those mostly likely to be used early on in the helping relationship to the more advanced skills and specialized training tools used later. However, each of these skills may be used at almost any stage in a helping relationship. Thus, our basic skills of listening and empathy are often needed late in the relationship, while the more advanced skills of advanced empathy or assessment of lethality may, at times, be used early on.

Chapter 3, Foundational Skills are those skills, perhaps we should say attitudes, that all helpers should provide early on in the relationship and are the prelude to the more focused helping skills. They include honoring and respecting the client, being curious, delimiting power and developing an equal relationship, non-pathologizing the client, and demonstrating the 3 C's: commitment, caring, and courteousness.

Chapter 4, Essential Skills are core skills that should be used in any helping relationship and often initiate movement toward goal identification and even goal achievement. They include silence and pause time, listening skills, reflecting feelings and content, paraphrasing, and basic empathy.

Chapter 5, Commonly Used Skills help the client move toward solving problems. Although all of them will not be used in every helping relationship, they are skills we often find exhibited by helpers. They include affirmation giving, encouragement, and support; offering alternatives, information giving, and advice giving; modeling; self-disclosure; collaboration; and advocacy.

Chapter 6, Information Gathering and Solution-Focused Questions distinguishes between these two important types of questions which may be used in the helping relationship. The information gathering skills covered include open questions, closed questions, tentative questions, and why questions, while the solution-focused questions examined include preferred goals questions, evaluative questions, coping questions, exception-seeking questions, and solution-oriented questions.

The last chapter of this section, *Chapter 7: Advanced Skills and Specialized Training,* are methods and tools selectively used based on the needs of the clients. They include the advanced skills of advanced empathy; confrontation: challenge with support; interpretation; and cognitive-behavioral responses; and the specialized training skills of assessment for lethality: suicidality and homicidality; crisis, disaster, and trauma helping; token economies; positive helping; and coaching. (See Figure 1)

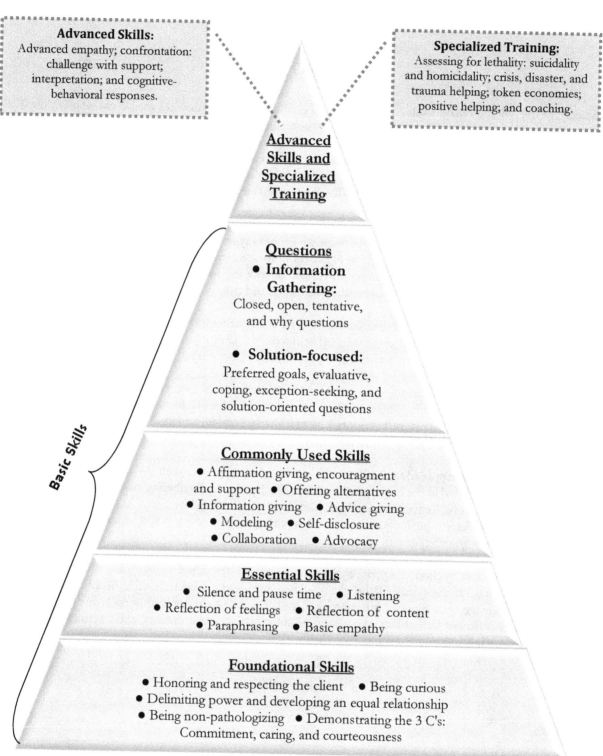

Figure 1: Sequence of Helping Skills

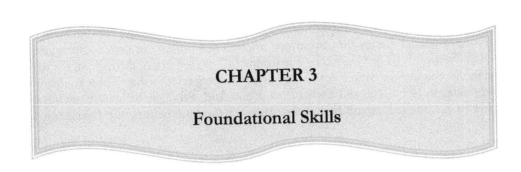

CHAPTER 3

Foundational Skills

LEARNING OBJECTIVES

1. Understand the role that foundational skills play in developing a healthy therapeutic alliance.

2. Examine a number of important foundational skills, all of which are precursors to the skills utilized in the helping relationship.

3. Define and understand the foundational skills of:

   a. Honoring and respecting the client

   b. Being curious

   c. Delimiting power and developing an equal relationship

   d. Being non-pathologizing

   e. Demonstrating the 3 C's: commitment, caring, and courteousness

INTRODUCTION

This first skills chapter identifies and demonstrates beginning foundational skills. Although the characteristics of the effective helper and the factors that contribute to creating a positive or negative initial experience with an agency (found in Section I , "The Counseling Environment") are important throughout the relationship, the skills discussed in this chapter are critical to the start of any helping relationship. These foundational skills are just that—the foundation or basis to all of what is to come. And, although basic in many ways, they are the mark of whether or not the helper will be helpful. They set the tone of how the helper will be within the relationship.

In many ways, foundational skills highlight ways of being with a client as opposed to specific techniques that one can teach. However, in this chapter we will attempt to deconstruct each of these skills and see if we can give some examples of how they can be demonstrated by helpers. Much of what is discussed in this chapter are common sense skills that all too often are not embraced by helpers but are nevertheless critical to a successful helping relationship.

Let's take a look at the skills of honoring and respecting the client, being curious, delimiting power and developing an equal relationship, non-pathologizing, and demonstrating the 3 C's: commitment, caring, and courteousness. These skills are the prelude to the rest of the techniques to be discussed in the chapters to come including essential skills, commonly used skills, use of questions, and advanced skills and specialized training (see Figure 3.1).

Figure 3.1: Sequencing of Helping Skills

HONORING AND RESPECTING THE CLIENT

Going perhaps one step further than *acceptance* and *unconditional positive regard*, honoring and respecting clients has to do with acknowledging and demonstrating that you appreciate the unique path clients have taken and will take in life (Sung & Dunkle, 2009). Honoring and respecting a client is the cornerstone of many ethical codes:

> The fundamental values of the human services profession include respecting the dignity and welfare of all people; promoting self-determination; honoring cultural diversity; advocating for social justice; and acting with integrity, honesty, genuineness and objectivity. (National Organization of Human Services, [NOHS] 2015, Preamble)

> The primary responsibility of counselors is to respect the dignity and promote the welfare of clients. (American Counseling Association, 2014, Section A.1.a)

> Social workers treat each person in a caring and respectful fashion, mindful of individual differences and cultural and ethnic diversity. (National Association of Social Work, 2008, para. 4, Section on Ethical Principles)

Honoring and respecting your client often starts with a *professional disclosure statement* that reflects important values of the helping relationship which are also upheld in ethical codes (e.g., ACA, 2014; Jansson, 2016; NASW, 2008; NOHS, 2015). Such a written statement is given to clients when first meeting them. In part, a professional disclosure statement (1) provides information about credentials, (2) suggests the purpose of the helping relationships, (3) offers a synopsis of a helper's theoretical orientation or way of working with clients, (4) supports the client's unique diversity and denotes the importance of the client in the helping relationship, (5) states that the helper will keep promises made to clients, (6) acknowledges and ensures that the helper is committed to the client, (7) underscores that the helping relationship is confidential under all but certain circumstance (e.g., danger to self or others), (8) encourages and supports the client's self-determination, (9) suggests agency rules and legal issues to be adhered to, and (10) provides information about limits to and boundaries of the helping relationship (Corey, Corey, Corey, & Callanan, 2015; Remley & Herlihy, 2014) (see Experiential Exercise 3.1). (See further discussion in Chapter 8).

Experiential Exercise 3.1: Writing a Professional Disclosure Statement

A professional disclosure statement ensures that clients feel welcomed in the helping relationship, are knowledgeable about what is to occur, and understand the process of such a relationship. Using the ten items noted above, develop your own professional disclosure statement. Share your written disclosure statements with the rest of your class.

Honoring and respecting a client means that when a client first comes to see a helper, he or she has appreciation for and unconditional acceptance of where the client is in his or her life. (Gold, 2008; Jansson, 2016). In that sense, the resistant client is honored as the helper tries to understand the reasons for the defiance. In this context, the client is not labeled as a "difficult" client, but a client who has faced some challenging circumstances that have led to resistance. Similarly, the depressed client's sadness is acknowledged and seen as a message to the person about his or her life, not a sign that there is something inherently wrong or that he or she can never get better. Or, the cynical client is seen as a person who has a reason for having a skeptical attitude and the helper's goal is to understand why he or she has this attitude. Honoring the client is accepting the client in all of his or her feelings and attitudes, understanding the context in which the client has come to be, and having a desire to help (see Reflection Exercise 3.1).

Reflection Exercise 3.1:
Honoring Resistance

Years ago, I went to a workshop entitled "Working with Resistant Adolescents." Known to be a difficult population to work with, I was interested in how this workshop leader would help us understand resistant adolescents who seem to not want our help. I was initially startled at the beginning of the workshop, and then enlightened, when I heard the workshop leader say, "There are no resistant adolescents, there are only resistant helpers." The point he was making was that it's not the adolescent's job to *not* be resistant. Instead, it is the helper's responsibility to understand and honor the resistant adolescent, as well as understand and respect how he or she has come to show such behavior. He suggested that helpers should not play the "blame game" by making the "resistant adolescent" be the person with the problem. The problem is with the helper who cannot reach the adolescent.

Think about times when you have had friends, clients, or acquaintances that you were quick to label—perhaps you saw them resistant to change, depressed, or even psychotic. Would you be able to change that attitude and replace it with honor and respect instead? Would you be able to understand them? Discuss your experiences in small groups.

One of the ways we can show our clients that we honor and respect them is through the questions we ask when they first come in. The following are a few examples:

- Tell me what brings you here today?
- I'm so glad you were able to come here today, and I hope you feel comfortable with me.
- So, it seems like you've had a difficult time. I hope I can help in some way.
- I can tell you really don't want to be here, but maybe there's some way that I can help make your time worthwhile.
- What do you think would be most helpful for you during your time here?
- How can I best help you?
- I really want to understand how you have come to feel the way you feel.
- I want to be helpful in the best ways possible. Let me know if what I'm doing is working for you.

There are many questions or statements that you can make to show clients you honor and respect them and want to understand their predicament. Using the theme of accepting the client in all of his or her feelings and attitudes, understanding the context in which clients have come to be, and having a desire to help the client, write in other types of questions or statements. Try to formulate questions that show the client that the helper is a positive force in the client's life and honors the client. Then do Experiential Exercise 3.2.

1. _____
2. _____
3. _____
4. _____
5. _____

Experiential Exercise 3.2:
Practicing Honoring and Respecting Clients

The following are two clients who are having a difficult time in their lives. Using some of the responses we made above, or coming up with some new responses, show how you might respond to "Helena" and "William" in ways that demonstrate honor and respect.

Example 1: Helena is new to the agency and is seeing you for the first time. She is angry, cynical, and doesn't want to be with you. Her first conversation follows.

> *I don't know why I have to be here. I shouldn't have to beg for anything from you. And, your office staff sucks. They were the rudest to me. Meanwhile, my kids are in the car, and I need to get out of here. Can you help me quickly or not?*

One person role-play Helena while someone else role-play the helper. How might the helper respond in a way that honors and respects Helena?

Example 2: William just lost his job, is depressed, and feels hopeless. He has come to your employment agency hoping you can help but is too depressed to do anything besides walking in your office.

> *I thought my job would be permanent. I had it for 9 months, and I liked everyone at the place. I was shocked when they let me go. They said they just couldn't justify my job no more. What am I going to do? I doubt you can help me.*

One person role-play William and the other role-play a helper. How might the helper respond in a way that honors and respects William?

<u>*Possible Responses:*</u> After you have made some possible responses to Helena and to William, examine some of the examples at the end of the chapter. In small groups or as a class, how do your responses compare to mine?

BEING CURIOUS

Successful helpers are naturally curious about others (Rice, 2015). How did he happen to end up like this? What made her react like that? What tragedies has he faced? What childhood traumas did she go through? How did she feel when that happened? These are just a few of the many questions that go through the mind of a curious helper. However, successful helpers are not just thinking about these questions; they are also willing and wanting to ask their clients these questions. They are naturally interested in the lives of others. As you might imagine, successful helpers are comfortable inquiring about a client's life while simultaneously honoring and respecting him or her as an individual.

Curious and effective helpers do not avoid subjects, because they know that inquiring about clients' lives can be the initial path to helping clients resolve important life concerns. Although the type and depth of questions will vary depending on the setting the helper works in, successful helpers, at the very least, have the desire to ask questions. They are curious about their clients and they want to know more. Some of the types of statements and questions that can be used when showing curiosity include:

- I'm curious to know more about that.
- How do you feel about sharing more about that?
- Can you tell me how that happened?
- That is so interesting, please go on.
- Tell me more, if you can.
- I'm really interested in what you are saying!
- What you're saying intrigues me. Keep going.

Obviously, the above just represent a few of the questions or statements that can be asked by a helper who is interested in the client and curious to know more. Experiential Exercise 3.3 can help you practice this important skill. See if you are willing to encourage the role-play client to reveal aspects of himself or herself beyond what might normally be uncovered in a conversation.

Experiential Exercise 3.3: Practicing Being Curious

Pair up with another person in your class, or practice this at home with a friend. The other person should have some kind of problem to discuss (real issues work best, but role-play situations work too). As the "client" is talking, see how many statements or questions you can ask that show that you are curious about the client's life. Consider how you can help the client deepen his or her understanding of self through your curiosity.

If possible, have a third person observe the role-play and make notes about the types of questions you asked or statements you made and if they were successful in encouraging the client to talk. Remember to honor and respect your client while doing this.

DELIMITING POWER AND FORMING AN EQUAL RELATIONSHIP

> Most counselors, of course, probably experience themselves as partners with their clients in the treatment process, not as "truth bullies" who beat down clients' perspectives with their superior views. (Hansen, 2006, p. 295)

Usually in helping relationships, the helper has some amount of legitimate power over the client. For instance, consider the following helper-client relationships and reflect on the kind of power that the helper holds over the client.

- The helper works for Temporary Assistance of Needy Families (TANF) and determines what aid the client can receive.
- The helper works for employment services and can refer the client to different job settings.

- The helper works for a domestic violence shelter and helps the client find shelter and obtain a restraining order.
- The helper works at a homeless shelter and determines who can be placed in transition housing.
- The client is severely depressed, and the helper is charged with counseling the client.

You can see that in every situation above, the helper has some amount of power; that is, the helper is in a position where, to some degree, he or she can impact the client's future.

In the past, the helping relationship was seen as one in which the helper was the expert who had some knowledge to reveal to the client. Although helpers often do have information for clients (e.g., how to apply for food stamps; where to find information on birth control, etc.), in recent years it has been increasingly common for helpers to see themselves as equal partners with their clients in the helping relationship (Harrison, 2013). No longer are they separate, objective, prescriptive experts that stand apart from their clients and tell them what to do. Instead, while acknowledging that some power imbalances are inherent due to the relationship, today's helpers increasingly attempt to provide a relationship which is viewed as an equal and joint journey with their clients.

If you were like me, and probably like most people, when growing up you learned that helping people involved giving advice. Although advice giving has its time and place (see Chapter 5), if provided too frequently and if offered authoritatively it can lead to power disparities in the helping relationship. Ultimately, this can result in the client feeling dependent, disempowered, and even angry at the helper (Egan, Owen, & Reese, 2014) (see Reflection Exercise 3.2).

> ### Reflection Exercise 3.2:
> ### Differentiating Equal and Power Relationships
>
> Think about the different relationships you have had in your life. Which ones would you consider "power relationships," and which might you put into the category of "equal relationships."? Write down some of the attributes that predominated in each of the power and equal relationships. Discuss your list in a small group, and make a master list in class that differentiates between the two types of relationships.

How does the helper build an equal relationship with shared power? It begins with honoring and respecting the client, but also entails monitoring one's responses so they do not appear overly authoritative, prescriptive, or bossy. For instance, look at the two responses to a young pregnant woman who is considering her options to her pregnancy:

Helper 1: You better decide quickly and make the right decision for yourself. You know, this is going to follow you around for the rest of your life, and however you decide, it better be the right decision!

Helper 2: You certainly have a dilemma facing you, and I'm here for you as you reflect on this very important decision for yourself.

Clearly, Helper 1 is considerably more authoritarian and prescriptive than Helper 2, who views the relationship on a more equal basis (see Experiential Exercise 3.4). You can imagine the different types of dynamics that would occur due to a Helper 1 response in contrast to a Helper 2 response.

> ## Experiential Exercise 3.4:
> ## Developing Equal Relationships
>
> Using those qualities and kinds of responses identified earlier when honoring and respecting your client, and integrating some of the attributes you identified in Reflection Exercise 3.2, find a partner in class and role-play with that person an equal relationship. When you have finished, discuss in class the level of difficulty you had with developing such a relationship.

NON-PATHOLOGIZING

Many human services clients are marginalized in society, angry at the system, or feel as if there is something wrong with them (Gallagher & Street, 2012). When a helper sees a client and treats that person as if he or she has a problem, is defined by a diagnosis, or is less than human, the helper is often feeding into an already existing worldview of the client. Such an attitude detracts from the client's humanness, sets the helper up as a judge of others, and lessens opportunities for client growth.

Pathologizing others is not unusual. We have all done it. Have you ever called a person a name—either to their face or under your breath? Have you ever been in a relationship in which you began to "diagnose" the other person? Oh, that "blankity blank" person is psychotic, or "OCD," or a "borderline personality," or simply "crazy." When people are not happy with others, they will sometimes find a way of diagnosing others in an effort to dismiss what the other person is saying and uplift their own sense of self-righteousness. Unfortunately, such a diagnosis dehumanizes the person and can cause serious fractures within the helping relationship (Glasser, 2013; Pickersgill, 2013) (see Reflection Exercise 3.3).

> ## Reflection Exercise 3.3:
> ## Pathologizing Others
>
> We've all done it—thought that another person was, or told another person that he or she was, "diagnosable" in some way. Think back on your relationships and consider when you may have "diagnosed" a person; that is, tried to define him or her as a particular formal or informal mental disorder ("crazy," "stupid," "overly anxious," "clinically depressed," "bipolar," etc.). Write down times you may have done this and discuss your list with other students in your class. Did you have positive outcomes when you did this? What were some of the negative consequences of your responses? How did such responses, on your part, make the other person feel? How did it make you feel? If you were to do it again, might you have a better way of responding?

In line with honoring and respecting the client and not setting oneself up as the expert, when one de-pathologizes the helping relationship, the client increasingly becomes an equal to the helper and is more likely to feel comfortable, safe, and trusting within the relationship. William Glasser, who developed *reality therapy* and *choice theory*, suggested that helpers should develop *caring habits* by using language that is supportive, encouraging, accepting, trusting, and respectful and not use language that will pathologize, diagnose, blame, or criticize the client (Glasser & Glasser, 2007; van Nuys, 2007) (see Experiential Exercise 3.5).

Experiential Exercise 3.5:
Having, not BEING a Diagnosis

Today, the *Diagnostic and Statistical Manual-5th edition (DSM-5)* is used to help mental health professionals find diagnoses for mental disorders. Although the DSM can be helpful in conceptualizing client problems, treatment planning, making decisions about medication, and more, it sometimes results in the client feeling as if he or she IS the diagnosis as opposed to a person who has some qualities OF the diagnosis (Corey et al., 2015; Pickersgill, 2013). Although using DSM-5 may be important at times, it is equally important that when clients are diagnosed, they are not treated as if they ARE the diagnosis.

In class, with the help of your instructor and using the DSM-5, choose two or three diagnoses. Then, using one of these diagnoses, have one individual role-play a helper who treats the client with dignity, honor and respect, and does not attempt to pathologize the client despite the fact that the client acts as if he or she IS the diagnosis; that is, acts like his or her identity is defined by the diagnosis. In other words, the helper should treat the client as if he or she is a worthy human being who is *not* defined by the diagnosis. After role-playing with the first client, you may want to do this a couple more times, using one or two additional diagnoses.

After role-playing for 10-15 minutes, discuss the positive results of treating a person as if their identity is not defined by a diagnosis. Do you think you can do this with clients? If time allows, each person in the class should practice such role-plays with others.

DEMONSTRATING THE 3 C's: COMMITMENT, CARING, & COURTEOUSNESS

Already mentioned in many ways throughout this chapter, it is always important for human service professionals to remember that they should be committed, caring, and courteous. Being committed means that you follow up on promises that you make to clients and that you are there for your clients when they need you. It means that when they don't show up for an appointment, you contact them and encourage them to come in. It is a never-ending dedication you have to the well-being of your clients—even when they might not have it for themselves. It shows them that you are a rock in their sometimes shaky lives.

Being courteous means that you continually treat your clients respectfully and with appropriate politeness, Furthermore, it means you are aware of your clients' customs and defer to them when appropriate (e.g., knowing what religious customs a person might have; using the proper name designation, etc.). Being caring— well, we all know what that is. It is one's ability to show concern to others, have regard for others, and be there for them in times of need.

We all know the 3 C's. We can describe them, feel them, and produce them when appropriate. To a large degree, these attributes are moral imperatives that all helpers should strive to achieve (Levitt & Aligo, 2013). All too often, however, I have seen human service professionals not care, not be courteous, and not follow-up on their commitments with clients. Don't become one of those! (see Experiential Exercise 3.6).

Experiential Exercise 3.6:
Practicing the 3 C's: Commitment, Caring, and Courteousness

Find a partner, and take turns role-playing a helper with his or her client. Focus on being committed, courteous, and caring. Have a third person make notes every time you make a response that shows one of the 3 C's. The observer can also notate other, less helpful responses. Role-play for about 10 minutes, and then change roles with a different person being the helper. Discuss your role-plays after you are finished with particular attention to what the observer has noted. Make sure each person gets to be the helper.

CONCLUSION

This chapter examined foundational skills necessary when working in the client-helper relationship and included honoring and respecting the client, being curious, delimiting power and developing an equal relationship, being non-pathologizing, and demonstrating the 3 C's: commitment, caring, and courteousness. All of these skills should be demonstrated throughout the helping relationship; however, as their name implies, they are the cornerstone of the helping relationship and as such, are most important when you first meet a client. In contrast to the other skills that you will learn about in Chapters 4, 5, 6 and 7, these skills are a bit more akin to attitudes that one should embrace. Thus, throughout the chapter we discussed ways to embody the foundational skills and gave you examples of how they have been used. As you continue to learn about other skills in the following chapters, never forget your foundational skills—without them, the other skills will crumble (see Reflection Exercise 3.4).

Reflection Exercise 3.4:
Remembering Your Foundational Skill

A couple of years ago I was diagnosed with kidney cancer. Luckily, it was found very early, and I am now fine. Soon after being diagnosed, I realized that there were ways in my life that I was behaving that I wanted to change. Mostly, I wanted to try and be more thoughtful and kind to people—all people. However, living a life in which this had not been my primary goal meant that I had to constantly remind myself that I needed to change. I therefore bought myself a special ring that I could look at during the day to remind myself that this was my primary goal. Is it a perfect fix? No. However, it does help to remind me of a very important goal in my life.

Consider the foundational skills discussed in this chapter. Are there some skills that you could work on? Are there some skills that do not come naturally to you? Like my ring, are there ways to remind yourself that that these are skills that are important in your life—certainly with clients, and probably with people you love? How might you remind yourself of these important skills in your life?

SUMMARY

This first chapter of Section II explored the foundational skills of honoring and respecting the client, being curious, delimiting power and developing an equal relationship, being non-pathologizing, and demonstrating the 3 C's: commitment, caring, and courteousness. Noting that these skills are the cornerstone of developing a trusting and safe relationship, we highlighted the fact that these skills are more attitudes one has in the helping relationship as opposed to skills you can describe and learn, like the ones that will follow in Chapters 4, 5, 6, and 7. Near the beginning of the chapter, a graphic was shown that demonstrated the order that the skills are generally exhibited in the helping relationship and how these skills lay the groundwork for other skills that follow.

Starting with honoring and respecting the client, we noted that this skill is partly related to some of the values upheld in the ethical codes of professional relationships. We then noted that one way of honoring and respecting a client is to provide a professional disclosure statement and obtain informed consent. Some aspects of a professional disclosure statement we highlighted, included (1) providing information about credentials, (2) suggesting the purpose of the helping relationships, (3) offering a synopsis of a helper's theoretical orientation or way of working with clients, (4) supporting the client's unique diversity and indicating the importance of the client in the helping relationship, (5) stating that the helper will keep promises made to clients, (6) acknowledging and ensuring that commitments made to clients will be kept, (7) underscoring that the helping relationship is confidential under all but certain circumstance (e.g., danger to self or others), (8) encouraging and supporting the client's self-determination, (9) suggesting agency rules and legal issues to be adhered to, and (10) providing information about limits to and boundaries of the helping relationship. We then went on to highlight the idea that regardless of how the client presents him or herself, the effective helper is able to honor and respect the client and work with him or her without judgment. Some examples of questions and statements that suggest honoring and respect were given.

Being curious was the next skill that was highlighted. It was suggested that all helpers have a natural curiosity about clients, but the skilled helper is not afraid of his or her curiosity, knows what questions to ask when inquiring about the client's world, and is not afraid to ask the tough questions.

Delimiting power and forming an equal relationship was the next set of skills important to the helper. We noted that helpers generally have a certain amount of power in helping relationships because they usually can impact the client's world in a negative or positive manner. We pointed out that in recent times, helpers have moved away from a relationship earmarked by an authoritative and prescriptive approach to one in which the helper shares power with the client and sees the relationship as a joint journey. We suggested that helpers monitor their responses to ensure they are developing equal relationships and are not being authoritative, prescriptive, or bossy.

Not pathologizing clients was the next skill we highlighted in this chapter. We noted that it is not unusual for individuals to pathologize others, especially when in close relationships. We warned that this is generally not helpful and is particularly destructive to helping relationships. We pointed out the importance of using language and "caring habits" that can build a comfortable, safe, and trusting relationship, such as those suggested by William Glasser. We noted that although the DSM-5 can be helpful in case conceptualization, treatment planning, medication decisions, and more, the helper should not see the client as the diagnosis. Instead, the helper must understand that although clients may have some diagnostic qualities, they are much more than the diagnosis.

The final skills we encouraged you to embrace included the 3 C's: commitment, caring, and courteousness. Committed helpers follow through on promises, courteous helpers are polite and are aware and respectful of client customs, and caring helpers show concern for their clients. We noted that these three skills are moral imperatives for helpers.

The chapter concluded with a brief reminder that we should all work on ways of continually remembering the foundational skills if we are to have effective and solid long-term relationships with our clients.

KEY WORDS AND TERMS

Acceptance

Being curious

Caring habits

Delimiting power and developing an equal relationship

Demonstrating the 3 C's: commitment, caring, and
    courteousness

Diagnostic and Statistical Manual-5th edition (DSM-5)

DSM-5

Honoring and respecting the client

Non-pathologizing of the client

Pathologizing

Professional disclosure statement

Reality therapy and choice theory

Unconditional positive regard

William Glasser

Possible Responses To Helena And To William In Experiential Exercise 3.1

Example 1 (Helena): I don't know why I have to be here. I shouldn't have to beg for anything from you. And, your office staff sucks. They were the rudest to me. Meanwhile, my kids are in the car, and I need to get out of here. Can you help me quickly or not?

> *Helper:* It sounds like today has been really frustrating, and I want you to know that I am here to help in any way.

> *Helper:* I want to help you as quickly as possible. It sounds like it's been really difficult so far at the agency.

> *Helper:* How about you bring the kids in with you? Or, if you want, we can have them sit in the waiting room and one of the staff can watch them. What do you think?

Example 2 (William): I thought my job would be permanent. I had it for 9 months, and I liked everyone at the place. I was shocked when they let me go. They said they just couldn't justify my job no more. What am I going to do? I doubt you can help me.

> *Helper:* That must really be discouraging, and I want you to know that I am here to help you in any way possible.

> *Helper:* You've been through a lot; let's see what we can do to make things a bit better for you.

> *Helper:* I guess I hear how important a good job is for you and that says a lot about who you are as a person. Let's see how we can help you.

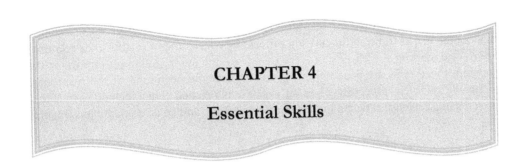

CHAPTER 4

Essential Skills

LEARNING OBJECTIVES

1. Understand the importance of essential skills in establishing the relationship, building trust and rapport, and starting the client's process of self-examination.

2. Examine how to respond to clients using the essential skills, including:

   a. Silence and pause time

   b. Listening

   c. Reflection of feelings

   d. Reflections of content

   e. Paraphrasing

   f. Basic empathy

INTRODUCTION

Although the foundational skills noted in Chapter 3 are critical to establishing the relationship, the following essential skills allow the helper to begin the helping process by continuing to establish the relationship, building trust and rapport, and starting the client's process of self-examination. Although important throughout the helping relationship, these skills are generally most crucial near the beginning of the relationship. Still, they should be continually revisited, especially when an impasse is reached. They include silence and pause time, listening skills, reflecting feelings, reflecting content, paraphrasing, and basic empathy (see Figure 4.1).

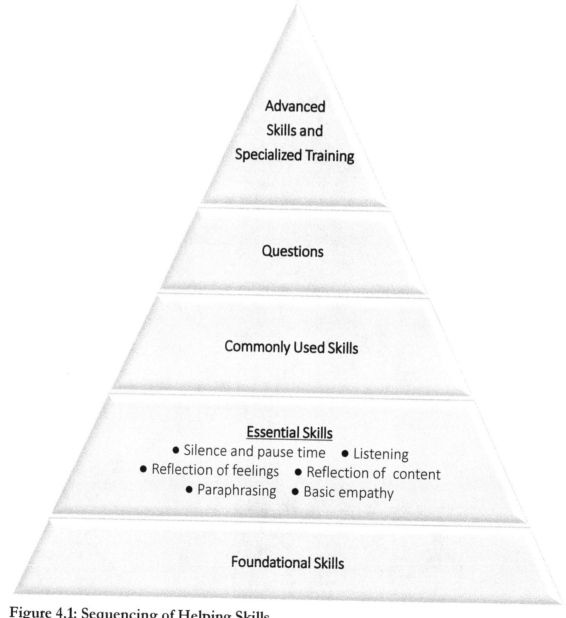

Figure 4.1: Sequencing of Helping Skills

SILENCE AND PAUSE TIME

When   is   empty   space   facilitative,   and   when   does   it   become
a   bit   much?

Silence is a powerful tool in the helping relationship that can be used for the client's benefit (Linnell, Bansel, Ellwood, & Gannon, 2008; Sommers-Flanagan & Sommers-Flanagan, 2015). Silence allows the client to reflect on what he or she has been saying, enables the helper to process the session and formulate his or her next response, says to the client that communication does not always have to be filled with words, and gives the client an opportunity to look at how words can sometimes be used to divert the client from his or her feelings.

Silence is powerful. It will sometimes cause the client to feel anxious, which may have either good or bad outcomes. On one hand, a client may react to anxiety by continuing to talk and process a particular topic, while on the other hand, a client could become so unsettled that he or she drops out of the helping relationship. To be an effective listener, you must be able to maintain the amount of silence that can be facilitative, not destructive. I once had a professor who suggested waiting 30 seconds before responding to a client. Thirty-seconds is a REALLY long time. Complete Experiential Exercise 4.1 and see how much silence might feel comfortable to you.

> ### Experiential Exercise 4.1:
> ### How Much Silence is Right for You?
>
> Pair up with another student in class and have one role-play a helper while the other role-plays a client. The client should begin to role-play a counseling situation and continue talking for about one minute, at which point the instructor should yell out "stop." After the instructor shouts "stop," the helper should formulate a response to the client but not say it until the instructor says "go," 30 seconds later. After making the response, the "helper" and "client" should discuss how it felt to wait this relatively short amount of time. You may want to do this a few times with different amounts of "pause times." Also, make sure each student gets to be the helper.

I'm sure that after completing Exercise 4.1, you will agree that 30 seconds is a long time to wait before making a response. Although waiting that long is unusual, you probably found that such a pause allowed the helper to formulate his or her response, gave the client the opportunity to think about what he or she said, and allowed the client to consider what to say next. How long of a pause works best for you? Do you think it would be helpful to work on making your pauses longer?

Cultural background may influence an individual's use and interpretation of silence, as well. Research has found that silence manifests differently among various cultures (Hendrix, 2001; Levitt, 2001; Zur 2007). For instance, Native Americans have sometimes been labeled as withdrawn, or even resistant to treatment, because they are simply more comfortable with longer pauses than other cultural groups. As a helper, you may want to consider your pause time to discover your comfort level, while recognizing that your client's pause time might vary as a function of his or her culture.

LISTENING

First there is the hearing with the ear, which we all know; and the hearing with the non-ear, which is a state like that of a tranquil pond, a lake that is completely quiet and when you drop a stone into it, it makes little waves that disappear. I think that [insight] is the hearing with the non-ear, a state where there is absolute quietness of the mind; and when the question is put into the mind, the response is the wave, the little wave. (Krishnamurti, cited in Jayakar, 2003/1986, p. 328)

Before actually talking about the importance of listening and how to listen effectively, let's take a quick quiz to see what kind of listener you are. Complete Experiential Exercise 4.2.

Experiential Exercise 4.2: Listening Quiz

Take the following listening quiz by placing a "U" next to the response if you think a person "Usually" should respond in that manner, an "S" if you think a person "Sometimes" should respond in that manner, and an "R" if you think a person should "Rarely" respond in that manner. Compare your answers to the answers that can be found at the end of this chapter.

____1.   When listening, I try to determine what should be talked about during the interview.

____2.   When listening to someone, I prepare myself physically by sitting in a way in which I can make sure that I hear what is being said.

____3.   I try to be "in charge" and lead the conversation.

____4.   I usually clear my mind and take on a nonjudgmental attitude when listening to another.

____5.   When listening to another, I try to tell that person my opinion of what he or she is doing.

____6.   I try to decide from the other's appearance whether or not what he or she is saying is worthwhile.

____7.   I attempt to ask questions if I need further clarification.

____8.   I try to judge from the person's opening statement whether or not I know what is going to be said.

____9.   I try to listen intently to feelings.

____10. I try to listen intently to content.

____11. I try to tell the other person what is "right" about what he or she is saying.

____12. I try to "analyze" the situation and give interpretations.

____13. I try to use my experiences to best understand the other person's feelings.

____14. I try to convince the other person the "correct" way to view the situation.

____15. I try to have the last word.

Although easy to define, listening is one of the most difficult skills for Americans to learn, as we are rarely taught how to hear another person. In fact, ask an untrained adult to listen to another, and usually he or she will end up interrupting and giving advice (see Reflection Poem 4.1). Effective listening, however, helps to build trust, convinces the client that he or she is being understood, encourages the client to reflect on what he or she has said, ensures the helper that he or she is on the right track, and is an effective way of collecting information from a client without the potentially negative side effects of using questions (Neukrug, & Schwitzer, 2006).

Reflection Poem 4.1:
Listen to Me

When I ask you to listen to me and you start giving me advice, you have not done what I asked.
When I ask you to listen to me and you begin to tell me why I shouldn't feel that way, you are trampling on my feelings.
When I ask you to listen to me and you feel you have to do something to solve my problem, you have failed me, strange as that may seem.
Listen: All that I ask is that you listen, not talk or do—just hear me.
When you do something for me that I can and need to do for myself, you contribute to my fear and inadequacy.
But when you accept as a simple fact that I do feel what I feel, no matter how irrational, then I can quit trying to convince you and get about this business of understanding what's behind these feelings.
So, please listen and just hear me.
And, if you want to talk, wait a minute for your turn—and I'll listen to you.

(Author Unknown)

Hindrances to Effective Listening

Even when one "knows" how to listen, a number of factors can prevent a person from listening effectively. Work through Experiential Exercise 4.3 and explore some of the hindrances to listening. I suspect your list of "hindrances to listening" created in Experiential Exercise 4.3 has items similar to those I have listed below.

1. *Preconceived Notions:* Having preconceived ideas about the person based on how he or she is dressed, or other factors, leads you to make assumptions about what the person has said—sometimes incorrect assumptions.

2. *Anticipatory reaction:* Anticipating what the person is about to say prevents you from actually hearing what he or she has said.

3. *Cognitive distractions:* Thinking about what you are going to say blocks you from hearing what the person is actually saying.

4. *Personal Issues:* Having your own unfinished business or personal issues preoccupies your mind and inhibits your ability to listen.

5. *Emotional Response*: Having a strong emotional reaction to the person's content prevents you from being able to hear the person accurately.

6. *Distractions*: Being distracted by such things as noises, temperature of the room, hunger pains, and so forth makes your mind wander.

Experiential Exercise 4.3:
Hindrances to Listening

In class, get into groups of three students. Within your group, each person will take the number 1, 2, or 3. Number 1, you choose any of the topics listed below and start presenting the pro side of the situation while Number 2 listens. Then, Number 2, you present the con side while Number 1 listens. Keep going back and forth for a few minutes. Number "3," you are the objective person—help out as needed and take notes concerning each person's ability to reflect accurately. Also note any important body language you notice. Offer feedback when the role-play is completed. When you have finished the first situation, have numbers "2" and "3" role-play the second situation, and then numbers "3" and "1" role-play the third situation with the "other" person being the "objective helper."

Once you have finished, the instructor will ask for feedback concerning what prevented each of you from hearing the other person. Make a list these "hindrances to listening." Make sure you discuss some of the following items: preoccupation, defensiveness, emotional blocks, and distractions.

Some Possible Topics: Abortion, torturing of suspected terrorists to gain information, racial profiling by police, capital punishment, national health care (Obamacare), free college tuition, or other topics of your choosing.

Good Listening

Good listening is an active process, is intimately related to client outcomes, and involves the following (Egan, Owen, & Reese, 2014; Ivey, Ivey, & Zalaquett, 2016):

1. Talking minimally
2. Concentrating on what is being said
3. Not interrupting
4. Not giving advice
5. Not expecting to get something from the relationship
6. Hearing the speaker's content
7. Hearing the speaker's affect
8. Using good non-verbals to show you are hearing the person, such as having good and appropriate eye contact, using head nods, saying "uh-huh," and so forth.
9. Asking clarifying questions such as "I didn't hear all of that, can you say it again" or "Can you explain that in another way so I'm sure I understand you?"
10. Not asking questions (other than clarifying questions).

Preparing for Listening

When you are ready to listen, the following practical suggestions should assist you in your ability to hear a client effectively (Egan et al., 2014; Ivey, et al., 2016).

1. *Calm yourself down.* Prior to meeting with your client, calm yourself down-meditate, pray, jog, or take deep breaths.

2. *Stop talking and don't interrupt.* You cannot listen while you are talking.

3. *Show interest.* With your body language and tone of voice, show the person that you're interested in what he or she is saying.

4. *Don't jump to conclusions.* Take in all of what the person says and don't assume you understand the person more than he or she understands himself or herself.

5. *Actively listen.* Many people do not realize that listening is an active process that takes deep concentration. If your mind is wandering, you are not listening.

6. *Concentrate on feelings.* Listen, identify, and acknowledge what the person is feeling.

7. *Concentrate on content.* Listen, identify, and acknowledge what the person in saying.

8. *Maintain appropriate eye contact.* With your eyes, show the person you are listening; however, be sensitive to cultural differences in the amount of eye contact given.

9. *Have an open body posture.* Face the person and show the person you are ready to listen through your body language but be sensitive to cultural differences.

10. *Be sensitive to personal space.* Be close enough to the client to show him or her that you are ready to listen but have a sense of the amount of personal space that is comfortable to your client.

11. *Don't ask questions.* Questions are often an indication that you are not listening (you have an agenda). Try to avoid questions unless they are clarifying ones (e.g., "Can you tell me more about that?").

Listening comes with practice. Experiential Exercise 4.4 is a good beginning point.

Experiential Exercise 4.4:
Practicing Listening

Pair by threes to practice your listening skills. Have one person role-play a client while the other listens. The third person will observe and give feedback regarding how well the listener heard what the "client" said. The listener should first prepare for listening as just noted. Then, he or she should make sure that there are as few hindrances to listening as possible. Next, this person should try to listen actively by paraphrasing what his or her partner has said. After the first role-play, have different students play the client, listener, and observer. Then, do a third role-play giving the last student an opportunity to be the listener.

REFLECTION OF FEELINGS, REFLECTION OF CONTENT, AND PARAPHRASING

These three basic forms of responding, *reflection of feeling*, *reflection of content*, and *paraphrasing*, are important for the beginning of the helping relationship. However, use them too much, and the client will think you're a novice who can only parrot back what he or she has said. Used judiciously, however, they can be very helpful in ensuring that the client will keep talking.

Reflection of Feelings

As the term implies, reflection of feeling relies on "concentrating on the feelings the client is stating and repeating them back to the client with either the same feeling word the client used," or a word that is similar to the one the client used (e.g., the client says "sad" and you respond with "down"). Generally, such reflections use statements such as:

> I think you might be feeling ......
> It sounds like you're feeling ......
> ..... is the feeling I'm hearing from you.

Your ability to discern a feeling is critical to being able to reflect feelings accurately and be empathic (discussed later) (see Experiential Exercise 4.5).

Experiential Exercise 4.5:
Practicing Reflection of Feelings

Pair up with two other students. One be the helper, one the client, and one an observer. The client should discuss a problem or situation, and the helper should only reflect feelings using the framework just discussed. The observer monitors the effectiveness of the reflections and gives feedback to the helper when the role-play is over. Do this for a few minutes. Then switch roles. Make sure each person has a chance to be the helper.

Appendix B offers a list of feeling words. If you need practice discerning feelings, then go through the list and make sure you understand each word's meaning. Then, spend some time talking about each of these words with individuals so you are clear on the different feeling words. Practice reflection of feelings with friends and classmates on your own, using this list.

Reflection of Content

Like reflection of feelings, reflection of content focuses on repeating back to the client specific statements the client has made, but instead focuses on the content, instead of the feelings. Similar sentence stems highlighted in the section on reflection of feelings can be used when one is reflecting content; however, instead of using the word "feeling," use the word "saying" (e.g., I think that you're saying....; I sounds like you're saying...). Here are some additional stems that can be used when reflecting content (these stems can also be used for reflection of feelings, but use the word "feeling" rather than "saying," "suggesting," or "stated that"):

> I hear you saying that....
> I think you're suggesting that....
> What most stands out for me is when you stated that.... (See Experiential Exercise 4.6).

> ## Experiential Exercise 4.6:
> ## Practicing Reflection of Content
>
> Pair up with two other students: one be the helper, one the client, and one an observer. The client should start discussing a problem situation, and the helper should only reflect content, using the examples above or other, similar types of responses. The observer monitors the effectiveness of the reflections and gives feedback when the role-play is over. Do this for a few minutes, and then switch roles. Have each person be the helper.

Paraphrasing

In a sense, paraphrasing is combining the reflection of feeling and content. It is the ability to reflect back the general feelings and information expressed by the client. This can be done by parroting the client's actual statements; however, if you repeat back verbatim to clients too often, they may get annoyed with the repetition. Therefore, it is usually suggested that one take the general meanings and feelings of clients' statements and reflect them back to them. This can be especially difficult if the client has made a rather long statement. Obviously, you can't reflect back everything. Here are some rules you might consider when paraphrasing what a client has said:

1. Listen for the feelings.
2. Listen for the content.
3. If the client talks for a relatively long time, pull out the feelings and content that seem most poignant and reflect back only those items.
4. Use words and feelings that are synonyms or similar to what the client said, rather than the exact words and feelings the client used (see Experiential Exercise 4.7).

> ## Experiential Exercise 4.7:
> ## Practicing Paraphrasing
>
> Pair up with two other students: one person be a helper, one a client, and one an observer. The client should start discussing a problem situation and the helper should practice paraphrasing. The observer monitors how effective the paraphrasing has been and gives feedback to the helper when the role-play is over. Do this for a few minutes, and then switch roles. Make sure each person has an opportunity to be the helper.

BASIC EMPATHY

Listed as one of the important helper qualities in Chapter 1, empathy is also an important skill in the helping relationship. Highlighted, for centuries, as an important quality to embrace (Gompertz, 1960), it wasn't until the twentieth century that empathy was formally incorporated into the helping relationship. Probably the person who has had the greatest impact on our modern understanding and use of empathy is Carl Rogers.

> The state of empathy, or being empathic, is to perceive the internal frame of reference of another with accuracy and with the emotional components and meanings which pertain thereto as if one were the person, but without ever losing the "as if" condition. (Rogers, 1959, pp. 210-211)

Empathy is the act of showing the client that he or she has been heard, and numerous research studies have indicated that good empathic ability is related to client progress in the helping relationship. Showing empathy can be done in many ways, including the use of reflective listening techniques and paraphrasing, like we just discussed. The popularity of Rogers's work during the twentieth century eventually led to the development of a five-point scale to measure empathy. The Carkhuff scale, named after its developer Robert Carkhuff, is a widely used instrument in the training of helpers (Carkhuff, 2009; Cormier, Nurius, & Osborn, 2013; Lam, Kolomitro, & Alamparmabil, 2011).

The Carkhuff scale ranges from a low of 1.0 to a high of 5.0, with .5 increments. Any responses below a 3.0 are considered subtractive or non-empathic, while responses of 3.0 or higher are considered empathic. Empathic responses that are around a level 3 are often called "Basic Empathy" and responses over 3.0 are called "additive" or advanced empathic responses (see Figure 4.1). *Advanced empathy* will be examined in Chapter 7: Advanced Skills and Specialized Training.

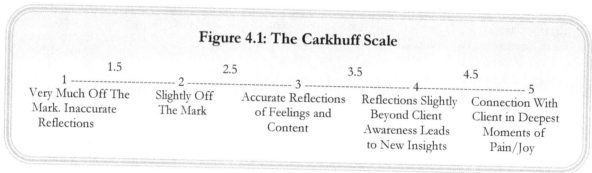

Figure 4.1: The Carkhuff Scale

1.5	2.5	3.5	4.5
1 ------- 2 ------- 3 ------- 4 ------- 5			
Very Much Off The Mark. Inaccurate Reflections	Slightly Off The Mark	Accurate Reflections of Feelings and Content	Reflections Slightly Beyond Client Awareness Leads to New Insights	Connection With Client in Deepest Moments of Pain/Joy

As is obvious in Figure 4.1, the Carkhuff scale defines level 1 and level 2 responses as detracting from what the person is saying (e.g., advice giving, reflecting inaccurate feelings or content), with a level 1 response being way off the mark and a level 2 only slightly off. For instance, suppose a client said, "I can't seem to get along with anybody. People at work seem to avoid me, and my family, well, they just are judgmental and yell at me. Life really sucks." A level 1 response might be, "Well, why don't you do something to make your life better—like try harder to get along with people!" (advice giving and being judgmental). A level 2 response might be, "You are having kind of bad time right now" (does not reflect the intensity of the feeling and is not specific enough about the content). On the other hand, a level 3 response accurately reflects the affect and meaning of what the client has said. Using the same example as above, a level 3 response might be, "Well it sounds like the criticism and yelling at home, as well as people avoiding you at work, are making for a really bad time for you right now."

Level 4 and level 5 responses, sometimes called advanced empathy, reflect feelings and meaning beyond what the person is saying and add to the meaning of the person's outward expression. For instance, in the above example, a level 4 response might be, "It sounds like you're feeling isolated from everybody at home and at work and pretty low. This expresses a new feeling—"isolated"—which the client didn't outwardly state, but is indeed feeling. And, as soon as the helper reflects this feeling, the client becomes aware of it. This is not a hypothesis or a guess; it is a feeling that the helper actually experiences from the client, and one in which the client is on the verge of experiencing himself or herself. Level 5 responses are usually made in long-term therapeutic relationships with expert helpers. They express to the client a deep understanding of the emotions (e.g., intense pain or joy) he or she feels as well as recognition of the complexity of the situation.

Usually, in the training of helpers, it is recommended that they attempt to make basic or level 3 empathic responses. A large body of evidence suggests that such responses can be learned in a relatively short amount of time and are beneficial to clients (Carkhuff, 2009; Cormier, et al., 2013; Lam, et al., 2011). Basic empathy responses need to be mastered prior to the advanced empathic responses, which are considered value added responses; that is, although not critical to the helping relationship, they can lend depth and breadth to client understanding of self. These responses will be examined in Chapter 7: Advanced Skills and Specialized Training.

For effective empathic responding, it is not only crucial to "be on target" with the feelings and the content, but also to reflect these feelings at the moment when the client can absorb the helper's reflections. For instance, you might sense a deep sadness or anger in a client and reflect this back to him or her. However, if the client is not ready to accept these feelings, then the timing is off and the response is considered subtractive. Fact Sheet 4.1 provides some guidelines for making an effective basic empathy, or level 3, response.

Fact Sheet 4.1: Keys to Making Basic ("Level 3") Empathic Response

1. Reflect back feelings accurately.

2. Reflect back content accurately.

3. If client talks for a lengthy amount of time, reflect back most poignant feelings and content only.

4. Use paraphrasing and similar words as the client.

5. Use language attuned to the client's level of understanding.

6. Do not add new feelings or new content.

7. Do not respond with a question (e.g., Sounds like you're feeling bad about the situation?).

8. Do not make the response too lengthy (keep it to about one sentence or two short sentences).

9. Do not hypothesize or make guesses about what the client is saying.

10. If the client verbally or nonverbally says your response is "off," assume it is and move on.

11. Do not ask, "Is this correct?" (or something akin to that) at the end of your sentence. (However, listen to their response, you'll know if it's correct).

12. Don't get caught up thinking about the next response—you'll have trouble listening to the client.

Making Formula Empathic Responses

Often, when beginning helpers first practice empathic responding, it is suggested that they make a "formula response" to client statements. This kind of response generally starts with reflecting the feeling followed by paraphrasing the content. In fact, helpers often call these *reflections of feelings* or *active listening* responses. In the following example, note how the words "you feel" precede the feelings the client is expressing and the word "because" precedes the content of what the client is saying. After looking at the example below, do Experiential Exercise 4.8.

Client: My boyfriend has left me, and I just can't stop crying. I'm so depressed.

Helper: You feel <u>depressed</u> *because* <u>your boyfriend has left you.</u>

Experiential Exercise 4.8:
Making Formula Responses

Use a formula response to the scenarios below. In the first few scenarios, use the feeling words given to you by the client. However, as the scenarios continue, you will have to imply what the individual is feeling. Try to imply what is obvious; that is, don't try to read too much into the individual's feeling state.

1. Pregnant teenager to human service professional:

Client: I have to get an abortion. If my parents find out they're going to kill me. If they knew I've been sleeping with John, they'd throw me out for sure. I'm scared.

Helper: You feel _____ because _____.

2. Individual with a disability to human service professional:

Client: I'm pissed off. I know they didn't hire me because I'm disabled. I want to know what my legal rights are. Do you know what I can do?

Helper: You feel _____ because _____.

3. Minority client to human service professional:

Client: I'm really suspicious. I think I'm getting the shaft from my realtor. I keep telling her I want to move to this one community, and she can't find anything for sale there. I don't believe it!

Helper: You feel _____ because _____.

4. Teenager to human service professional:

Client: I'm not worried. My boyfriend doesn't use condoms. Why should he? He's not going to get AIDS—he doesn't sleep around. I'm the only one who sees anyone else!

Helper: You feel _____ because _____.

5. Abused older person to human service professional:

Client: I guess I deserve to be hit. I can't remember where I keep anything anymore. Besides, my daughter really loves me.

Helper: You feel _____ because _____.

Experiential Exercise 4.8:
Making Formula Responses (Cont'd)

6. *Accused person to human service professional:*
Client: I didn't do nothing. Those charges are trumped up. They just want to get me because they know I've been in trouble before!

Helper: You feel _____ because _____.

7. *Pro-life person to human service professional:*
Client: I refuse to let any more babies die. I'll do anything to close down those murdering abortion clinics.

Helper: You feel _____ because _____.

8. *Pro-choice person to human service professional:*
Client: I believe a woman has a right to choose what to do with her body, and I'm sick and tired of these pro-lifers interfering with other people's right to choose!

Helper: You feel _____ because _____.

9. *Estranged wife to human service professional:*
Client: My husband wasn't faithful to me, so I left him. Now I want him back. I miss him so much, but I can't let him back for what he did to me.

Helper: You feel _____ because _____.

10. *Drug user to human service professional:*
Client: I can stop using. This stuff is not that important to me. If you find me a job, I'll quit!

Helper: You feel _____ because _____.

Making Natural Empathic Responses

As helpers become more comfortable with formula responses, they can begin to make empathic responses using more natural conversational tones. These natural responses maintain the reflection of feeling and the paraphrasing of content but aren't as stilted as the formula responses. For instance, in the following example, look at the "natural" response made to the client.

Client: I'm at my wit's end. I'm as depressed as ever. I keep trying to change my life and nothing works. I try communicating better, I change my job, I change my looks. I even take antidepressants, but nothing helps.

Helper: You keep trying to change your life, but nothing seems to be helping. You're still as down as you've ever been.

In the above example, you can see how the feeling word is still reflected and the basic content is still included, but it is said in a more conversational tone. Now, using the same scenarios as you used earlier, make natural responses to the situations in Experiential Exercise 4.9.

Experiential Exercise 4.9:
Making Natural Responses

In contrast to the formula response, natural responses are more conversational; however, they still have the basic elements of reflection of clients' feelings and content. See if you can make natural responses to the same situations in which you earlier made formula responses:

1. Pregnant teenager to human service professional:
Client: I have to get an abortion. If my parents find out they're going to kill me. If they knew I've been sleeping with John, they'd throw me out for sure. I'm scared.

*Natural Response:*_____
_____.

2. Individual with a disability to human service professional:
Client: I'm pissed off. I know they didn't hire me because I'm disabled. I want to know what my legal rights are. Do you know what I can do?

Natural Response: _____
_____.

3. Minority client to human service professional:
Client: I'm really suspicious. I think I'm getting the shaft from my realtor. I keep telling her I want to move to this one community, and she can't find anything for sale there. I don't believe it!

Natural Response: _____
_____.

4. Teenager to human service professional:
Client: I'm not worried. My boyfriend doesn't use condoms. Why should he? He's not going to get AIDS—he doesn't sleep around. I'm the only one who sees anyone else!

Natural Response: _____
_____.

Experiential Exercise 4.9:
Making Natural Responses (Cont'd)

5. *Abused older person to human service professional:*

Client: I guess I deserve to be hit. I can't remember where I keep anything anymore. Besides, my daughter really loves me.

Natural Response: _____ .
_____

6. *Accused person to human service professional:*

Client: I didn't do nothing. Those charges are trumped up. They just want to get me because they know I've been in trouble before!

Natural Response: _____ .
_____

7. *Pro-life person to human service professional:*

Client: I refuse to let any more babies die. I'll do anything to close down those murdering abortion clinics.

Natural Response: _____ .
_____

8. *Pro-choice person to human service professional:*

Client: I believe a woman has a right to choose what to do with her body, and I'm sick and tired of these pro-lifers interfering with other people's right to choose!

Natural Response: _____ .
_____

9. *Estranged wife to human service professional:*

Client: My husband wasn't faithful to me, so I left him. Now I want him back. I miss him so much. But I can't let him back for what he did to me.

Natural Response: _____ .
_____

10. *Drug user to human service professional:*

Client: I can stop using. This stuff is not that important to me. If you find me a job, I'll quit!

Natural Response: _____ .
_____

Practicing Empathic Responses

Most people don't grow up knowing how to make empathic responses, and that is why learning empathy is much like first learning to ride a bicycle—the more you practice, the better you'll get. Experiential Exercises 4.10, 4.11, and 4.12 give you an opportunity to practice this very important skill.

Experiential Exercise 4.10:
Practicing Empathic Responding: Victoria

The following is a scenario of a client named Victoria. For each of Victoria's statements, make a formula and a natural response. When you have finished, share your responses in small groups and/or in class.

1. *Victoria: I wanted to see you today because I felt like my life is falling apart.*
Formula Response: You feel _____ because _____.
Natural Response: _____
_____.

2. *Victoria: Well, since I dropped out of college, I just can't seem to pull things together--not that they were really together when I was in college. But, I can't get a good job, my parents hardly talk with me, and my partner, well, she's always pissed at me.*
Formula Response: You feel _____ because _____.
Natural Response: _____
_____.

3. *Victoria: I've been seriously thinking of just leaving the area and starting all over. Leaving my parents. Leaving Sierra, and leaving it all. Just a fresh start. What do you think?*
Formula Response: You feel _____ because _____.
Natural Response: _____
_____.

4. *Victoria: I guess I'm ambivalent about everything. Maybe I should start college again and try to make amends with Sierra. And, maybe I should sit down and just have a talk with my family. On the other hand . . . I don't know. I just don't know what to do.*
Formula Response: You feel _____ because _____.
Natural Response: _____
_____.

Experiential Exercise 4.10: Practicing
Empathic Responding: Victoria (Cont'd)

5. *Victoria: Well, I guess I shouldn't be making any rash decisions right at the moment. Perhaps I should just give myself some time and try to sort this out in counseling. Yes, I think that's a good idea.*
Formula Response: You feel _____ because _____.
Natural Response: _____
_____

6. *Victoria: I appreciate you listening to me today. I really feel that I at least have a little bit of a sense of where I'm going. Should I come back next week?*
Formula Response: You feel _____ because _____.
Natural Response: _____
_____

Experiential Exercise 4.11:
More Practice with Empathy: Jake

The following is a scenario of a client named Jake. For each of Jake's statements, make a formula and a natural response. When you have finished, share your responses in small groups or in class.

1. *Jake: I don't care what you think, I'm not going to go back to that house. My parents just don't understand me. And I won't go back to school either; all they do there is put me in detention all the time. I'm going to fail no matter what I do, so why should I go back!*
Formula Response: You feel _____ because _____.
Natural Response: _____
_____

2. *Jake: I didn't start that fire, and I didn't steal that car. I get blamed for it all. Nobody ever believes me, and neither will you.*
Formula Response: You feel _____ because _____.
Natural Response: _____
_____

3. *Jake: I was out cruising with some friends when one of my buddies saw that car. It had the keys in it, and it was running. He just jumped in it and started driving it. I just went along for a ride. What kind of f-king idiot leaves a car like that running anyway? He deserved it to be stolen.*
Formula Response: You feel _____ because _____.
Natural Response: _____
_____

Experiential Exercise 4.11: More
Practice with Empathy: Jake (Cont'd)

4. Jake: So, if you want to get anywhere with me, you'll just leave me alone. No need to do this talking. You won't get anything out of me.
Formula Response: You feel _____ because _____.
Natural Response: _____
_____.

5. Jake: What will I get out of this talking anyway? Tell me, what do I get out of it? Like, if you pay me, maybe I'll say something here.
Formula Response: You feel _____ because _____.
Natural Response: _____
_____.

6. Jake: The detention center sucks. My parents keep coming to visit me-as if they care. Even my sister comes to see me. It's dark and . . . (begins to get teary-eyed).
Formula Response: You feel _____ because _____.
Natural Response: _____
_____.

7. Jake: Well, I guess I'd like to get out of here. Maybe you could help me get a job or something once I get out. What do you think?
Formula Response: You feel _____ because _____.
Natural Response: _____
_____.

Experiential Exercise 4.12:
Empathic Bombardment

Here's a fun exercise to practice empathic responding. Your instructor will sit in the middle of the classroom. Form two circles around him or her. The instructor is the client while those in the first circle are the "helpers." In the second circle are the "observers" who will rate the responses of the helpers. So all of you "observers," make sure you have a pencil and a piece of paper with you. The instructor will role-play a situation and any person in the first circle can respond, but only with an empathic response. The instructor will turn to the "helper" who is responding, and meanwhile, the observers will write down the response and rate it on the Carkhuff scale. After you have done this exercise for a few minutes, observers can share their ratings of the various responses. Then, do another role-play with the observers and helpers switching roles.

Conclusion

Empathy is probably the most important helping skill for the human service professional. It is critical in the development of a strong working relationship, is crucial for maintaining a bond with the client, and can help the client understand deeper parts of himself or herself. Basic empathy can be learned rather quickly, can help clients understand themselves, and is generally considered the most important response a helper can make to a client in the helping relationship. Although advanced empathy can deepen the relationship even further, it is not considered an essential skill. Instead, advanced empathy is considered a value-added skill, which will be discussed in Chapter 7: Advanced Skills and Specialized Training.

SUMMARY

This chapter examined the important foundational skills of silence and pause time; listening; reflection of feelings, reflections of content, and paraphrasing; and basic empathy. We noted that silence is a very powerful skill that allows the client and the helper to review what has been said in an interview. By being silent, clients will sometimes want to fill the void and continue to talk about a topic. Too much silence, however, could push a client out of the helping relationship. We reminded you that when one is not silent, one is not listening. Related to silence, pause time is the amount of time a helper allows between responses, and the length of pause time that a client feels comfortable with may depend on his or her cultural background. Therefore, helpers should be sensitive to the amount of pause time clients are comfortable with.

Listening, one of the most important helping skills, does not come easily to many individuals. A number of hindrances to listening were highlighted in the chapter, including preconceived notions, anticipatory reactions, cognitive distractions, personal issues, emotional responses, and distractions. Several practical suggestions for listening were noted, including talking minimally, concentrating on what is being said, not interrupting, not giving advice, being able to give without expecting to get, accurately hearing content and feelings, using good non-verbal communication to show attentiveness, asking for clarification when necessary, and not asking questions. A number of suggestions were also made when preparing for listening, including calming yourself down, not talking and not interrupting, showing interest, not jumping to conclusions, actively listening, concentrating on feelings, concentrating on content, maintaining eye contact, having an open body posture, being sensitive to personal space, and not asking questions.

Next in the chapter, three forms of basic responding were highlighted, including reflection of feeling, reflection of content, and paraphrasing. Specific ways to reflect feelings and content were noted and practiced. Paraphrasing, which, in many ways, is the combination of the reflection of feeling and reflection of content, was also noted and practiced in the chapter.

Empathy, the ability to perceive the internal world of the client as if one were that person "without losing the 'as if' feeling," is probably the helper's most important skill and was the next focus of the chapter. Although empathy has been discussed for centuries, during the 20th century it was popularized for helping professionals by Carl Rogers and was operationalized by Carkhuff, who developed a five-point scale to measure a helper's effectiveness. It was noted that helpers who make a level 3 or higher empathic response are generally helpful to clients; those who make less than a level 3 response may be harmful. A level 3, or "basic empathy" response, was defined as one that accurately reflects the affect and content of what the client is saying. Advanced empathic responses are Level 4 or Level 5 responses. Level 4 reflects feelings and meaning beyond what the client is aware of, and level 5 responses express deep understanding of a client's emotions, as well as recognition of the complexity of the client's situation. On the contrary, Level 1 or 2 responses are judgmental or off the mark in reflecting affect and meaning.

We noted that usually, in the training of helpers, it is recommended that they attempt to make basic or level 3 empathic responses. We pointed out that a large body of evidence suggests that such responses can be learned in a relatively short amount of time and are beneficial to clients. Basic empathic responses need to be mastered prior to the advanced empathic responses, which are considered value added responses; that is, although not critical to the helping relationship, they can lend depth and breadth to client understanding of self. These responses will be examined in Chapter 7: Advanced Skills and Specialized Training.

KEY WORDS AND TERMS

Active listening
Advanced empathy
Basic empathic responses
Carkhuff, Robert
Carkhuff Scale
Empathy
Formula responses
Good listening
Hindrances to effective listening
Listening

Natural responses
Silence and pause time
Paraphrasing
Pointing out conflicting feelings or thoughts
Preparing for listening
Reflecting deeper feelings
Reflection of content
Reflection of feeling
Rogers, Carl
Self-disclosure

Answers to Exercise 4.2

Usually: 2, 4, 9, 10; Sometimes: 7, 13; Rarely: 1, 3, 5, 6, 8, 11, 12, 14, 15

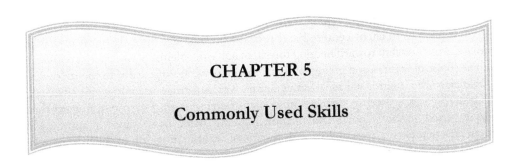

CHAPTER 5

Commonly Used Skills

LEARNING OBJECTIVES

1. Highlight the more commonly used skills in the helping relationship.

2. Learn the important role that commonly used skills play in the helping relationship, including

   a. Affirmation, encouragement, and support

   b. Offering alternatives, information giving, and advice giving

   c. Inadvertent and intentional modeling

   d. Content and process self-disclosure

   e. Collaboration

   f. Advocacy

INTRODUCTION

The commonly used skills in this chapter go beyond the non-directive skills thus far talked about. While all the skills in Chapters 3 and 4 were client-centered and focused on building the helping relationship, the skills in this chapter move the relationship toward helping the client solve problems. Skills used to reinforce goal seeking behaviors, such as support, affirmation giving, and encouragement, are discussed in the following pages. Ways of suggesting change to the client, such as offering alternatives, information giving, and advice giving, are also examined. Modeling is a skill used to develop new client behaviors as they move toward their goals. Self-disclosure may be used to both build the relationship and offer new ways of approaching problems. Collaboration ensures that clients are satisfied with their goal-seeking direction in the helping relationship, and advocacy is a tool taught to clients, or conducted by helpers, to ensure that clients' rights are being upheld. All of these skills are engrained in the helping relationship and tend to emerge once a working alliance has been established (see Figure 5.1).

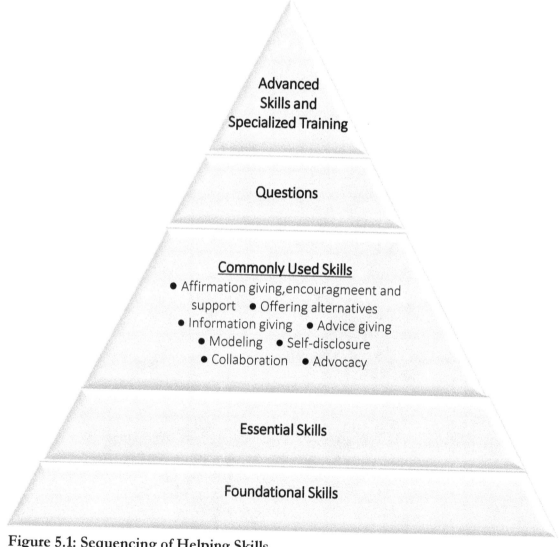

Figure 5.1: Sequencing of Helping Skills

AFFIRMATION GIVING, ENCOURAGEMENT, AND SUPPORT

The human services professional may improve the client's sense of love and belonging, and, ultimately, raise his or her self-esteem, by affirming, encouraging, and supporting the client throughout the helping process (Steinem, 1992). Let's examine these critical skills in the helping relationship (Dean, 2015; Trice-Black & Foster, 2011).

Affirmation Giving

Whether called "reinforcement" or a "genuine positive response," affirmation is an important aspect of positively acknowledging a client's way of being in the world which acts as a significant tool for raising a client's self-esteem. Statements like "Good job," "You are lovable and capable," or "You are a good person" help the client feel supported and worthwhile. Other statements and behaviors, such as saying "Well done!" "I'm happy for you," and giving caring hand-shakes, warm hugs, and approving smiles, are other effective ways of communicating affirmation. In point of fact, it is the rare helper who does not affirm his or her clients in some manner. Occasionally, when helpers become cynical or burnt out, or have simply lost their sense of caring for their clients, they are not able to impart meaningful affirmations. As a result, the helper could unintentionally create a negative atmosphere that is more damaging than beneficial to the client's well-being.

Unfortunately, many families in the United States do not freely hand out affirmations. If you did not grow up in an affirming environment, then you may have difficulty affirming others. Reflection Exercise 5.1 and Experiential Exercise 5.1 can help you look at whether or not you have been affirmed in your life and provide ways of how to practice affirming others.

Reflection Exercise 5.1:
Have You Been Affirmed?*

Part 1: On the left side of a piece of paper, write down five things you are good at. Then, on the right side, write down who, if anyone, has affirmed you for what you wrote down. If you have not been affirmed for a particular activity on the left side of the paper, then write "No One" on the right side (see my example below). When you have finished, form groups of four to eight students and move on to Part 2.

Things I'm Good At	People Who Have Affirmed Me
Writing	My Students, Colleagues, My Wife
Running	No One
Discussing Issues	Friends
Being a Dad	My Wife, My Daughter, My Mom-in-Law
Being an Administrator	My Dean, My Colleagues

Part 2: Pick one of the items you listed in Part 1 (if there was any item to which you were not affirmed, pick that one). Now sit in the middle of your group and tell your fellow group members how you are good at that item. Then, have each group member go around and affirm you in that area. When each member of your group has finished, join the rest of the class to discuss the following (see next page).

Continued on Next Page

Reflection Exercise 5.1:
Have You Been Affirmed?* (Cont'd)

1. How did it feel to be affirmed by others?
2. Did you have an easy or difficult time affirming others? Why or why not?
3. Do you find that you are often affirmed in life?
4. Do you think that affirming others, especially clients, would feel genuine?
5. Do you believe that affirmations can really raise a person's self-esteem?
6. Do you think you can increase the numbers of affirmations you give?

*Note: Part 1 may be used with clients if you are seeing them individually. Parts 1 and 2 may be used with clients if you are running a group.

Experiential Exercise 5.1:
Giving and Getting Affirmations

Part 1: In small groups or as a class, students may be given the opportunity to tell others something positive to raise others' self-esteem. Statements could be in the form of an acknowledgement of the way one interacts in class, how one dresses, how one presents oneself, and so forth. See how it feels to offer other persons an affirmation. After you've done this for a few minutes, talk about how it felt to give and receive affirmations

Part 2: The instructor may develop some mechanism for students to give anonymous affirmations throughout the semester. For instance, each student's name could be written on an envelope and posted on the wall so students can leave affirmations for one another. Or, students could visit a website where they are able to share affirming posts with one another. There is no harm in allowing students to identify who wrote their affirmations, although this is not necessary or mandatory. One important rule is that the statement must be positive. Periodically, the instructor can process the kinds of affirmations students are receiving and how they feel about receiving (or not receiving) affirmations.

Encouragement

Similar to affirmations but focused more on helping a client achieve a specific goal, encouragement can also be a vital tool for raising a client's self-esteem. Encouragement includes statements, such as "I know you can do it," "Just keep trying," "You've made a great start," and so forth. Within the helping relationship, encouragement is generally focused on being a cheerleader for a client while he or she attempts to reach identified goals. Exercise 5.2 gives you practice in using encouragement.

Support

Somewhat more allusive than affirmation and encouragement, "offering support" is a general term acknowledging that one role of the helper is to help the client feel as if there is someone in his or her corner. Support may come in many forms, depending on the setting in which the helper works. For instance, a client

Experiential Exercise 5.2:
Encouraging Encouragement

Part 1: Get together in pairs and have one student be the helper and the other be the client. The client should discuss a personal goal which he or she is having difficulty accomplishing (e.g., losing weight, finding a job, communicating more with a loved one). The helper should encourage the client by saying things like, "I know you can do it," "You have the inner strength to accomplish this" "Keep trying and I know you'll accomplish this," and so forth. After a few minutes, switch roles. After you have completed the exercise, form groups of six to eight students and discuss how it felt to be encouraged by another person.

Part 2: Remaining in your groups, have one student agree to share a current problem he or she is dealing with. That person should sit in the middle of the group and share how he or she has been working toward fixing the problem. When appropriate, any group member can practice giving affirmation and encouragement to help the student reach his or her goal. Students should only say something if it feels genuine. If time allows, other members of the group can sit in the middle and share their personal issues. After the exercise is completed, any individual who sat in the middle of the class should discuss how it felt to receive such encouragement.

may feel supported by a helper emotionally, may know that the helper is available if he or she is in crisis, and may be able to count on the helper to advocate on his or her behalf.

Although support is an important part of the helping relationship, there may be ethical concerns depending on the type of support one is offering. Read the following ethical standard, and then complete Reflection Exercise 5.2. Try to determine which types of support might be crossing ethical boundaries.

> Human service professionals recognize that multiple relationships may increase the risk of harm to or exploitation of clients and may impair their professional judgment. When it is not feasible to avoid dual or multiple relationships, human service professionals should consider whether the professional relationship should be avoided or curtailed. (NOHS, 2015, Standard 5)

Final Thoughts

Over the years, some have warned that too much affirmation, encouragement, and support could cause the client to become dependent on the helper (Kinnier, Hofsess, Pongratz, & Lambert, 2009). However, such responses have become part of the helper's repertoire of skills, as helping relationships have taken on an increasingly humane interpersonal focus compared to the somewhat antiseptic, objective focus many helpers have used in the past. By offering such responses, the helper hopes that clients will realize that affirmation, encouragement, and support have been lacking in their lives. Such insight can be the predecessor for clients taking their first steps in developing an increased self-affirming approach to life—one in which they are open to finding new relationships that are more affirming, encouraging, and supportive.

Reflection Exercise 5.2:
The Limits of Support

In small groups, discuss whether you think each of the following helper behaviors would be ethically acceptable as a means of supporting your client. Consider how your response may vary depending on your work setting.

1. Lending money to your client.
2. Finding time for your client when he or she is in crisis.
3. Driving your client to a homeless shelter.
4. Helping your client who is struggling with poverty, paint his or her apartment.
5. Calling the school of your client's child to ensure the child gets needed services.
6. Paying your client to do a small job (e.g., fix your car).
7. Giving your client extra time during a session when he or she is dealing with an emotionally charged situation.
8. Spending time, after work, helping your client learn parenting skills.
9. Picking up your client's children and taking them to an after-school program, because your client is working and the children have no other way of getting there.
10. Having a cup of coffee, off hours, with a client to ensure he or she is doing okay.

OFFERING ALTERNATIVES, INFORMATION GIVING, AND ADVICE GIVING

Offering alternatives, information giving, and advice giving are helper-centered skills in the sense that they are ideas, originated by the helper, to assist the client in solving problems (Anderson, 2012; Ivey, Ivey, Zalaquett, 2016; Kirschenbaum, 2015; Neukrug & Schwitzer, 2006). Although these skills can be helpful in problem-solving, each carries the potential to damage the helping relationship. Clients may feel judged or become overly dependent, as such responses may lead them to believe their relationship with the helper is the answer for most of their problems (see Figure 5.2). Let's take a closer look at the skills of offering alternatives, information giving, and advice giving.

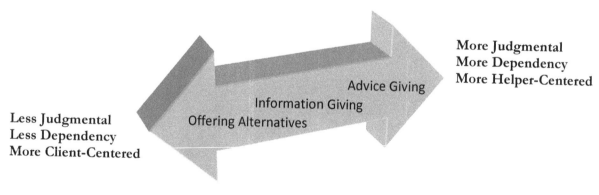

More Judgmental
More Dependency
More Helper-Centered

Advice Giving
Information Giving
Offering Alternatives

Less Judgmental
Less Dependency
More Client-Centered

Figure 5.2: Potential Damaging Effects of Skills

Offering Alternatives

Offering alternatives suggests to the client that there may be a number of ways to tackle a problem and provides a variety of alternatives from which the client may choose. Compared to information giving and advice giving, offering alternatives has the least potential for harm. This is because it does not presume there is one solution to the problem, it has the least potential for setting up the helper as the final expert, and to some degree, it allows the client to pursue various options while maintaining a sense that he or she is directing the session (see Figure 5.2). See Experiential Exercise 5.3 to learn about offering alternatives.

Experiential Exercise 5.3:
Practicing Offering Alternatives

Form triads, and in each group have one student be a helper, one a client, and one an observer who will assist the helper, if necessary. The client should talk for a few minutes about a real or made-up problem, and the helper is to offer possible alternatives. It is probably best if you first use your basic listening and empathy skills in an effort to fully understand the problem being presented. After you understand the problem, offer alternatives.

If the helper is having difficulty coming up with alternatives, the observer can make suggestions. After a few minutes, if time allows, switch roles. If even more time allows, you can switch roles again. After you have finished, discuss in your triad the questions listed below. Students in each triad may want to share their responses with the whole class.

1. Was it easy for the helper to come up with alternatives?
2. Did the client already know the alternatives being offered?
3. Was offering alternatives helpful?
4. How did the client react to being offered alternatives?
5. Do you think another skill would have been more helpful than offering alternatives? Why or why not?

Information Giving

Information giving offers the client important "objective" information (Ivey et al., 2016; Neukrug & Schwitzer, 2006). Since clients often know more than helpers might suspect, the key to making a successful information-giving response is to offer information of which the client is truly unaware. Thus, the information offered should be seen as useful and likely to be used by the client. However, since information-giving responses assume the helper has some valuable information the client needs, such responses tend to set up the helper as the expert, increasing the potential for the client to become dependent on the relationship. Exercise 5.4 can help you see the pitfalls of information giving.

Advice Giving

When advice giving, the helper offers expert opinions and hopes the client will follow through on the suggestions. This kind of response has the potential for developing a dependent relationship, as the client could end up relying on the helper for problem-solving. In addition, advice giving may mimic control issues from the client's family of origin (e.g., parents giving advice) and thus, can be seen as a value-laden response.

Experiential Exercise 5.4:
Giving Unnecessary Information

Get into pairs and have one student be the helper and the other the client. The helper should give the client information of which the client is already aware. You can use one of the scenarios listed below or come up with one of your own (make sure the client is already familiar with the chosen topic and has information that may be given by the helper). The client may respond in any way he or she wishes. For example, some clients might respond politely but think to themselves that they are already aware of the information being offered. Other clients might become belligerent, and tell the helper, "I already know about that; you're not helping me." After you've role-played for a few minutes, switch roles. When you are finished role-playing, get into small groups to discuss how it felt to be offered alternatives on a topic you already knew thoroughly.

Possible Scenarios:

1. A client is concerned about becoming HIV-positive. Thus, the helper decides to give information on how one can acquire HIV.
2. A client is concerned about becoming pregnant. Therefore, the helper decides to give information on different kinds of birth control.
3. A client is worried about saving money for his children, and the helper gives information on how to budget money.
4. A client is interested in majoring in human services (or psychology, sociology, etc.), and the helper gives information on what that entails.
5. "Other" scenario of your choice.

Because of this, some consider advice giving a response that should be avoided (Anderson, 2012; Ivey, et al., 2016). For instance, it is not unusual for parents of teenagers to tell their children a wide range of ways to live in the world (e.g., how to study, who to date, what to do with their future). However, many teenagers will be highly offended by such advice. Although our clients may not act like teenagers, there is a little bit of teenager in all of us, and most people look askew at advice giving—especially advice giving that is already thought about on their own. However, if given gently and if the advice is something the client has not already thought of, this response can assist a client in finding solutions quickly. Remember, there are many ways to give advice, and a helper need not act like a tyrant while doing so (see Experiential Exercise 5.5).

Final Thoughts

Offering alternatives, information giving, and advice giving can offer valuable ways of helping clients problem solve. They also have some potential for being destructive to the relationship, however. Thus, the helpfulness of these responses always needs to be balanced with their potential for damaging the helping relationship (Ivey et al., 2016; Orlinksy, Ronnestad, & Willutzki, 2004). The helper must judge whether or not these responses are helpful to the client based on a careful understanding of the client's needs, and whether an alternative response could be more effective. When the helping relationship is most effective, clients are more likely to brainstorm alternatives independently or ask the helper for advice prior to the helper actually offering it.

Experiential Exercise 5.5:
Levels of Advice Giving

Have one student sit in the middle of three concentric circles. The student in the middle is to role-play a client problem. The innermost circle is to offer advice in a gruff, authoritarian manner. For instance, students in this circle might start responses with statements like, "You should . . . !" or, "It's imperative that you . . . !" The middle circle is to offer advice in a milder form, but still with a dogmatic tone. Some examples of how these students might start responses include "Why don't you . . . " or, "You might want to . . ." The outermost circle is to offer advice in a mild, tentative way, while attempting to not be authoritarian. Students in this circle might start their responses with statements like, "I've been wondering if you ever thought about . . ., "or "Have you ever given thought to . . . "

You may want to have a few students take turns sitting in the middle of the circles. After you have done this exercise for 10 or 15 minutes, the students who sat in the middle should share how they experienced each of the circles. Also, individuals in the circles might want to share how they experienced the exercise. In the future, when you are in the role of an advice giver, consider the different ways that you might give such advice.

MODELING

In all varieties of helping relationships, helpers will act as models for their clients *whether or not they want to be* (Bussey, 2015; Cooper, Heron, & Heward, 2007; Martin & Pear, 2015). Sometimes called *social learning, imitation,* or *behavioral rehearsal,* helpers constantly model for their clients. For instance, when helpers are empathic, clients may learn how to listen to loved ones more effectively. When helpers model assertiveness, clients may learn how to positively confront someone in their lives. And when helpers model being effective mediators, clients may learn new ways of dealing with conflict. Helpers are change agents when they model for clients, which may occur either *inadvertently* or *intentionally.*

Inadvertent Modeling

Clients tend to look up to helpers and even idealize them. Such admiration creates the perfect condition for the development of inadvertent modeling, or unconsciously performing another person's qualities and attributes. This process has the potential to powerfully effect and dramatically influence the client's change process (Bussey, 2015; Zur, 2016).

When the helper models inadvertently, he or she does not purposefully set out to change specific client behaviors (Bussey, 2015). Instead, this helper acts as a model by simply using helping skills within the relationship. For instance, if a helper is showing empathy toward a client, the client might learn how to exhibit this important skill with others as a result of experiencing empathy from the helper. Similarly, a client might learn effective nonverbal attending behavior, such as eye contact and the use of silence, by being attended to in that manner by the helper. Inadvertent modeling occurs in all helping relationships and should never be underestimated! You can see how the helper's ability at making effective responses may greatly impact his or her clients' lives. Reflection Exercise 5.3 helps you look at how others have inadvertently modeled for you.

Reflection Exercise 5.3:
Models That Influenced You

On the top row of the grid below are the names of individuals whom I have modeled or would like to model. In the second row, I have filled in qualities I have adopted from these significant others in my life. In the third row are qualities I have observed from others that I would like to adopt in my own life. See how I completed the grid, and in the second grid, fill in the appropriate spaces. If you have additional names you would like to add, create a new grid on a blank piece of paper.

NAME OF PERSON YOU MODELED

	My Father	Roger: My First Counselor	Wife	?????
Qualities You Modeled From That Person	Integrity: My father was always honest and thoughtful. I have always tried to show integrity to others and see my father in my mind's eye when I do.	Empathy: Roger was great at exhibiting empathy, and I learned how to be empathic from experiencing it from him.	Patience: I watched my wife with my children and learned how to be patient with them when they did not do what I wanted them to do.	
Qualities You Viewed and Would Like to Adopt	Thoughtfulness: My father always took time before making major decisions or responding to others' opinions. I find myself doing the same at times.	Pausing—Roger had a great ability at pausing prior to responding to people.	My wife has the ability to not worry about things. I would like to worry less about some things, such as health of myself and of my children.	

NAME OF PERSON YOU MODELED

Qualities You Modeled From That Person				
Qualities You Viewed and Would Like to Adopt				

Intentional Modeling

Many helpers use intentional modeling as an important tool in their arsenal of change methods. By providing multiple ways of helping clients change targeted behavior (Ivey et al., 2016; Neukrug, 2016), intentional model can occur (1) through deliberate displays of specific behaviors on the part of the helper (e.g., deliberately expressing empathy, being nonjudgmental, or being assertive hoping the client will pick up such traits), (2) through role-playing with the client and displaying models of specific behaviors (e.g., the helper might role-play job interviewing skills), and (3) through teaching the concept of modeling to clients and encouraging them to identify individuals who have positive characteristics they would like to emulate in their everyday lives (e.g., a person who has a fear of public speaking might choose an orator he or she admires and view the person live, on YouTube, etc.).

Intentional modeling involves a two-part process that includes first observing a targeted behavior and then practicing it. Thus, clients need to have appropriate models to imitate and practice the desired behavior inside or outside the session. With intentional modeling, any targeted behaviors the client wishes to acquire need to have a high probability of being adopted. For instance, an individual who has a fear of making speeches would first need to find a model to emulate. After observing this model, a hierarchy could be devised whereby the client would first make a speech to his or her helper, then to some trusted friends, then to a small group, and so forth, perhaps asking for feedback along the way to sharpen his or her performance. Using these baby steps helps to assure a high probability that targeted behaviors will be adopted by the client (in this case, making speeches).

Intentional modeling is a powerful tool that may be used by helpers to effectively change client behavior. While inadvertent modeling occurs throughout the helping relationship regardless of whether the helper and client realize it, intentional modeling requires the client to make a deliberate attempt to practice new behaviors with the consultation of the helper. This kind of modeling requires a trusting relationship, should be carefully and deliberately planned, and demands a thorough assessment of the client's needs to ensure the appropriate choice of targeted behaviors. Therefore, intentional modeling does not generally take place at the beginning of the helping relationship. It requires the helper to first take time to build rapport with the client and establish an accurate assessment of the client and his or her situation. Work through Exercise 5.6 for practice in intentional modeling.

SELF-DISCLOSURE

Generally defined as when helpers purposefully or unwittingly help clients by revealing something about themselves to the client (Bloomgarden & Mennuti, 2009; Ivey et al., 2016), self-disclosure is often seen as a mixed bag that can result in positive or negative outcomes. On the one hand, it can lead to increased client-self-disclosure, can be a way of expressing empathy by demonstrating that one understands the client's experience due to having been in similar situations, and can be a method of demonstrating new skills (e.g., the helper may describe behaviors that were beneficial in his or her life, hoping that the client may try similar behaviors) (Forrest, 2010; Zur, 2009). On the other hand, self-disclosure can make a client feel uncomfortable, as some clients will feel like it is inappropriate for the helper to share information about his or her life. In extreme cases, it can be considered an unethical practice, especially when the helper is focusing more on his or her own needs instead of the needs of the client (see Reflection Exercise 5.4).

Generally, two types of self-disclosure have been identified: content self-disclosure, in which helpers reveal personal information about themselves; and process self-disclosure, in which helpers reveal moment-to-moment information about their experience in the relationship with their clients.

Experiential Exercise 5.6:
Intentional Modeling

In the provided space, list the qualities you would like to adopt from Reflection Exercise 5.3. Then write specific ways you could practice acquiring them. In small groups, share and discuss your qualities and specific plans. Some groups might want to meet on an ongoing basis to encourage the acquisition of the qualities. How might these qualities work positively for you as a helper?

Qualities You Would Like to Acquire

1.

2.

3.

4.

Mechanism for Acquiring the Qualities Listed

1.
2.
3.

1.
2.
3.

1.
2.
3.

1.
2.
3.

Reflection Exercise 5.4:
Self-Disclosure Gone Awry

One of my former students was in therapy with a psychiatrist who, over time, increasingly began to disclose his problems to her. One day, she heard that he hanged himself. Following his death, she revealed to me her feelings of intense guilt for not having saved his life. What a legacy to leave this student! Clearly, the psychiatrist's self-disclosure was unhealthy and unethical. (Ironically, the comedian Sarah Silverman appears to have seen the same psychiatrist and also experienced the negative results of his suicide! [The Week Staff, 2010]).

Despite the situation described above, there are circumstances where self-disclosure may be appropriately used to help a client open up and may also serve as a model of positive behaviors. What do you think is the appropriate amount of self-disclosure in the helping relationship?

Content Self-Disclosure

Content self-disclosure, or the helper's revelation of some personal information to enhance the helping relationship, can have a number of positive results. For instance, such disclosure can show the client that the helper is "real," and can create a stronger alliance between the client and the helper. In addition, such disclosure can create deeper intimacy, which ultimately could foster deeper self-disclosing by the client. This kind of self-disclosure can act as a type of empathic response, such as when it is used to show a client that a helper is listening and understanding:

> *Helper:* When I went through my divorce, I felt sad and depressed. I think I'm hearing that's how you're feeling.

Finally, self-disclosure of this kind can offer the client new positive behaviors that a client can model:

> *Helper:* After my divorce, when I was ready, I decided to get back into the dating scene which upped my spirits some. Do you think you might be ready for that?

In the above examples, notice how the helper keeps the disclosures to a minimum and immediately focuses back on the client. After all, the intent of this kind of self-disclosure is to enhance the client's experience of rapport and trust, be an empathic response, or offer a solution for the client. It should not be used to give helpers an opportunity to talk about themselves. Even if self-disclosure is being used to benefit the client, some may feel put off by self-disclosure and think that helpers should keep their life stories out of the relationship, or feel that the helper's revelation of his or her own struggle is an indication of weakness. Thus, using content self-disclosure should be done with great care, and only after consideration of the client's needs.

Process Self-Disclosure

Similar to the concept of *immediacy*, process self-disclosure involves sharing the helper's moment-to-moment experience of self in relation to the client (Ivey, et al., 2016; Sackett, Corrine, Lawson, & Burge, 2012). Such process comments can have a number of positive effects. For example, they can help clients see the impact they have on a helper and make connections between how this impact is similar to the way they affect others in their lives. Also, clients may learn how moment-to-moment communication can enhance relationships. For instance, a helper might say the following to a client:

> *Helper:* You know, right now I really feel connected with you. You seem to be really opening up.

This "immediate" sharing of one's feelings models how to share feelings and thoughts in a relationship and will hopefully be followed up by an "immediate" response from the client. Such models of self-disclosure can be generalized as a new form of communicating with those who are important in the client's life. Similar to the Rogerian concept of genuineness, process self-disclosure is a mechanism that allows the helper to be real with his or her feelings toward the client. On the other hand, helpers should not confuse such disclosure with the unethical practice of sharing their feelings with a client in an effort to work through their own issues or to achieve catharsis (Rogers, 1957).

Some helpers suggest using care in sharing moment-to-moment feelings with clients. Rogers (1957) pointed out that clients are rapidly changing as they shared deeper parts of themselves, and as they change, the helper's feelings toward them will quickly change, as well. Instead of sharing moment-to-moment feelings, Rogers suggested that it is often more important to share persistent feelings, as these are more meaningful to the relationship.

When to Use Self-Disclosure

> I try not to make a fetish out of not talking about myself. If a client, on the way out the door, asks in a friendly and casual way, "Where are you going on your vacation?" I tell where I'm going. If the client were then to probe, however ("Who are you going with? Are you married?") I would be likely to respond, "Ah ... maybe we'd better talk about that next time." (Kahn, 2001, p. 150)

Self-disclosure needs to be done sparingly, at the right time, and as a means for promoting client growth rather than satisfying the counselor's needs (Harrison, 2013). A general rule of thumb that I use is: "If it feels good to self-disclose, don't." If it feels good, you're probably meeting more of your needs than the needs of your client. Some general guidelines for the use of self-disclosure, include:

1. Use self-disclosure sparingly and only if the client seems comfortable with it.

2. Use self-disclosure to build the relationship, to reveal new possible avenues of behavior for clients, or to show empathy.

3. Don't self-disclose to have one's own needs met.

4. Never self-disclose when it leads to blurred boundaries, and particularly don't self-disclose on personal topics, such as sexual issues and intimacy.

5. Consider if other responses might be more effective. (See Experiential Exercise 5.7).

Experiential Exercise 5.7:
Self-Disclosure

First, students should pair up based on whether they have had one of the following problem situations in their lives (or other common problems).

1. Divorce	5. Trust issues with friend
2. Getting fired	6. Financial problems
3. Being "dumped" by a significant other	7. Marital problem
4. Problem pregnancy	8. Disliking parent(s)

In your dyad, have one person be the helper while the other plays the helpee. The helpee should talk about the chosen situation for 5 to 10 minutes, during which the helper should attempt to make at least one self-disclosing response that relates to the situation. If possible, the response should be given in a manner that would facilitate the client's exploration of self. After you have finished, if time allows, switch roles. In class, address the following questions:

1. Was the helper's self-disclosure helpful to the client?
2. Did the helpee and helper develop a greater alliance as a result of self-disclosure?
3. Did the self-disclosure change the focus of the session in any manner?
4. Were there better possible responses than self-disclosure?

COLLABORATION

Collaboration is the intentional practice of making time to talk with your client about how much progress has been made in the helping relationship (Miller, Hubble, & Seidel, 2015; Sommers-Flanagan & Sommers-Flanagan, 2015). Collaboration shows respect for clients' feedback about their perceptions of progress and shows a willingness, on the part of the helper, to change strategies if clients are not content with what has occurred. Collaboration should be deliberate and occur at multiple, evenly distributed points during the relationship. More frequent collaboration can occur if a client is clearly unhappy with progress. Some general ways of offering collaboration, include:

1. The use of basic listening and empathy skills to offer a summary of what has occurred and provide time for the client to respond.

    Helper: So, it seems like, thus far, you believe that the helping relationship has been beneficial to you and that you are looking forward to making more progress in the future.

2. Using questions to ask clients their thoughts on progress to date.

    Helper: What are your thoughts about how things are going thus far?

3. Using questions to ask clients about new directions they would like to take.

    Helper: So, what ideas do you have about where you would like to take these discussions in the future?

4. Using helper self-disclosure to reveal what progress the helper believes has occurred so far.

    Helper: You know, overall you have made some significant changes, although it does seem like you're somewhat stuck in resolving some issues regarding your wife.

5. Using helper self-disclosure to provide ideas for future direction.

    Helper: My sense is that you have made some good progress, and I'm now wondering if you would like to try some new ideas on working through some of your concerns. For instance….

6. Having an honest discussion concerning discrepancies between clients' and helpers' beliefs about current progress and direction in the future.

    Helper: It seems like I'm seeing some progress being made in your relationship with your children, but you do not. Let's talk about that. For instance, I think you have really been able to work on how you discipline them. What are your thoughts on that?

    Client: Well, yes, I have made some progress, but it seems like it's just too little too late. I'm wondering if we can maybe find some other things that might work more quickly.

Collaboration is a powerful tool that can only occur if the helper has the willingness to hear constructive feedback from the client. If helpers are too fragile and defensive about their skills, then they may find this important skill difficult.

ADVOCACY

Due to the nature of human service work, advocacy is an important skill that human service professionals should know and practice. Advocacy occurs in numerous ways and is often considered part of a *social justice* focus; that is, it is assumed that one's advocacy work is focused on taking active steps to heal a societal wound (Wark, 2008), especially when the helper is advocating against prejudices the client is facing or is advocating on a systemic level to make changes in the broader system (Simpson, Abadie, & Seyler, 2016). Toporek, Lewis, and Crethar (2009) suggest that advocacy can include empowering clients to advocate for themselves, advocating directly for clients, advocating for community change, and advocating for change in the society. Advocacy is also an important theme in the Ethical Standards for Human Service Professionals (NOHS, 2015):

- Human service professionals are aware of local, state, and federal laws. They advocate for change in regulations and statutes when such legislation conflicts with ethical guidelines and/or client rights. Where laws are harmful to individuals, groups, or communities, human service professionals consider the conflict between the values of obeying the law and the values of serving people and may decide to initiate social action. (Standard 12)

- Human service professionals stay informed about current social issues as they affect clients and communities. If appropriate to the helping relationship, they share this information with clients, groups and communities as part of their work. (Standard 13)

- Human service professionals are aware of social and political issues that differentially affect clients from diverse backgrounds. (Standard 14)

- Human service professionals provide a mechanism for identifying client needs and assets, calling attention to these needs and assets, and assisting in planning and mobilizing to advocate for those needs at the individual, community, and societal level when appropriate to the goals of the relationship. (Standard 15)

- Human service professionals advocate for social justice and seek to eliminate oppression. They raise awareness of underserved population in their communities and with the legislative system. (Standard 16)

The following offers some examples of how human service professionals can advocate for and with clients.

Empowering Clients to Advocate for Themselves

This occurs when the helper teaches the skills and resources needed to enable clients to learn how to advocate for themselves.

Example: A client who is battered by her husband, and feels worthless, learns through the helping relationship that she is worthwhile and is encouraged to become involved with local services to assist other women in her situation. Eventually, her new empowered self is able to stand up for her rights and seek the needed services in her community to ensure that she will no longer be abused.

Advocating Directly for Clients

Sometimes clients feel so vulnerable that they have little power to make change. Other times, there is an immediate need to attend to a particular situation. Clearly, in these cases there is little time to help clients learn how to advocate for themselves. Here, it is appropriate for helpers to advocate for their clients.

Example: A client is raped and wants to report the rape to the police. However, she feels so devastated, that she currently does not have the wherewithal to take action on her own. In this case, it is appropriate for the helper to go with the client to the police station, help her file a report, and assist her in her dealing with the police and with others (e.g., hospital staff, if taken to the hospital).

Advocating for Community Change

The Black Lives Matter movement, a response to abuses directed towards Black people in some police departments and city governments, speaks to embedded problems and racism in established governmental systems. With such injustices, it may be incumbent for the human service professional to take action and assist in making positive community change in an effort to lessen, and hopefully, end these problems.

Example 1: After the United States Attorney General's office declares that there has been embedded racism in your local police department that has negatively impacted some of your clients, you decide to join a local protest movement that is advocating for more transparency in the department and for more minority hires.

Example 2: After the United States Attorney General's office declares that there has been embedded racism in your local police department, your agency reaches out to the local police department to conduct training with them on how they can utilize community policing, become more aware of their own prejudices and biases, and work more closely with the community.

Advocating for Societal Change

Clearly, there are society-wide problems that negatively impact certain client groups more than others. In these cases, human service professionals may decide to become actively involved in political movements to address these systemic problems.

Example 1: Despite the fact that Blacks are less likely to deal drugs than Whites, they continue to get arrested for drugs at rates alarmingly higher than Whites (Ingraham, 2014). With this in mind, a human service professional joins a national organization to make non-violent drug crimes a misdemeanor and to push for the release of tens of thousands of African Americans who have been imprisoned for non-violent drug crimes.

Example 2: You work for a family planning clinic, and as an agency, the staff decide to support a national candidate for president who supports the goals of the clinic. Literature is handed out at the agency in support of this candidate, and the staff commit to work for the election of this person during their off hours.

Advocating through local protest movements or by assisting other agencies and systems in making change is a responsibility of all human service professionals, but it is often not an easy task. When working for an agency— an agency that is part of a community or political system—how willing would you be to push for change in the broader system? Often, this takes being outspoken, and could even cause problems for the human service professional at work. Are you willing to be an advocate and advance causes that you believe will positively impact your clients? (See Experiential Exercise 5.8).

> First they came for the Communists but I was not a Communist so I did not speak out. Then they came for the Socialists and the Trade Unionists but I was not one of them, so I did not speak out. Then they came for the Jews but I was not Jewish so I did not speak out. And when they came for me, there was no one left to speak out for me. (Martin Niemoeller, German anti-Nazi theologian and Lutheran pastor)

Experiential Exercise 5.8:
Advocating for Clients

In small groups, come up with:
1. Situations in which you might want to advocate for clients.
2. Situations where you might want to advocate for changes in your community.
3. Situations where you might want to become politically active toward changes nationally.

How might advocacy in the above situations look? Do you think that taking an advocacy position in any of the above situations might cause you problems at work? Why or why not? Would you be willing to be an advocate?

CONCLUSION

A variety of skills have been highlighted in this chapter and the preceding two chapters. To a large degree, they were discussed in the order generally displayed in the helping relationship; that is, one usually starts with the foundational skills, moves onto the essential skills, and then moves on to the commonly used skills. Keeping this in mind, Experiential Exercise 5.9 is your chance to practice many of these skills. Remember to keep your use of questions to a minimum, if used at all (remember, we have not even discussed questions yet).

Experiential Exercise 5.9:
Practicing Skills

Chapters 3, 4 and 5 offered a number of helping skills that should be beneficial in the helping relationship. Here's your chance to practice what you've learned thus far. Find a partner and record a 30- to 60-minute session. Try to use a variety of the skills you have learned from the chapters during that session. At the end of the session, make sure that you conclude with a collaboration statement. Then, at home, write out each of your responses, identify what kind of skill you made, and make a note about whether you think you used the appropriate skill and whether you could have been sharper in the manner in which you used the skill. Your instructor may want you to hand in the recording and your responses, or just talk about your responses in class. Keep in mind that the next chapter focuses on questions, so do your best to *not* ask any questions at this point in time. Questions are often easily made by students and it's good to practice *not* using them. You probably want to keep a copy of Figure 5.1 near you to ensure that you use a number of the skills discussed in Chapters 3, 4, and 5.

SUMMARY

Chapter 5 focused on some of the more commonly used helping skills of human service professionals. Starting with the basic skills of affirmation giving, encouragement, and support, we noted their importance to raising a client's self-esteem. We noted that affirmation giving sustains and feeds a client, encouragement reinforces a client's efforts toward established goals, and that support is a general term that means the helper shows, in various ways, that he or she is "in the client's corner."

Moving on to offering alternatives, information giving, and advice giving, we stressed that all three skills can result in the client feeling judged by the helper or create a dependent relationship. However, we noted that offering alternatives is less likely to do this than information-giving, and information-giving is less likely than advice giving. We then demonstrated ways these skills may be used so they are more likely to be accepted by the client.

Modeling, we noted, can be conducted in two ways. Inadvertent modeling occurs as a by-product of the helping relationship and takes place when the client, due to the importance of the helping relationship, unconsciously picks up important skills that the helper is exhibiting. In contrast, intentional modeling is deliberate and can involve the display of specific behaviors on the part of the helper in hopes that clients will emulate those skills, role-playing specific skills with clients during the session so they can practice new skills, or teaching clients about the modeling process so that they can find models to emulate outside of the helping relationship.

Self-disclosure, or the revelation of something about the helper's life to the client, can be conducted purposefully or unwittingly. We noted that content self-disclosure, or the sharing of information about the helper, can be conducted in many ways and has a number of purposes. For instance, it can involve discussing personal information about the helper in an effort to build the relationship, be used to show the client that you understand him or her, be a manner of fostering deeper self-disclosure on the part of the client, and be used as a model for the development of potentially new behaviors. Process self-disclosure, sometimes called immediacy, is the sharing of the helper's moment-to-moment experience of self in relation to the client. This type of self-disclosure teaches clients new behaviors relative to genuineness in relationships. It was stressed that self-disclosure is a skill that should be used sparingly. A number of guidelines to using self-disclosure were provided.

We next reviewed collaboration, which focuses on checking in with the client to ensure that the client is satisfied with the direction of the helping relationship. Collaboration shows respect for client feedback and should be used throughout sessions. A number of different ways to be collaborative were noted.

The last skill discussed in this chapter was advocacy. We noted that advocacy can include empowering clients to advocate for themselves, advocating directly for clients, advocating for community change, and advocating for change in the society. A number of examples of advocacy were offered, and we discussed how difficult advocacy can be, especially when it entails a human service professional being outspoken at his or her workplace.

KEY WORDS AND TERMS

Advice giving
Advocacy
Advocating directly for clients
Advocating for societal change
Advocating for community change
Affirmation
Behavioral rehearsal
Collaboration
Content self-disclosure
Empowering clients to advocate for themselves
Encouragement

Imitation
Inadvertent modeling
Information giving
Intentional modeling
Modeling
Offering alternatives
Process self-disclosure
Self-disclosure
Social justice
Social learning
Support

CHAPTER 6

Information Gathering and Solution-Focused Questions

LEARNING OBJECTIVES

1. Understand the purpose and use of questions.

2. Learn the differences between information gathering and solution-focused questions.

3. Learn the purpose of and how to use the following information gathering questions in the helping relationship:

    a. Closed questions that delimit content and affect
    b. Open questions that delimit content and affect
    c. Tentative questions
    d. "Why" questions

4. Understand when it is best to use closed, open, tentative and "why" questions.

5. Learn the purpose of and how to use the following solution-focused questions:

    a. Preferred goals questions
    b. Evaluative questions
    c. Coping questions
    d. Exception-seeking questions
    e. Solution-oriented questions

INTRODUCTION

- What purpose do questions serve?
- Can questions be used to gather information quickly?
- Can questions be used to help increase client insight?
- Can questions be used to help clients reach their goals?
- Can questions interfere with the helping process?
- Can questions make a person defensive?
- Can other techniques be used in lieu of questions?
- At what point should one use questions?

Although questions are sometimes viewed negatively in training programs, they are an important tool for the helper. For instance, questions may help uncover historical patterns, reveal underlying issues, and challenge the client to change. Also, questions have the potential to determine and establish goals, encourage clients to deepen their self-exploration, examine which behaviors have been successful for the client in the past, and more. Questions come in many forms, and how and when they are asked will often determine their effectiveness as a helping skill. Some of the more popular forms of questions are listed in Figure 6.1. The first part of the chapter will examine information gathering questions while the second part will focus on solution-focused questions (see Figure 6.1).

Figure 6.1: Sequence of Helping Skills

INFORMATION GATHERING QUESTIONS

Information gathering questions are helpful when one is concerned about obtaining information to help solve the client's problems or address the client's concerns. These questions tend to be *helper-centered*, as they are developed from what the helper believes is important, not necessarily what the client sees as critical (although sometimes the helper and client might agree on what is important). They include *closed questions, open questions, tentative questions*, and *"why" questions*.

Closed Questions

Closed questions limit the types of responses clients are likely to make (e.g., "Do you like mom or dad better?") (Egan, Owen, & Reese, 2014; Hill, 2014; Ivey, Ivey, & Zalaquett, 2016) This type of question may prompt a "yes" or "no" response (e.g., "Do you like cheesecake?") or seek very specific information ("Tell me who is in your family"). This type of inquiry is helpful when the interviewer needs to obtain information quickly from clients, as in an intake interview or when the helper is pressured by time constraints. They should be used gingerly in a long-term counseling relationship as they tend to set up the helper as the expert authoritarian, or even interrogator, and can make the client feel defensive (see Quick Points 6.1). Two types of closed questions include closed questions that delimit content and closed questions that delimit affect.

> ### Quick Point 6.1:
> ### Features of Closed Questions
>
> **Positive:** Closed questions can be helpful when gathering information quickly—information that may be important in making decisions about a client's future.
>
> **Negative:** Closed questions can sometimes cause a client to feel defensive, if the helper barrages the client with questions and sets himself or herself apart as the expert.

Closed Questions That Delimit Content. Questions focusing on the content of a person's life that limit a client's choices are called closed questions that delimit content. A *yes/no closed question* or *forced choice closed question* simply means that the client is being asked to respond with a "yes" or with a "no" or with a limited number of options (e.g., "Have you tended to be an active parent or one who is disengaged?," or "Does your job entail a lot of administrative duties?," or "Do you see yourself as mildly, moderately, or severely argumentative with your children?" A *direct closed question* limits the responses a client is likely to make (e.g., "How many times did your parents hit you?" or "Who in your family is the most irritating?").

Although such questions can be helpful in gathering information quickly, they sometimes lend themselves to choices that may not accurately represent the client. For instance, in the above examples, the client may have a more nuanced answer than "yes" or "no" to the question about administrative duties, or perhaps the client falls somewhere in between being an active or disengaged parent, or maybe knowing about the times the client was hit would give more insight to a client's situation than only knowing how many times he or she was hit. Clients often have more involved, complex ways of understanding their situations and forced-choice responses tend to push them to respond in a manner that might not truly reflect how they see themselves.

Closed Questions That Delimit Affect. Closed questions that limit a client's choices and focus on a client's feeling state are called closed questions that delimit affect. An example of an affect limiting "yes/no" closed question might be: "Do you feel sad about the loss of your pet?" A "forced choice" closed question that delimits affect might be "Do you feel sad or angry about the loss of your pet?" (See Experiential Exercise 6.1). In general, the closed question is less facilitative than the open question, which will be discussed next.

Experiential Exercise 6.1:
Practicing Closed Questions

Break up into groups of three. One person role-play a client, the second a helper, and the third an observer. The observer should help out when needed. The client should role-play a person with a problem, and the helper should try to only respond with closed questions. The observer should make a note of the different kinds of closed questions that were asked. After you have role played for about 5 or 10 minutes, switch roles, and then switch roles a third time so everyone gets to practice. After each role play, have the observer share the different kinds of closed questions made by the helper. Finally, as a group, discuss how effective the closed questions were in eliciting information from the client.

Open Questions

In contrast to closed questions, open questions enable the client to have a wide range of responses and require more than a "yes" or "no" or forced choice response (Egan et al.; Hill, 2014; Ivey et al., 2016). Like closed questions, open questions can be focused on content or on affect. For instance, a client could be asked a content focused open question such as, "How did you meet your spouse?" or "What is it about your family that is unique?" Or, a client might be asked an affect focused open question, such as "So, how did you feel about that?" Or, "What were your feelings when that happened?"

Open questions can be powerful, as they allow clients the freedom to respond in a multitude of ways. This creates an environment in which the client has more leeway in directing the focus of the session. Thus, this type of question is seen as less helper-centered (more *client-centered*) than a closed question (see Experiential Exercise 6.2, then 6.3).

Experiential Exercise 6.2:
Practice with Open Questions

Your instructor should break the class into groups of three. Within your triad, identify a helper, client, and observer. The client should discuss a real or made up problem, and the helper should respond by asking only open questions. The observer is there to assist the helper, should she or he have difficulty with the task. Also, if the observer believes the helper did not respond with an open question, he or she should stop the interview and the three students should discuss what open questions could be asked. Then, resume the exercise. After doing this for 5 to 10 minutes, change roles and have the client be the helper, the observer be the client, and the helper be the observer. Then, after another 5 to 10 minutes, do the exercise one last time, changing roles again. In class, discuss the relative ease or difficulty of making open questions.

Experiential Exercise 6.3: Contrasting Closed Questions and Open Questions with Empathic Responses

Have a student volunteer talk about a topic of his or her choice that involves some kind of dilemma or difficulty. The rest of the class should create two circles around the student. The first circle is to only ask closed questions and the second circle is to only ask open questions. Have the student discuss the dilemma or difficulty for about five minutes while the first circle only responds with closed questions. Then, for the next five minutes, the second circle should only respond with open questions. Finally, for five more minutes, anyone should respond with only empathic responses. When you have finished, discuss the following questions as a group.

1. How did the student experience the first part of the exercise?
2. How did the student experience the second part of the exercise?
3. How did the student experience the last part of the exercise?
4. Was it easier for the helpers to ask closed questions, open questions, or to make empathic responses?
5. Did questions need to be asked at all?
6. Do you think it would be better to ask a good question or to make a good empathic response?

Open or Closed Questions—Which to Use?

Generally, open questions are more useful than closed questions in facilitating a deeper helping relationship. For instance, if a helper wants a client to talk at length about his or her family, a simple question, like "Can you tell me more about your family?" can be quite useful. In contrast, the use of a closed question is important when the helper wants to gather specific information quickly. For instance, if the helper wants to know the relative positions of various members in a family, a quick question, like "Who is in your family and what are their ages?" could be important. Or, if a helper wants to quickly assess a client's feelings about his or her family, the helper might ask the closed question, such as "Overall, do you think your family was dysfunctional or functional?" The down side to questions like these is that they may direct the session in a manner that is not particularly relevant to what the client wishes to discuss, and they can limit the range of discussion. Thus, the human service professional needs to consider the purpose of the question—is it to gain information quickly through the use of a closed question, or is it to allow the client to discuss a topic broadly while also building on the helping relationship through the use of open questions?

Tentative Questions

Regardless of the type of question used, it can often be asked in a tentative manner that suggests the helper is testing the waters. For instance, rather than asking "What are the names and ages of the people in your family?" one could ask "Would you mind telling me about your family members-their names and ages?" Or rather than asking the question "How sad do you feel about your divorce?" a helper could ask the tentative question "I'm wondering if you might be feeling sad right now about your divorce?' Or, rather than saying, "How are you feeling about the divorce?" one could ask, "I would guess that you might have some feelings about the divorce." Sometimes helpers will add a small question at the end of a sentence, such as, "Is that true?" to make a question sound more tentative. Tentative questions lessen the harshness sometimes found with the use of closed and even open questions and gives the client an easier opportunity to back out of responding to the question if feeling uncomfortable.

91

Sometimes, the tentative question is hardly a question at all and is more akin to an empathic response. For instance, in the example above, rather than saying, "I would guess that you might have some feelings about the divorce," the helper could say, "It seems like you're having some feelings about the divorce." Tentative questions tend to "sit well" with clients. They're easier to hear, help the session flow smoothly, help to create a nonjudgmental and open atmosphere, and are generally responded to positively by clients. Experiential Exercise 6.4 helps to identify how you can make tentative questions and Experiential Exercise 6.5 helps you to practice your skills with tentative questions.

Experiential Exercise 6.4:
Developing Tentative Questions

In class, come up with different beginning phrases that might start a tentative question. For instance, in the previous examples, I began the responses by stating, "I wonder if you . . . ", and with, "I would guess that you . . . ".

Think of a number of different ways one might begin a tentative question. Write them in the space provided and share your various responses in class.

1. _____.

2. _____.

3. _____.

4. _____.

5. _____.

6. _____.

Experiential Exercise 6.5:
Making Responses Using Tentative Questions

Break up into groups of threes. One person role-play a client, the second a helper, and the third an observer. The observer should help out when needed. The client should role-play a person with a problem, and the helper should try to only respond with tentative questions. The observer should make a note of the different kinds of tentative questions that were asked. After you have role played for about 5 or 10 minutes, switch roles, and then switch roles a third time so everyone gets to practice. After each role play, have the observer share the different kinds of tentative questions made by the helper. Then, as a group, discuss how effective the tentative questions were in eliciting information from the client.

"Why" Questions

Have you ever been asked the question, "Why do you feel that way?" Did it make you feel self-protective, suspicious, cautious, or distrustful? "Why" questions tend to make a person feel defensive. Generally, it is recommended that helpers use other kinds of questions or make empathic responses (De Jong & Berg, 2013; Grant & O'Connor, 2010; Ivey et al., 2016). If one could honestly answer "why," "why" questions would be the most powerful question used in the helping relationship. However, clients use the helping relationship to find the answer to "why." If they knew, they wouldn't be in the helper's office. I have found that after I've formed an alliance with a client, I might periodically slip in a soft "why" question and say something like, "Why do you think that is?" However, if I use this type of question at all during a session, I use it sparingly.

When to Use Closed, Open, Tentative, and "Why" Questions

Although questions can be helpful in uncovering patterns, inducing self-exploration, and challenging the client to change, their overuse can set up an atmosphere that some clients find degrading—one in which the client feels humiliated and put on the spot, as the helper acts as the superior expert. Some also note that this kind of atmosphere can lead to dependence on the helper as the helpee increasingly assumes the helper is taking the lead in the helping relationship (Cormier, Nurius, & Osborn, 2013). These effects lead some to suggest that the empathic response should often be considered as an alternative to the question (Neukrug, 2016; Neukrug, Bayne, Dean-Nganga, & Pusateri, 2012; Rogers, 1942). For instance, suppose a client said the following:

Client: I come in for help from this place and all I get is a lot of nonsense. No one really wants to help me. No one cares about me, my kids, my family!

A helper could respond with this question:

Helper: What makes you feel that way? Why do you think we don't care?

Although the above response might be made from a sincere and thoughtful place, it may make the client feel defensive and even angry. However, look at the following response:

Helper: It seems like no one here is helpful or cares about you and your family.

Generally, if one is not needing to quickly gather information and has unlimited time with a client, it is effective to use an empathic response. Given the limited human resources of social service agencies, however, the unlimited time option is simply not available. In either case, you may want to consider if you are relying too much on using questions. *Questions tend to come easy to people, while empathic responses take work.* Although much more can be said about the different uses of questions in the interviewing process, remember to be careful whenever you ask questions. Some guidelines for the use of questions include:

1. Are you aware that you are asking a question?
2. Under the current situation, is asking a question the best response you can come up with?
3. Are you using the type of question most amenable to the situation at hand?
4. Have you considered alternatives to asking questions?
5. Will the question you are about to ask inhibit the flow of the interview? If so, do the benefits of using it (e.g., gathering specific information quickly) outweigh the drawbacks of not using it?

After reviewing Fact Sheet 6.1, complete Experiential Exercise 6.6 so that you can practice the use of questions thus far examined in the chapter.

Fact Sheet 6.1:
Information Gathering Questions

Type of Question	Definition	Examples	Advantages/ Disadvantages
Closed Questions Delimiting Content	Questions that focus on a particular topic or point of view and force the client to pick between "yes" or "no" answers, forced choice answers, or direct the client in a manner that limits his or her response.	"Do you think you will live with your parents or on your own after the child is born?"	Useful when needing to gather information quickly. They can set up an atmosphere in which the helper is seen as an authoritarian figure. Client elaboration is limited.
Closed Questions Delimiting Affect	Questions that force the client to pick between "yes" or "no" or forced choice feeling choices.	"Did you feel happy or sad when you found out that you were pregnant?"	Useful when needing to gather information quickly. They can set up an atmosphere in which the helper is seen as an authoritarian figure. Client elaboration is limited.
Open Questions	Questions that allow the client to respond in a myriad of ways.	"How do you feel about being pregnant?"	Less repressive than closed questions and allows the client to respond in a wide range of ways. Not as client-centered as tentative questions or empathic responses.
Tentative Questions	Questions asked in a gentle manner that often allow for a large range of responses from the client.	"Is it that you have a lot of mixed feelings about being pregnant?"	The least helper-centered (most client-centered) although the content of what is being talked about is still picked by the helper.
Why Questions	A question that seeks a deep thoughtful response, but often results in defensiveness on the part of the client.	Why do you think your parents were so mean to you?	The most potentially damaging question as individuals tend to respond to such questions defensively. However, if asked at right moment and time, could be facilitative of deep exploration.

Experiential Exercise 6.6:
Asking Effective Questions

Examine the following and see if they tend to be closed, open, tentative, or why questions. Also, consider whether some questions could be a combination of these. Finally, decide if an empathic response can be made in its place or if there might be a better type of question to use. Share your "better responses" in class.

Type of Question

<u>Example:</u> *Did you feel sad or angry about your daughter running away?*   *Closed*
<u>Better Response:</u> *It sounds like you had some strong feelings about your daughter's behavior*

<u>Question 1:</u> Did you feel good or bad about the breakup?   _____
Better Response: _____.

<u>Question 2:</u> How did you feel about the death of your father?   _____
Better Response: _____.

<u>Question 3:</u> How angry were you at your brother for not helping you out?   _____
Better Response: _____.

<u>Question 4:</u> How many times have you been to the unemployment office?   _____
Better Response: _____.

<u>Question 5:</u> Is it that you were feeling pretty upset about being lied to?   _____
Better Response: _____.

<u>Question 6:</u> How often during the day do you cry about the breakup?   _____
Better Response: _____.

<u>Question 7:</u> Would you like to tell me more about that situation?   _____
Better Response: _____.

<u>Question 8:</u> Might you have some strong feelings about the accident?   _____
Better Response: _____.

<u>Question 9:</u> Will it take two or three months to get over this?   _____
Better Response: _____.

<u>Question 10:</u> How often have you been in counseling and who were your counselors? _____
Better Response: _____.

<u>Question 11:</u> Why do you think your parents divorced?   _____
Better Response: _____.

SOLUTION-FOCUSED QUESTIONS

> Suppose that one night, while you were asleep, there was a miracle and this problem was solved. How would you know? What would be different? (de Shazer, 1988, p. 5)

Like the famous *miracle question* above, solution-focused questions have become a staple for many helpers in recent years. These questions are focused on quickly identifying what behaviors have worked in a client's life, determining where the client wants to be in the future, and helping the client get to his or her desired goals (Bannink, 2010; De Jong & Berg, 2013; de Shazer et al, 2007; Trepper et al., 2014). Solution-focused questions are seen as building on client strengths, do not focus on client problems, view the client in a manner that is non-pathologizing, and helps the client move toward finding solutions not rehashing past concerns and issues. Such questions can generally be classified into one of five areas: (1) *preferred goals questions*, that examine what the client is hoping his or future will look like; (2) *evaluative questions*, that involve an assessment of whether client behaviors have been productive toward reaching client goals; (3) *coping questions*, that are used to identify behaviors which the client has successfully used in the past to deal with his or her problems; (4) *exception-seeking questions*, that identify times in the client's life when he or she has not had the problem and focus on what the client was doing during those times; and (5) *solution-oriented questions*, that broadly ask the client how his or her life would be if the problem did not exist. Vignette 6.1 offers a scenario concerning Antonne, who has sought counseling due to ongoing depression and anxiety. This scenario will be used to exemplify how different kinds of questions might be used.

Vignette 6.1:
Antonne

Antonne, a 29-year-old single male, is severely anxious and has suffered with anxiety and depression most of his adult life. He is the oldest of three children and describes growing up in a family that was highlighted by a lot of screaming, chaos, and few boundaries. He notes that his parents had an "on and off" loving relationship that seemed to match the chaos that was prevalent in the family. Being the oldest, he states that he had a lot of rules placed on him, that he was judged much more harshly than his younger siblings, and that he was often given the responsibility of taking care of his younger brother and sister. He was often told that he "better do well in school" or his future would be "hell." He grew up wanting to have more stability in his life, a steady job, a "quiet family," and a sense that his life had purpose. However, despite obtaining his associates degree in psychology, he has had trouble obtaining a job and states he has had no luck in the dating scene. He is afraid he will always be searching for a job, a partner, and stability. In an effort to feel better, some of the things that Antonne has tried, include: reading self-help books, taking anti-depressant medications, exercising, and being in in-depth, long-term counseling.

Preferred Goals Questions

While the traditional use of questions have often focused on problems, preferred goals questions are future oriented and help clients identify how their lives would look if identified goals were to be reached (de Shazer, 2007; Trepper et al., 2014). Some preferred goals questions that we could apply to Antonne's situation include the following:

- Antonne, if this were to be the best helping session you ever had, can you imagine what goals you would identify to focus upon and how you might try to reach them?
- How would you act differently in the future, Antonne, if coming here has been worthwhile for you?
- If your life was better in one month, six months, or a year, what would be happening? What might you be doing differently Antonne?
- Antonne, if you were getting closer to reaching your goals and things were getting better, how might you be acting different?

You can see that you can replace Antonne's name with anyone's name and use the exact same preferred goals questions.

Evaluative Questions

Evaluative questions focus on whether behaviors that clients have used have helped them achieve their goals (De Jong & Berg, 2013; Franklin, et al., 2012). Their purpose is to identify what has worked, so that the client can do more of it, and to identify what has not worked, so clients will not spend endless amounts of energy focusing on less productive behaviors. For instance, in Antonne's case, the following questions might be asked:

- Antonne, what has worked for you in trying to alleviate your depression?
- How helpful was the use of anti-depressants, Antonne?
- What aspects of "depth" therapy were helpful to you, Antonne?
- Antonne, you've mentioned that you have been exercising a lot lately. How has that worked for you in helping you feel better?
- What about reading self-help books, Antonne? Have they helped you with your depression and anxiety?
- Out of all the ways you've tried, what was the most effective in alleviating your anxiety and depression, Antonne?

Notice how evaluative questions are not focused on the depressive and chaotic family atmosphere, as such questions would be problem-focused, not solution-focused. In addition, the questions are almost exclusively focused on what has worked, not on what hasn't worked. Focusing on what has not worked would be a waste of time and energy and considered a useless rehash of past failures. For instance, if Antonne says, "long-term therapy made me feel worse," then a discussion about it should be limited, although it would be okay to ask a question like, "Although overall, long-term therapy was not helpful, what aspect *was* helpful for you?" With this question there is an assumption that although long-term therapy was not productive overall, a small aspect of it was helpful, and if you can identify what was helpful, you can do more of it. Overall, the helper should focus on those behaviors that have worked and have expanded discussions around those responses so that those behaviors can be used in solution building.

Coping Questions

Coping questions ask clients to think about and describe times when they successfully dealt (coped) with their problems (De Jong & Berg, 2013; Franklin, Trepper, Gingeric, & McCollum, 2012). In the past, helpers would often ask something like: "Have there been times when you were able to cope with (the problem)?" However, because some clients view their problems as so overwhelming they are not able to see times when they did cope successfully and quickly respond with, "No." Instead, a solution-focused helper assumes there were times when the client was successful and, in a positive manner, asks "What ways have you found to cope with (the problem)? In Antonne's case, a helper might ask some of the following coping questions:

- So, tell me Antonne, in what ways have you been successful in coping with your depression in the past? What about the anxiety?
- Antonne, what other ways have you tried that were successful in alleviating your depression and anxiety?
- I know you had trouble getting out of bed this morning because you were so depressed, Antonne. Tell me what you did do to get yourself up and going.
- Antonne, your depression seems to have impacted your eating, and you've lost some weight. When you have eaten, what enabled you to be able to eat?
- Antonne, when you think back on your life, can you identify things that you did that helped to alleviate your depression and anxiety?

Exception-Seeking Questions

Exception-seeking questions, one of the most well-known types of solution-focused questions, explore what is going on in a client's life when the client is not experiencing the problem (Bannink, 2010; De Jong & Berg, 2013; Franklin, et al., 2012). This type of question helps to quickly focus on the task at hand—finding solutions. As with coping questions, rather than asking *if* the client has exceptions, there is an assumption that the client *has* had exceptions in his or her life. In Antonne's case, the following questions could be used:

- I bet there have been times in your life, Anotonne, when you have not felt depressed. Can you describe them for me?
- What was going on in your life, Antonne, when you did not feel depressed?
- When undergoing hardships, people often have moments when they feel good. Antonne, can you describe times like that for me? What is going on with you during those times?
- You mentioned that you were less depressed and less anxious a couple of years ago, Antonne. What was going on in your life then that seemed to ward off your depression and anxiety?

Solution-Oriented Questions

Similar to preferred goals questions, solution-oriented questions also look at the client's future but have a broader focus, as they don't zero in on specific behaviors (Bannink, 2010; De Jong & Berg, 2013; Franklin, et al., 2012). However, both types of questions look at how things are different in the future. One kind of solution-oriented question, the Miracle Question, was noted at the start of this section. Here are some additional solution-oriented questions, applied to Antonne's situation:

- Antonne, how would your life look different if you were not depressed or anxious?
- Antonne, if you were given a magic pill that would somehow make everything better, how would your life look?
- If you could change anything in your life so you would feel better, Antonne, how would things be different?
- Antonne, if there was some deity that could suddenly make your life better, what would your life look like?

Final Thoughts About Solution-Focused Questions

Solution-focused questions are future oriented and steeped in the *positive psychology* tradition (McAuliffe, 2018; Terni, 2015). This means that they don't spend an inordinate amount of time talking about the past, avoid focusing on pathology, concentrate on those aspects of a person's life that bring contentment, and assume that clients have strengths that can help them overcome their current situations. In Antonne's situation, you can see how there was a limited focus on his upbringing and the problems in his family. Instead, there was a focus on his future goals, ways that he's been able to cope with his problems, and new behaviors he might be able to adopt that will help him ensure a positive outlook on life (review Fact Sheet 6.2, then do Experiential Exercises 6.7 and 6.8).

Fact Sheet 6.2:
Summarizing Different Types of Solution-Focused Questions

Types of Question	Definition	Examples
Preferred Goals Questions	Questions that assess what the client is hoping his or her future will look like.	"If the helping relationship was successful, what would you be doing differently?"
Evaluative Questions	Questions that involve an assessment of whether client behaviors have been productive.	"What behaviors are you doing these days that are helpful in making you feel better?"
Coping Questions	Questions that are used to identify behaviors which the client has successfully used in the past to deal with his or her problems.	"When you felt this way in the past, what worked best for you?"
Exception-seeking Questions	Questions that identify times in the client's life when he or she has not had the problem and focus on what the client was doing during those times.	"When you felt badly in the past, were there moments when things were going well. What were you doing during those moments?"
Solution-oriented Questions	Questions which broadly ask how the client's life would be if the problem did not exist.	"If you suddenly walked out this door and everything was better, what would your life look like?"

Experiential Exercise 6.7:
Helping Antonne

Form groups of six students. Have one student role-play Antonne while the other students each pick one of the five types of solution-focused questions. As Antonne talks about his life, take turns asking a type of question falling under the category you chose. You can use the question identified in the book, but better yet, try to come up with your own questions that match the category.

Experiential Exercise 6.8:
Practicing Solution Focused Questions

Pair up with another person in class and either role-play a made-up situation or share a personal life problem with your partner. The "helper" should try his or her best to mostly respond with solution-focused questions. However, to keep the dialogue moving, the helper may want to be a good listener and also respond empathically to his or her role-playing client. A third person, an observer, can note the different responses the helper is making and review them when the role-play is over.

INTEGRATING QUESTIONS INTO THE HELPING RELATIONSHIP

So far in the text, you have reviewed a number of critical skills useful in conducting an interview with a client. Here's your chance to practice them. To some degree, the sequencing of these skills occurs in the order in which they have been presented. Thus, the foundational skills are generally delivered first, followed by the essential skills, commonly used skills, and the use of questions. However, there are times when this is not the case, such as when it is critical for the human service professional to gather initial information from the client when he or she first enters an agency. In this case, the use of questions may parallel and even precede the use of the essential skills and commonly used skills (we hope the foundational skills always come first).

So, while keeping the basic structure in mind, here is your chance to practice these skills. Using Log Sheet 6.1 to help you remember the many skills you've learned and the basic sequencing of them, role-play with another student in class. As usual, a third student can be an observer. Spend between 30 and 60 minutes role-playing with the student so that you can practice as many skills as possible. The observer will make notes of the helper's responses on the Log Sheet. When you have finished, the three of you can discuss the helper's various responses, their efficacy, and whether they were made at an appropriate time. This assignment can also be done outside of class, as long as there is an observer to complete the log. Don't forget to embrace the eight characteristics of the effective helper and to be on top of your non-verbal behaviors when conducting the role-play.

LOG SHEET 6.1: ASSESSING SKILL USAGE			
TYPE OF SKILLS	**TRACKING RESPONSES**		
FOUNDATIONAL SKILLS	Time*	Key Words In Response	Effectiveness and Timing
Honoring and Respecting			
Being Curious			
Delimiting Power/Being Equal			
Non-pathologizing			
Being Committed			
Being Caring			
Being Courteous			
ESSENTIAL SKILLS			
Silence and Pause Time			
Listening			
Reflection of Feelings			
Reflection of Content			
Basic Empathy			
Advanced Empathy			
COMMONLY USED SKILLS			
Affirmation Giving			
Encouragement			
Support			

*Time: Time the response was made during the interview

LOG SHEET 6.1: ASSESSING SKILL USAGE (CONT'D)			
TYPE OF SKILLS	**TRACKING RESPONSES**		
COMMONLY USED SKILLS	**Time***	**Key words in response**	**Effectiveness and Timing**
Offering Alternatives			
Information Giving			
Advice Giving			
Modeling			
Self-Disclosure			
Collaboration			
Advocacy			
INFORMATION GATHERING QUESTIONS			
Closed			
Open			
Tentative			
"Why" Questions			
SOLUTION-FOCUSED QUESTIONS			
Preferred Goals			
Evaluative			
Coping			
Exception Seeking			
Solution-oriented			

*Time: Time the response was made during the interview

SUMMARY

This chapter examined the various types of questions often made in the helping relationship. Starting with information gathering questions, we noted that these responses are helpful when one is concerned about gathering information to help solve the client's problems or address the client's concerns. These questions tend to be helper-centered, as they are developed from what the helper believes is important, not necessarily what the client sees as critical. We noted that there were four types of such questions, including closed questions, open questions, tentative questions, and "why" questions. Closed questions are usually made when a helper needs to gather information quickly and generally require a "yes" or "no" or forced choice response by the client or a specific answer to a direct question. They can focus on the content or affect that the client is presenting. Open questions allow a wide range of responses to questions and are generally used when wanting a client to expand on the content or affect that the client is presenting. Tentative questions are used when one is wanting to make the question a bit more inviting and client-centered. In contrast to the other types of questions, it was suggested that "why" questions be avoided, because they can often make a client feel defensive. If a helper has developed a strong alliance, however, a "why" question might be slipped in periodically.

In addition to information gathering questions, in this chapter we focused on solution-focused questions. These types of questions are future oriented, non-pathologizing, and focus on client strengths. They examine what behaviors have worked in a client's life, identify where the client wants to be in the future, and develop ways of helping the client achieve his or her goals. We focused on five types of solution focused questions: (1) preferred goals questions, that examine what the client is hoping his or future will look like; (2) evaluative questions, that involve an assessment of whether client behaviors have been productive toward reaching client goals; (3) coping questions, that identify behaviors the client has successfully used in the past to deal with his or her problems; (4) exception-seeking questions, that identify times in the client's life when he or she has not had the problem and focus on what the client was doing during those times; and (5) solution-oriented questions, that broadly ask the client how the client's life would be if the problem did not exist. Finally, the chapter ended with a look at how questions are integrated into all of the skills talked about thus far in the book.

KEY WORDS AND TERMS

Client-centered
Closed questions
Coping questions
Evaluative questions
Exception-seeking questions
Forced choice closed questions
Helper-centered
Information gathering questions
Miracle question

Open questions
Positive psychology
Preferred goals questions
Solution-focused questions
Solution-oriented questions
Tentative questions
"Why" questions
Yes/no closed questions

CHAPTER 7

Advanced Skills And Specialized Training

LEARNING OBJECTIVES

1. Learn how to apply the advanced skills of:

   a. Advanced empathy

   b. Confrontation: Challenge with support

   c. Interpretation

   d. Cognitive-behavioral responses

2. Learn about specialized training in the following areas that are commonly practiced by human service professionals, including:

   a. Assessing for lethality: Suicidality and homicidality

   b. Crisis, disaster, and trauma helping

   c. Token economies

   d. Positive helping

   e. Life-coaching

INTRODUCTION

There are so many ways that skills are applied in human services that it's hard to decide which advanced skills and specialized training should be highlighted in this chapter. In fact, when recently editing an encyclopedia, I found there were about 300 theories responsible for the development of thousands of skills and literally hundreds more areas of practice which are not theory specific (Neukrug, 2015).

Deciding what kinds of advanced skills and specialized training to talk about, when there are literally thousands of them, is not an easy task. So, I based inclusion in this chapter on three important factors: (1) those advanced techniques that have been traditionally used by human service practitioners, (2) those advanced techniques that have become increasingly popular, and (3) areas of service that have been shown to be critical to the work of the human service professional. Using this rubric, I came up with a small number of advanced skills and areas of specialized training. In the first section of the chapter, I highlight a few advanced skills, including: advanced empathy, confrontation (challenge with support), interpretation, and cognitive-behavioral responses. In the second section, I present a few areas of service that have become increasingly important in human service work, including: assessing for lethality: suicidality and homicidality; crisis, disaster, and trauma helping; token economies; positive helping; and coaching (see Figure 7.1).

Figure 7.1: Sequence of Helping Skills

Perhaps what is also interesting is what I left out. First there are the "traditional" counseling theories—too many to list here. In addition, there are so many new techniques and trainings which I chose not to include, mostly because they involve some type of fairly involved advanced training. You may want to explore some of these on your own, however, as they have gained some popularity in recent years. Some of the more recent and popular approaches you might want to look into on your own include: acceptance and commitment therapy (ACT), alternative and integrative therapies, constructivist therapy, dialectical behavior therapy, eye movement desensitization response therapy (EMDR), feminist therapy, gender-aware counseling, motivational interviewing, multimodal therapy, neurocounseling, relational and intersubjectivity approaches, and self-psychology. These recommendations just represent a small number of the many advanced approaches out there. Let's start by looking at some of the advanced skills, and then later in the chapter, we will focus on important areas of service where specialized training is generally advised.

ADVANCED SKILLS

The skills addressed in this section are often used by human service professionals but go beyond the basic skills you learned about in chapters 3 through 7. If practiced at all, they should be carefully studied and preferably used when under supervision so that you can fine tune and nurture them. They include: advanced empathy, confrontation: challenge with support, interpretation, and cognitive-behavioral responses.

ADVANCED EMPATHY

If you remember from Chapter 4: Essential Skills, basic empathy is one of the most important skills a helper can use when working with clients. Advanced empathy takes off from where basic skills end. This advanced skill facilitates client awareness of underlying feelings and helps clients understand new ways to conceptualize their situations. Although not always necessary for the helping relationship, they are additive to the relationship in the sense that they offer something extra to clients that they would not normally have experienced.

Advanced empathy may reflect deeper feelings that were not directly stated by the client, may point out conflicting feelings or thoughts a client may be living with, may use metaphors or analogies to show the client that he or she was heard, can use self-disclosure as a means of demonstrating that the helper has a first-hand understanding of what the client is experiencing, or can use tactile responses (reflection of bodily sensations) to demonstrate understanding (Neukrug, Bayne, Dean-Nganga, & Pusateri, 2012). Advanced empathic responses can be anywhere from a level 3.0 or higher on the Carkhuff scale, although it's not unusual to find them in the 3.5 to 4.0 range (see Chapter 4: Essential Skills). Here are some examples:

Reflecting Deeper Feelings

Client: I'm at my wit's end. I'm so frustrated with my spouse. No matter what I do, nothing seems to work. I keep offering new ways to try and work things out, but he doesn't seem to care. I'm feel like throwing something at him.

Helper: Your frustration really shows—you've tried so many different things yet nothing seems to work. But most of all, I think I hear the sadness in your voice—sadness about the lack of connection you feel with your husband.

In the above example, look at how the helper first reflects the frustration the client is clearly feeling, but then moves on to reflect sadness. Not outwardly stated, this sadness was *subceived* ("felt/experienced": a word coined by Rogers) by the helper. If the helper is on target, the client will respond accordingly (see Reflection Exercise 7.1).

Reflection Exercise 7.1:
Reflecting Deeper Feelings Nonverbally

One time when I was in my own therapy, I looked at my therapist and I said, "You look so sad and distraught." He responded with: "I'm only reflecting what I see in you." At that point I began to sob.

Think about the different ways one can show a person the intense feelings he or she is experiencing without verbalizing one's interpretations outright. How might such reflections be helpful to the client? Discuss in small groups.

Pointing Out Conflicting Feelings or Thoughts

Client: You know, I love my wife so much that the thought of being without her is incredibly painful. She is my rock and makes my life so much easier.

Ten minutes later:

Client: I went out to lunch with my co-worker the other day, and I know she was flirting with me. I am so attracted to her; I am thinking of maybe acting on it.

Helper: Well, I guess I hear your mixed feelings. On the one hand, I know you love your wife and don't want to fracture that relationship. On the other hand, I hear that you have a really strong reaction to your co-worker.

Ah, if only life was simple! Alas, all of us have feelings and thoughts that conflict with one another. One important role of the helper is pointing these out to the client. Once these dilemmas are faced squarely by a client, they can be talked about and more fully understood. Otherwise, individuals go through life bouncing around from one conflicting thought or feeling to another—never making any sense of it all. Imagine what the conversation might be like if the above client talked about his conflicting feelings.

Metaphors or Analogies

Client: I'm at my wit's end. I'm as depressed as ever. I keep trying to change my life and nothing works. I try communicating better, I change my job, I change my looks. I even take antidepressants, but nothing helps. I'm just sinking into the depths of despair.

Helper: No matter what you do, it feels like you're re-arranging chairs on the Titanic.

In this example, the allusion to the Titanic tells the client that you understand how much the client is trying, but despite that, the client still feels as if he or she is sinking—nothing seems to help. Responses like this reach clients at different levels than the more traditional basic empathic response. Although metaphors and analogies are similar, there are some subtle differences. Metaphors are when one makes a broad abstract statement that reflects a person's situation ("Your life seems like it's just flying away from you"), whereas analogies reflect an analysis or comparison that makes logical sense.

Self-Disclosure

Client: I'm at my wit's end. I'm as depressed as ever. I keep trying to change my life and nothing works. I try communicating better, I change my job, I change my looks. I even take antidepressants, but nothing helps.

Helper: You know, there was a time in my life when I really struggled, and I remember how difficult it was for me to get through that time.

This example shows how a revelation about the helper's life can demonstrate to a client that the helper understands the client's level of difficulty. Also, notice the non-specifics of this response. The helper clearly doesn't want to reveal too much about his or her life. After all, this response is about the client, not the helper. Using self-disclosure should be done carefully and should only be conducted when one is trying to show a client that he or she is being heard—not because the helper gets something out of self-disclosing (see Chapter 5 for more on self-disclosure).

Tactile Responses

Client: I'm at my wit's end. I'm as depressed as ever. I keep trying to change my life and nothing works. I try communicating better, I change my job, I change my looks, and I even take antidepressants, but nothing helps.

Helper: When you just told me what you're going through, I felt my stomach twist and turn—I imagine this is how you must be feeling.

Here, the description of a physical reaction by the helper to the client's statement demonstrates that the helper has heard him or her deeply. These responses, although generally rare, can go far in demonstrating understanding of a client's situation.

Although beginning helpers are generally encouraged to try to stick to making formula or natural responses, as they become more proficient at these basic empathic responses, they can slowly begin to practice making the advanced responses. Experiential Exercise 7.1 will give you the opportunity to formulate some advanced responses.

CONFRONTATION: CHALLENGE WITH SUPPORT

Confrontation is generally defined as some type of hostile challenge in an attempt to change another person's point of view or perception of reality. However, within the context of the helping relationship, confrontation is thought of as a much softer challenge to the client's understanding of the world and offers the client an invitation to discuss discrepancies between a client's values and behaviors, feelings and behaviors, idealized self and real self, and expressed feelings and underlying feelings (Cormier, Nurius, & Osborn, 2013; Neukrug, Bayne, Dean-Nganga, & Pusateri, 2012; Strong & Zeman, 2010; Thompson, 2016).

To be effective, confrontation within the helping relationship first involves the building of a trusting and caring relationship, often through the use of one's listening skills and empathy. This is then followed by an invitation, on the part of the helper, to discuss the discrepancy (Egan, Owen, & Reese, 2014; Strong & Zeman, 2010). This process of support, followed by an invitation for dialogue and conversation, offers the best potential to change the client's perception of reality (Neukrug, 2017).

Experiential Exercise 7.1:
Making Advanced Empathic Responses

Form groups of four or five in your class. Using the same scenarios as were used in making basic empathic responses in Chapter 4, use any of the examples just discussed (reflecting deeper feelings, pointing out conflicting feelings or thoughts, using metaphors or analogies, using self-disclosure, or using tactile responses) as a group. See if you can make an advanced empathic response to each of the following client situations.

1. Pregnant teenager to human service professional:
Client: I have to get an abortion. If my parents find out they're going to kill me. If they knew I've been sleeping with John, they'd throw me out for sure. I'm scared.

Advanced Response: _____
_____.

2. Individual with a disability to human service professional:
Client: I'm pissed off. I know they didn't hire me because I'm disabled. I want to know what my legal rights are. Do you know what I can do?

Advanced Response: _____
_____.

3. Minority client to human service professional:
Client: I'm really suspicious. I think I'm getting the shaft with my realtor. I keep telling her I want to move to this one community, and she can't find anything for sale there. I don't believe it!

Advanced Response: _____
_____.

4. Teenager to human service professional:
Client: I'm not worried. My boyfriend doesn't use condoms. Why should he? He's not going to get AIDS-he doesn't sleep around. I'm the only one who sees anyone else!

Advanced Response: _____
_____.

5. Abused older person to human service professional:
Client: I guess I deserve to be hit. I can't remember where I keep anything anymore. Besides, my daughter really loves me.

Advanced Response: _____
_____.

Experiential Exercise 7.1:
Making Advanced Empathic Responses (Cont'd)

Form groups of four or five in your class. Using the same scenarios as were used in making basic empathic responses in Chapter 4, use any of the examples just discussed (reflecting deeper feelings, pointing out conflicting feelings or thoughts, using metaphors or analogies, using self-disclosure, or using tactile responses) as a group. See if you can make an advanced empathic response to each client situation that follow.

6. *Accused person to human service professional:*
Client: I didn't do nothing. Those charges are trumped up. They just want to get me because they know I've been in trouble before!

Advanced Response: _____
_____.

7. *Pro-life person to human service professional:*
Client: I refuse to let any more babies die. I'll do anything to close down those murdering abortion clinics.

Advanced Response: _____
_____.

8. *Pro-choice person to human service professional:*
Client: I believe a woman has a right to choose what to do with her body, and I'm sick and tired of those pro-lifers interfering with other people's right to choose!

Advanced Response: _____
_____.

9. *Estranged wife to human service professional:*
Client: My husband wasn't faithful to me so I left him. Now I want him back. I miss him so much. But I can't let him back for what he did to me.

Advanced Response: _____
_____.

10. *Drug user to human service professional:*
Client: I can stop using. This stuff is not that important to me. If you find me a job, I'll quit!

Advanced Response: _____
_____.

Four Types of Client Discrepancies

Sometimes, clients "hook" me, and I start bickering with them about a discrepancy I view in their life. This kind of confrontation is rarely helpful and almost always a result of unfinished business on the part of the helper. Effective helpers, however, can disengage from these emotional entanglements and are able to build relationships that offer the potential to challenge the client through an honest and thoughtful conversation concerning discrepancies in the client's life. As noted, four types of discrepancies include those between a client's values and behaviors, feelings and behaviors, idealized self and real self, and expressed feelings and underlying feelings.

1. Discrepancy Between a Client's Values and Behavior

When a client expresses a certain value and then his or her actions do not match that expressed value, there is incongruity in the client's life. For instance, suppose a client has been an anti-abortion advocate, and then tells you one day that her 15-year-old daughter is pregnant and she is "making her" get an abortion. Pointing out the discrepancy to the client might assist her in either reformulating her values or in changing her behavior (trying to make the daughter get an abortion). However, how the incongruity is presented to the client is important. For instance, one helper might say,

Helper: "You told me you were against abortion. Why are you doing this?"

Such a confrontation might make a client defensive (and notice the "Why" question!). However, another helper could say:

Helper: "That's interesting. I was under the impression that you were against abortion. Help me understand how you come to make sense of that.

2. Discrepancy Between a Client's Feelings and Behaviors

Sometimes a client might assert certain feelings and then act in a manner that seems to indicate otherwise. For instance, suppose a husband tells a helper that he loves his wife and then goes on to note how often he yells at her and cheats on her. As with discrepancies between values and behaviors, the helper can further client self-realization by noting such inconsistency.

Helper: So, I clearly hear your love for your wife, yet I'm confused by the yelling and the affairs. Can we talk about that?

Confronting the client in the above manner is an invitation for a discussion—*not* an invitation for an argument.

3. Discrepancy Between Idealized Self and Real Self

Some clients have lofty thoughts and fantasies about how they want to act (idealized self), but in reality, fall short from these self-imposed ideals (real self). For instance, a client might state that he wants to be more genuine in relationships:

Client: I'm going to be more real in my relationships, and honest with others about who I am and how I feel about them.

Now, imagine that the above statement is followed by a series of behaviors in which the client lies to his friends and his children about how he feels about their behaviors and about some of his own behaviors. The helper, could respond with:

Helper: So, the last time you were here you talked about the importance of being real in your relationships and how you were going to increasingly practice that. Yet, I think I hear that you didn't do that with your children and your friends. What do you think about that?

4. Discrepancy Between Expressed and Underlying Feelings

This last type of discrepancy is between a client's verbal expression of feelings and the underlying feelings a client won't admit to or is not currently aware of. For instance, as the client states the following (she seems to be holding back tears):

Client: My marriage is good, we live the kind of life that most married couples live—maybe we have a few problems, but nothing major.

In this case, the helper makes the following response:

Helper: As I'm hearing you talk, it seems like you're holding back tears. I'm thinking you have some deeper feelings about your marriage.

The above empathic response by the helper invites the client to talk about the underlying feelings. If you remember from the discussion of advanced empathy, this would be considered an advanced empathic response (above level 3) as it brings out feelings not outwardly expressed by the client.

Five Ways to Challenge Client Discrepancies

After building a strong foundation to the helping relationship, invitations to discuss a client's discrepancy can occur in a number of ways. Here, we offer a few examples, including you/but statements, inviting the client to justify the discrepancy, reframing, using satire, and using higher level empathy.

1. You/But Statements

When confronting a discrepancy in this manner, the helper verbally identifies the incongruence through the use of a "you said/but" statement and follows this with an invitation for a discussion. For instance, to a client who says he believes in honesty but is having an affair, the helper might state:

Helper: You say that you believe in honesty, but you seem to be hiding a serious matter from your wife. How do you make sense of that?

2. Asking the Client to Justify the Discrepancy

Another way of pointing out a discrepancy is to simply invite the client to discuss the contradiction so that the helper can better understand how the client makes sense of it. In this case, it is important that the helper truly feel like this is an invitation to the client, rather than an accusation or judgment of the client. For example, in the above example the helper might say:

Helper: Okay, I'm trying to understand how, on the one hand, you describe your relationship as one that's based on honesty, and on the other hand, you are hiding an affair from your wife? Can we talk about that?

3. Reframing

This way of highlighting the discrepancy offers the client an alternative way of viewing his or her situation followed by a discussion of this new reality. This is an invitation to discuss the discrepancy from a new frame of reference.

Helper: Even though honesty is important to you, sometimes other values override your desire to be honest. So, in this case, your value of protecting yourself and your wife from the pain of the affair may be more important than your value of being honest. Is that how you see it?

4. Using Satire

A fourth way a helper could point out a discrepancy is through the use of satire. Highlighting the contradiction in this way can be more confrontational than the other techniques and should be done carefully, if at all. With satire, the absurdity of the discrepancy is confronted. For instance, in the above example, you might say:

Helper: Well, I guess in this instance it's okay to be dishonest. After all, you're saving your wife from those painful feelings. Want to discuss this?

5. Higher-Level Empathy

The final way of challenging a client's discrepancy is through the use of advanced empathic responses. Any of the advanced empathic responses discussed earlier can be used to help bring new awareness to the client about discrepancies in his or her life. For instance, reflecting deeper feelings or pointing out conflicting feelings and thoughts exposes the client to deeper parts of himself or herself.

Reflecting Deeper Feelings and Pointing Out Conflicts:
Helper: As you are talking, I think I hear the guilt you're feeling about the affair. On the one hand, guilt, and on the other hand, exhilaration about this other person. That must be a difficult place to be.

Pointing out Conflicting Feelings and Thoughts:
Helper: You must be feeling quite conflicted. On the one hand you say you believe in honesty; on the other hand, you are hiding an affair. I guess I sense there is more to this story for you.

Now that we have discussed discrepancies and ways to confront them, use Experiential Exercise 7.2 to practice the art of confronting discrepancies in your helping relationships.

Experiential Exercise 7.2:
Confronting Sally

Sally, a thirty-six-year-old single female, makes about $80,000 a year working at a consulting firm. She loves her job, but is concerned that she is not making enough money to live the lifestyle that she wants to live. For three years, Sally has lived with her boyfriend Malik. She describes him as handsome and always concerned about her needs, except when he becomes abusive—which is about once a month. She notes that he has a very strong jealous streak, and he believes that Sally is often flirting with other men. At these times, he has gone into fits of rage and has even hit her. In addition, Sally would like to have children and is concerned she will soon be too old to conceive. Malik is steadfastly against having children.

Sally states she wants to end the relationship and can no longer take the abuse, despite the fact that Malik can be "as nice as pie" most of the time. However, she is worried that if she

Continued on Next Page

> ## Experiential Exercise 7.2:
> ## Confronting Sally (Cont'd)
>
> leaves Malik, she will not have the finances to support herself. Also, she is afraid that if she is alone, she will become depressed and start drinking again—like she did when she was younger. Despite having said that she wants to end her relationship with Malik, after six months of counseling, Sally has still not made any moves in that direction.
>
> *In small groups of 3 to 5, consider the different kinds of discrepancies in Sally's life. Then, one person role-play Sally, and using one or more of the previously described methods, confront Sally about the discrepancies you found. When you are done, switch roles and the other students can role-play Sally. Observers can notate the types of responses used. Discuss how it was to confront Sally using the techniques described earlier.*

INTERPRETATION

A client offers details about his significant other. Later, he shares details about his relationship with his parents. The helper hears similar themes and feelings running through these relationships, and says: "It seems like some of the issues you experienced with your parents are similar to those with your lover." The client shakes his head in agreement. Is this interpretation or is this empathy? Although some may consider this interpretation, this could very well be a high-level empathic response (Carkhuff Scale, above Level 3.0) for a number of reasons. First, it is a result of deep listening and concentration by the helper. Second, it is based on a deep understanding of the client's framework of reality. Third, the helper has reflected back an understanding of the client's predicament without adding material not produced by the client and without jumping to conclusions or making assumptions. And finally, the client agrees with the helper's assessment. The helper is "on target" with the response. This type of response is profound, reaches deep inside the client's soul, and speaks to the imaginary line between facilitating and leading a client (Neukrug, Bayne, Dean-Nganga, & Pusateri, 2012).

On the other hand, contrast the above helper response with the helper who states, "I believe your relationship with your lover is the result of deep seated anger stemming from your unresolved oedipal complex." This kind of interpretation is the analysis of a client from the perspective of the helper and is based on a preset model of counseling and psychotherapy that makes assumptions about how a person would react under certain circumstances.

Psychoanalysis uses interpretation as a major therapeutic intervention. For instance, psychoanalysts believe that dreams hold symbols to unresolved conflicts from our psychosexual development and can provide the client with understanding into his or her development (Bishop, 2015). A dream about a goat being a person's pet in an immaculately clean apartment could represent an underlying need to rebel against a repressive upbringing, the goat representing the archetypal oppositional animal. Similarly, some cognitive therapists assume that individuals with specific diagnoses would be expected to have certain kinds of underlying cognitive structures (ways of thinking) that can be interpreted to the client (Fefergrad & Richter, 2013). For example, it would be assumed that a person with an anxiety disorder has an underlying belief that the world is a fearful and dangerous place and underestimates his or her ability to deal with anxiety.

Whether one is psychodynamically oriented, cognitively oriented, or relying on some other theoretical approach, the timing of the interpretation is crucial. If all goes well, the interpretation will provide a deep understanding of why the client responds the way he or she does. The hope is that when this new understanding about the client is offered, it will lead to client change.

Although interpretations may assist the client in making giant leaps within the therapeutic context, there are risks involved in using this technique. For instance, interpretation sets the helper up as the "expert" and lessens likelihood of a genuine relationship occurring between the helper and client (Daniels, 2015). In addition, it lessens the here-and-now quality of the therapeutic relationship, while increasing the amount of intellectualizing that occurs during the session, as both the helper and client discuss the interpretive material (Resnick, 2015). Finally, the ability to measure the efficacy of interpretation and other psychoanalytic techniques has been called into question (Leuzinger-Bohleber & Target, 2002; Olson, Christopher, Janzen, Petraglia, & Presniak, 2011). It is for these reasons that Carl Rogers (1970), and others, vehemently opposed the use of interpretation.

> To me, an interpretation as to the cause of individual behavior can never be anything but a high-level guess. The only way it can carry weight is when an authority puts his experience behind it. But I do not want to get involved in this kind of authoritativeness. "I think it's because you feel inadequate as a man that you engage in this blustering behavior," is not the kind of statement I would ever make. (pp. 57-58)

When to Use and Not Use Interpretation

Your opinion regarding the use of interpretation most likely depends on your view of human nature. If you align yourself with a model of counseling that makes assumptions about human behavior external to the client's understanding of reality, then interpretation of client material will become an important tool for you. On the other hand, if you assume that client growth is based on client's obtaining a fuller understanding of themselves from their own view of reality, then interpretation is likely to be a useless tool for you in the helping process. Finally, if you believe interpretation can be a valuable tool in the helper's repertoire, then clearly it should be used only after a trusting relationship has been established and with a sound knowledge of the theoretical approach you follow. Now that you know what interpretation is and how it can be used incorrectly, examine how effective you think interpretation might be (see Experiential Exercise 7.3).

Experiential Exercise 7.3:
Practicing Interpretations

Break up into groups of four that include a helper, a client, and two observers. The client is to discuss a real or made-up problem situation. The helper is to first listen to the client carefully and then try to make an interpretive response. So, if the client says, "I'm having trouble with my girlfriend, she never wants to listen to me," you might say, "I'm thinking your parents may not have listened to you either." Make as many interpretive responses as possible. Meanwhile, observers should be writing down the different interpretations. When you are finished, respond to the following questions. If time allows, switch roles.

1. How easy was it to make an interpretive response?
2. Were the interpretations mostly "on-target" or not?
3. If the interpretation was on target, was it helpful for the client?
4. If the interpretation was not on target, how harmful was it for the relationship?
5. Do you think interpretation is something that would be helpful in your work as a human service professional?

Unlike many of the skills discussed in this text, if you use interpretation, I suggest you use it very carefully (if at all). First, the efficacy of interpretation is questionable. Second, to use interpretation effectively, helpers must have a thorough knowledge of the theoretical model on which the interpretation is based. Most human service professionals do not have that level of training. Finally, too many human service professionals use interpretation in a haphazard manner, making up their own interpretations as they go.

COGNITIVE-BEHAVIORAL RESPONSES

During the 1950s and 1960s Aaron Beck and Albert Ellis independently developed two theories of cognitive therapy that greatly impacted the way many people conduct counseling (Neukrug & Ellis, 2015; Weishaar, 2015). Although their theories had much in common, there were a number of differences. For instance, Beck believed we have what he called *core beliefs* (e.g., "I am powerless," I am helpless") that impact our *intermediate beliefs* (attitudes, rules and assumptions we make based on our core beliefs) that are responsible for developing our *automatic thoughts* (Rice, 2015). Automatic thoughts are fleeting thoughts we have all day long about how we are interacting in the world (e.g., "I shouldn't have said that," "I'm not good enough to do that," "That was a pretty good response," etc.). Although we all have automatic thoughts, and all of us can get in touch with them, some of us need a little practice to access them. Beck stated that our automatic thoughts affect how we feel, how we act, and our physiological responses (e.g., increase in stress hormones). So, if my core belief is one that says I am powerless, one resulting attitude might be, "life sucks, as I have no control over it," and a possible assumption could be, "I assume that things will more or less stay the way they are." These intermediate beliefs affect my reactions, so I might feel sad (feelings), stay at home all day and do nothing (behaviors), and have increased cortisol levels which is a factor in increasing stress levels (physiology).

If a helper can assist a client in accessing his or her automatic thoughts, he or she can work backwards and get a pretty good sense of one's intermediate thoughts and, eventually, one's core beliefs. Then, the helper can assist the person in changing those core beliefs (and, by default, the intermediate beliefs; the automatic thoughts; and the feelings, behaviors, and physiology). Like Beck, Ellis also focused on thoughts, but he stated there are three *irrational thoughts*, and that many of us abide by some of them (Ellis, 2015). They include:

1. "I *absolutely must* under all conditions do important tasks well and be approved by significant others or else I am an inadequate and unlovable person!"

2. "Other people *absolutely must* under all conditions treat me fairly and justly or else they are rotten, damnable persons!"

3. "Conditions under which I live *absolutely must* always be the way I want them to be, give me almost immediate gratification, and not require me to work too hard to change or improve them; or else it is *awful*, I *can't stand* them, and it is impossible for me to be happy *at all!*" (Ellis & MacLaren, 2005, pp. 32-33)

Ellis strongly noted that it is not an event that makes us feel and behave the way we do, but it is our thoughts about the event. He called this the "*A, B, and Cs,*" where A is the *activating event*, B is the *belief about the event*, and C is the *consequential feelings and behaviors*. If you know your "B" (which is being impacted by one of the three irrational thoughts), then you can pretty well guess what your "C" will be. So, if my partner breaks up with me and I become super depressed, it's not because he or she left me. Rather, it's because of what I believe about her leaving—which is related to one or more of the three irrational beliefs above.

Of course, Beck's and Ellis's theories is much more involved than the short descriptions I just offered. However, their basic ideas are this:

1. Our thinking impacts our feelings, behaviors, and physiology, sometimes in ways that are out of awareness.

2. It is relatively easy to gain awareness of the types of thoughts we are having that impacts our feelings, behaviors, and physiology.

3. By sharing our thoughts (e.g., automatic thoughts, irrational beliefs) with someone else, we can begin to see which thoughts are making us feel badly.

4. After we identify which thoughts are making us feel poorly, we can dispute and change those thoughts and develop new thoughts that result in good feelings.

5. In addition to identifying and changing our negative thoughts to positive ones, we can develop behaviors that reinforce new ways of thinking.

Although I don't expect the human service professional to be a full-fledged cognitive therapist, I do think this general approach can be used by the helper in working with many clients. Thus, when a human service professional has a client who is feeling down, anxious, or worried, he or she might consider a modified cognitive approach by asking the client to examine automatic thoughts or irrational thoughts. If the client can identify how his or her thinking makes the situation worse, the human service professional can help him or her work on developing new, more positive ways of thinking and, at the same time, work on changing some behaviors that would be in line with a more positive approach to living (see Reflection Exercise 7.2).

Reflection Exercise 7.2:
Practicing Cognitive Disputations

Part I: Use the below example of a client who just experienced the activating event of "my lover has left me." Then, examine the automatic thought, irrational belief(s), and possible consequences. Then go on to Part II on the next page.

Activating Event (A): My lover has left me.

Automatic Thought: I can't live in this world without her (or him).

Irrational Belief (B): Conditions under which I live *absolutely must* always be the way I want them to be, give me almost immediate gratification, and not require me to work too hard to change or improve them; or else it is *awful*, I *can't stand* them, and it is impossible for me to be happy *at all!*

Possible Consequence (C): *Feelings Consequence:* Depression, panic, isolation.

Behavioral Consequence: Need to immediately seek out another person, even if the relationship may not be healthy or positive. Or, isolation if depression is particularly bad.

Continued on Next Page

Reflection Exercise 7.2:
Practicing Cognitive Disputations (Cont'd)

Part II: Consider how you can dispute the client's irrational thoughts and help him (or her) develop new rational thoughts, as well as new behaviors that would result in a healthier way of living. When you are finished, discuss your responses with others in small groups and talk about the possibility that you might use this approach with clients.

Cognitive Disputations (disputing the irrational belief):

New, Rational Belief:

Behaviors to Support New, Rational Belief:

SPECIALIZED TRAINING

Although the human service professional is a generalist and can be found in a wide variety of settings doing a large array of activities, the practices highlighted in this section include skills that have become increasingly important or popular in human service work. They include assessing for lethality: suicidality and homicidality; crisis, disaster, and trauma helping; token economies; positive helping; and coaching.

ASSESSING FOR LETHALITY: SUICIDALITY AND HOMICIDALITY

At some point in their career, every human service practitioner will be faced with a client who is suicidal or homicidal, and it is extremely important to know what to do in such situations. Whether suicidal or homicidal, a client can be assessed along a similar continuum ranging from ideation (thinking about it), developing a plan, having a means to carry out the plan, preparing to implement the plan, rehearsing the plan, and finally acting on the plan (Resnick, 2011; Scott & Resnick, 2005) (see Figure 7.2). Establishing the client's placement on the continuum by asking pointed questions is helpful in determining risk level for harming self or others. Although not all individuals who are suicidal or homicidal follow this path, the vast majority do. Since there are high stakes involved with suicidal or homicidal thoughts and actions, it is important to assess for lethality whenever a human service professional suspects a client may be at risk.

Figure 7.2: Assessing for Lethality

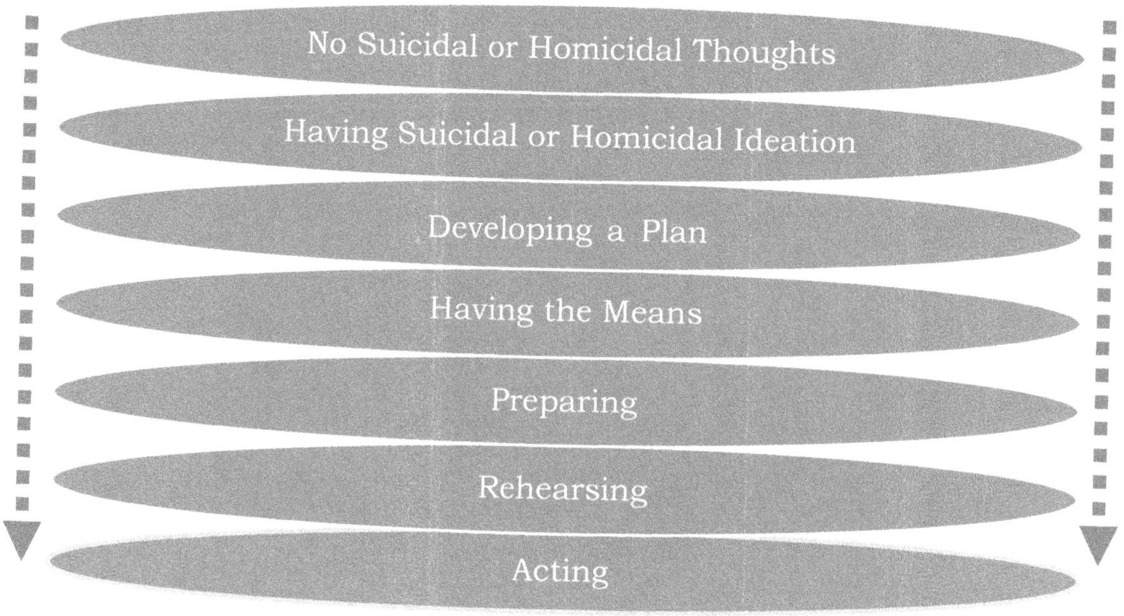

No Suicidal or Homicidal Thoughts

Having Suicidal or Homicidal Ideation

Developing a Plan

Having the Means

Preparing

Rehearsing

Acting

In addition to determining where on Figure 7.2 the person falls, there are a wide range of risk factors that can help a human service professional determine the likelihood of suicide, and to a lesser degree, homicide. Fact Sheet 7.1 identifies many of these risks.

In contrast to *risk factors*, there are a number of *protective factors* that seem to guard against the likelihood of a person committing suicide or homicide. Some of these include (ACA, 2011a; CDC, 2015; Juhnke, Granello, & Lebron-Striker, 2007; U.S. Department of Veteran Affairs, n.d.):

- Pregnancy
- Stable employment
- Medication compliance
- Children living at home
- Being connected with a therapist
- Easy access to clinical interventions
- Having children under the age of 18
- Strong family or community supports
- Positive coping and problem-solving skill
- Having strong religious or spiritual beliefs

Assessing for suicide or homicide risk is not an exact science (Pisani, Murrie, & Silverman, 2015), and the above gives you a quick sense of how to evaluate for suicidality and homicidality. However, having a thorough understanding of this important area requires supplementary materials and course work. You are encouraged to learn more about this important aspect of the human service professional's work.

Fact Sheet 7.1: Risk Factors and Signs for Suicide and Homicide

The following represent some risk factors and possible signs of suicidal or homicidal ideation. However, this is by no means an exclusive list. In addition, one can have just a few of these risk factors, and sometimes have none of these risk factors, and still be suicidal or homicidal.

- Prior attempts
- History of abuse
- Problems with anger
- Relationship breakup
- Wanting to seek revenge
- Family history of suicide
- Medication incompliance
- Alcohol/substance abuse
- Withdrawing from activities
- Extreme anxiety or agitation
- Recent loss of someone close
- Suddenly giving things away
- Impulsivity/lack of self-control
- History of significant problems
- History of psychiatric treatment
- Problems eating or eating too much
- Feeling trapped by current situation
- Active suicidal or homicidal ideation
- Problems sleeping or sleeping too much
- Dramatic shift of mood or feeling states
- Sudden poor performance in school or on the job
- Hopeless or lack of purpose or meaning in life
- Engaging in risky or impulsive behaviors without care of consequences
- Suddenly recovering from depressive symptoms or sudden positive outlook
- Having access to a lethal means (the more lethal, the more serious: e.g., having a gun)

Sources: American Counseling Association [ACA], 2011a; Centers for Disease Control and Prevention (CDC), 2015; Juhnke, Granello, & Lebron-Striker, 2007; Suicide Risk Assessment Guide, n.d.

CRISIS, TRAUMA, AND DISASTER HELPING

Unfortunately, as a result of helpers' sometimes inadequate responses to mass shootings, hurricane Katrina, the 9/11 attack, and thousands of veterans coming home from war with *post-traumatic stress disorder (PTSD)*, we have come to believe that helpers have not been well prepared to respond to a disaster, crises, or traumatic event (Craigen, Cole, Paiva, & Levingston, 2014; Scott, 2014; Selfridge, 2014). Thus, in recent years, human service professionals and other helpers have become better trained to do crisis counseling, work with people experiencing disasters, and understand and help those who have experienced trauma (Bowman & Roysircar, 2011). As a result, models of how to respond to crises, traumatic events, and disasters have been developed. For instance, the National Child Traumatic Stress Network and National Center for Post-Traumatic Stress Disorder (PTSD) (Brymer et al., 2009) delineate eight steps when responding to a crisis or disaster:

1. *Contact and Engagement:* Initiating caring, helpful, and compassionate contact with those in need.
2. *Safety and Comfort:* Ensuring that there are no further safety issues and providing psychological and physical comfort to those involved.
3. *Stabilization (if needed):* Helping orient survivors, providing a peaceful environment, and helping calm those who are emotionally overwhelmed.
4. *Information Gathering:* Understanding immediate concerns and needs by gathering information from the individual(s) and devising helping interventions based on the information gathered.
5. *Practical Assistance:* Addressing immediate concerns and needs through practical help to survivors.
6. *Connection with Social Supports:* Developing brief or ongoing contacts with family members, friends, and community resources.
7. *Information on Coping:* Reducing distress and encouraging healthy functioning by making available information on stress reactions to crisis and disaster situations.
8. *Linkage with Collaborative Services:* Ensuring that individuals faced with crisis and disaster situations have needed services now and in the future.

In general, crisis, disaster, and trauma counseling is seen as short term, built on client strengths, non-diagnostic oriented, and provided at agencies or where the crisis has occurred (Federal Emergency Management Agency, 2015). Many of the basic foundational, essential, and commonly-used skills noted in this text are core to the work of the crisis and disaster helper. However, in some cases the exposure to a horrific event can lead to long-lasting symptoms, such as in the case of those who suffer with PTSD. In these cases, more involved counseling needs to take place and advanced training would be needed.

TOKEN ECONOMIES

The behavioral technique of establishing a token economy has been successfully used with different client populations, particularly those with intellectual disabilities (Matson & Boijsoli, 2009). This technique is based on *operant conditioning*, a type of learning theory that uses *reinforcement contingencies* to change client behaviors. The token is considered a *secondary reinforcer* and can become quite powerful in changing client behaviors, because it is associated with a desired object for which the token is being exchanged (Hackenberg, 2009).

Typically, with this technique, a client is given a token for specific targeted behaviors that he or she is asked to exhibit. For example, a person might receive a token for successfully getting dressed in the morning, for exhibiting "appropriate" personal traits, for bathing himself or herself, and so forth. At the end of a specified amount of time, such as a week or a month, the individual can trade in his or her tokens for money or some other reinforcer such as candy or items in a gift shop.

Although token economies have been quite successful when applied to group homes for individuals with intellectual disabilities, they can also be highly motivating for other populations, including children, the mentally ill, and even college students (see Reflection Exercise 7.3).

Reflection Exercise 7.3: James's Day at the Group Home: A Token Economy

James wakes up in the morning, and after successfully dressing himself, is given a token. He has a special pouch where he keeps his tokens, and he beams proudly upon receiving one. After dressing, he eats breakfast with other members of the group home and then completes his tasks for the day, which may include doing the dishes, taking out the garbage, or clearing the table. When he completes each task, he is given another token. James's day is very structured and includes specific activities, depending on the day of the week. Since this is a Monday, James attends a reading group in the morning where volunteers read stories to members of the group home. Sometimes, some group members read stories to one another.

After lunch, James and the other group members will go on their weekly walk, picking up trash along the side of the road near their group home. They have a special sign on the road that notes that the street is kept clean by their group home. They are all very proud of this sign. Throughout the day, James can continue to receive tokens for assisting with the meals and for exhibiting appropriate behaviors. Tokens are never taken away from group members, but all group members know that if they do not behave in the "right way," they will not receive a token. James usually receives about eight tokens a day, and every Saturday he exchanges tokens for a gift. The group home has a designated area with a number of gifts the members can view. They range from things like stuffed animals, to books, to calculators, to healthy snacks.

After having read the above scenario, with a partner or in small groups, discuss how effective you think a token economy is with individuals with intellectual disabilities. Then, brainstorm other populations with which you think this might work. Share your thoughts with the larger class.

POSITIVE HELPING

If you remember from Chapter 6, a large section of the chapter focused on solution-focused questions. These questions are the bedrock to what some have called positive helping, or the positive psychology movement, that has emerged over the past twenty-five years (Lopez, Pedrotti, & Snyder, 2015). Positive helping assumes that we have choices in our lives relative to our mental, physical, and spiritual states; we are not determined by early childhood or other factors; and that we need to be careful when labeling or diagnosing a person, as such labels can result in negative attributions, or self-statements, by individuals including the person being labeled. As such, positive helping is optimistic, future-oriented, strength-based, and focused on a large number of human contexts. One does not just become positive by thinking in a positive manner; it is a purposeful and deliberate method of choosing how we live all aspects of our lives. Researchers suggest that having a positive focus can lead to greater resilience, a longer life, a decrease in physical health problems, and can increase creativity, engagement in life, and a personal sense of meaning (Bolier et al., 2013; Rankin, 2013) (see Reflection Exercise 7.4).

Reflection Exercise 7.4:
Your Positivity Ratio

Some research indicates that a healthy positivity ratio is 3 to 1, which means that our positive thoughts and actions should outweigh our negative ones to that degree. Here you can assess your positivity ratio. After taking the instrument at the website designated below, consider if you need to do some things in your life to become more positive. Also consider how you can use an instrument like this with your clients.

Positive ratio website: https://www.positivityratio.com/

Having a positive outlook on life is intimately related to various aspects of our wellness. For instance, in their Indivisible Self Model, Myers and Sweeney (2008) identify five factors that can be reflective of a positive outlook that also take into account an individual's context. The factors, which include the creative self, coping self, social self, essential self, and physical self (and contexts), are described in Reflection Exercise 7.5.

The bedrock of working with clients from a positive focus is using your essential and foundational skills. and applying solution-focused questions to help your client make positive changes in the future. A positive helping focus is a natural fit for the human service professional because it does not rely on in-depth knowledge of psychological theory or require the client to be involved in long-term therapy to implement. Instead, positive helping is accessible and pragmatic, as it focuses on:

1. Identifying how the person would like to change.
2. Identifying the different realms of a person's life to focus upon.
3. Being a cheerleader and support person for your client.
4. Focusing on how things can be different in the future.
5. Being committed to the client to ensure that there is follow-through.

LIFE-COACHING

In recent years, life-coaching (sometimes just called coaching) has become another mechanism for clients to develop healthy habits and fits nicely into the model of positive helping just discussed (Labardee, Williams, & Hodges, 2012). In contrast to counseling, coaching spends little time examining the past or focusing on problems. Rather, coaching relies on a short-term focused helping relationship in which the coach uses solution-focused questions to identify one or more issues on which to concentrate, collaboratively sets goals, affirms and encourages the client to work on goals, and helps to ensure continued follow-up after goals have been reached to ensure maintenance of goals (Shallcross, 2011). A whole host of concerns that tend to be short-term and not based on deeply held problems or deep client wounds can be focused upon in this process, such as weight loss, finding a job, communication skills, developing an exercise regime, managing one's budget, and so forth.

Coaching eschews diagnosis, does not generally rely on third-party (insurance) payments, and is viewed as less stigmatizing than the more traditional helping relationship. Life coaching will not likely replace counseling and therapy, but rather will offer an additional venue in which some clients can participate.

Reflection Exercise 7.5:
Assessing Your Wellness

Score yourself, from 1 to 5, on each of the following five factors, with 5 indicating the area you most need to work on. Then, find the average for all of the five factors (creative self, coping self, etc.). Next, write down the ways you can better yourself in any of the factors for which your scores seem problematic (probably scores between a 3 and 5). You might also want to consider how your scores may change as a function of the context in which you find yourself.

FACTORS

Creative Self: This is related to our uniqueness in our interpersonal relationships and how we come to make sense of our place in the world. It is highlighted by our ability to be mentally sharp and open minded (thinking), being in touch with our feelings (emotions), being intentional and planful and knowing how to express our needs (control), being effective at work and using our skills successfully (work), and having the capacity to deal with life as it comes at us (positive humor).

Coping Self: This is related to our ability to deal with life's events and to effectively cope with negative situations. It is composed of developing leisure activities (leisure), successfully coping with stress (stress management), valuing ourselves and having good self-esteem despite problems (self-worth), and having the capacity to be imperfect while recognizing it is unrealistic to think we can be loved by all (realistic beliefs).

Social Self: The social self is related to how we are connected to others through our friendships, intimate relationships, and through familial bonds. It is composed of the ability to connect with others in supportive, emotional, and sometimes sexual ways (friendship and intimacy). Additionally, it is the part of us that can share deeply with others and be mutually respectful and appreciative (love).

Essential Self: This has to do with how we make meaning in our relationships with ourselves and others. It is recognizing the part of us that is beyond our mind and body (spirituality), feeling comfortable in the way we identify with our gender (gender identity) and with our culture (cultural identity), and being able to care for ourselves through self-care and by minimizing harm in our environment (self-care).

Physical Self: This part of ourselves is reflected through our biological and physical self and is related to ensuring that we have adequate physical activity in our lives (exercise) and that we eat well, have a good diet, and avoid being overweight or underweight (nutrition).

CONTEXT
Context has to do with systems in which we live, such as family, community, social and political systems, work environment, and global system. When assessing yourself on the five factors, consider how your sense of self changes based on the context in which you find yourself.

Drawbacks to coaching include the fact that it may not be conducive to digging up underlying core issues, and the fact that few, if any, health insurance companies cover coaching services (Shallcross, 2011). In addition, because coaching sacrifices depth in favor of efficiency, it probably has limited efficacy in treating more serious mental health issues (Ley, 2014). Today, coaching has become its own specialty area and human service professionals can become a Board Certified Coach (BCC) through the Center for Credentialing and Education (CCE, 2015). In coming years, we will have a better sense of the popularity of life-coaching and whether coaching will move into the mainstream of helping services (see Experiential Exercise 7.4).

Experiential Exercise 7.4:
Coaching a Partner

Pair up with another student, and using the helping skills you learned in chapters three through six, assist that person with a life problem or issue. However, because coaching is not therapy, make sure this is not a long-term emotional or psychological problem, but a life problem which the "client" can more easily tackle (e.g., reducing stress, increasing physical health, talking more effectively with one's spouse or children, etc.). While coaching, the helper may want to focus upon the following:

1. Initially focus upon your foundational and essential skills to build the relationship.
2. Early on, using open questions, determine what to focus upon.
3. Use solution-focused questions to help the person identify goals and strategies for change.
4. Highlight goals and strategies and set dates for change.
5. Encourage and affirm your client along the way.
6. Remember to have a positive focus, build on client's strengths, be committed, be encouraging and affirming, and gently nudge your client to work on identified goals and strategies for change.

After role-playing for 20 to 30 minutes, discuss the coaching process with each other. Was it helpful? Do you think that coaching could be beneficial long-term? What are some of the positive and negative aspects of coaching?

SUMMARY

This chapter explored those advanced skills and specialized trainings that are widely used or becoming ever more important for the human service professional's work. Starting with advanced skills, we first looked at advanced empathy. We identified five types of advanced empathy, including reflecting deeper feelings, pointing out conflicting feelings or thoughts, the use of metaphors or analogies, self-disclosure, and tactile responses. We noted that advanced empathic responses can range from a level 3.0 to a level 5.0 on the Carkhuff scale, although it's not unusual to find them in the 3.5 to 4.0 range. We stressed that although such responses are not always essential for the helping relationship, they are additive in the sense that they offer a more complex understanding of the client's experience and a deeper awareness of one's feeling states.

The next skill we examined was confrontation: challenge with support. We noted that confrontation begins with building a trusting and caring relationship, followed by an invitation to discuss discrepancies. Four types of discrepancies we outlined included those between a client's values and behaviors, feelings and behaviors, idealized self and real self, and expressed feelings and underlying feelings. Five ways of inviting discussions about discrepancies included you/but statements, asking the client to justify the discrepancy, reframing, using satire, and using higher level empathy.

Interpretation was the third advanced skill we looked at. Interpretation is the analysis of a client's understanding of the world from the perspective of the helper and is based on a preset model of counseling. It should be used cautiously but could offer large movement in the helping relationship. However, if off base, it can damage the relationship. Psychodynamic oriented helpers use interpretations to make leaps about a person's behaviors, and cognitively oriented helpers sometimes develop treatment plans based on a client's symptoms and the assumptions (interpretations) about underlying cognitive structures.

The last type of advanced skills were cognitive-behavioral responses. Beck talked about the relationship between core beliefs, intermediate beliefs, automatic thoughts and the resulting feelings, behaviors, and physiological responses. Ellis talked about the A B C's of thinking, noting that it is not the activating event ("A") that causes consequences ("C"), such as negative feelings; it is the beliefs ("B") about the activating event that impact consequences ("C"). Ellis noted that irrational thoughts often drive "B." We suggested that the human service professional could use cognitive-behavioral responses when working with clients by helping them change cognitions and adopt behaviors that match the new, healthier ways of thinking.

Moving on to specialized training, we first touched on how to assess for suicidality and homicidality. We offered a continuum of lethality assessment that ranges from ideation (thinking about it), developing a plan, having a means to carry out the plan, preparing to implement the plan, rehearsing the plan, and finally acting on the plan. We highlighted some possible risk and protective factors to suicide or homicide.

We next highlighted crisis, disaster, and trauma helping and offered one model that delineates eight steps to responding to a crisis: contact and engagement, safety and comfort, stabilization, information gathering, practical assistance, connection with social supports, information on coping, and linkage with collaborative services.

Token economies, we noted, have been successfully used with different populations and are based on operant conditioning, a type of learning theory that uses reinforcement contingencies to change client behaviors. Here, a token that is a secondary reinforcer, is given to clients and traded in, at a later date, for food or a gift. Token economies have been successfully used with individuals with intellectual disabilities and other populations.

Positive helping, we noted, assumes that we have choices in our lives relative to our mental, physical, and spiritual states; that we are not determined by early childhood or other factors; and tends to focus on strengths, not pathology. Positive helping is also optimistic, future-oriented, affirming, and focused on a large number of human contexts. We highlighted one model of wellness that can be used in positive helping, the Indivisible Self Model, which looks at five factors in helping a person assess his or her level of wellness: the creative self, coping self, social self, essential self, and physical self. We also offered some steps that might be helpful when working with clients from a positive helping lens.

The last area of specialized training we included was life-coaching, or just "coaching." We noted that coaching spends little time examining the past or focusing on problems. Instead, it focuses on identifying goals and finding solutions, views the helping relationship as a partnership rather than a therapeutic relationship, is strength-based, and is often conducted in a less-structured environment than counseling. We explained that one can become a Board Certified Coach (BCC) through the Center for Credentialing and Education.

KEY WORDS AND TERMS

A, B, and Cs
Activating event
Advanced empathy
Assessing for lethality: Suicidality and homicidality
Automatic thoughts
Beck, Aaron
Belief about the event
Board Certified Coach
Center for Credentialing and Education
Creative self
Coaching
Cognitive-behavioral responses
Confrontation: Challenge with support
Consequential feelings and behaviors
Coping self
Core beliefs
Crisis, disaster, and trauma helping
Discrepancy between client's values and behavior
Discrepancy between client's expressed and underlying feelings
Discrepancy between client's feelings and behaviors
Discrepancy between client's idealized self and real self
Ellis, Albert

Essential self
Indivisible Self Model
Intermediate beliefs
Interpretation
Irrational thoughts
Life-coaching
Metaphors or analogies
Operant conditioning
Physical self
Pointing out conflicting feelings or thoughts
Positive helping
Post-traumatic stress syndrome (PTSD)
Protective factors
Reflecting deeper feelings
Reinforcement contingencies
Risk factors
Secondary reinforcer
Self-disclosure
Social self
Subceive
Tactile responses
Token economies

SECTION III

TREATMENT ISSUES

The last section of the book examines a variety of treatment issues when working with clients in the helping relationship. *Chapter 8* reviews a broad range of case management concerns, which are issues related to the overall process involved in maintaining the optimal functioning of clients. Thus, we review the process of providing informed consent and professional disclosure statements; conducting assessment for treatment planning; developing, evaluating, and monitoring progress toward client goals; writing process notes, monitoring the use of psychotropic medications; case notes and reports; ensuring the security and confidentiality of records; managing and documenting client contact hours; making referrals; conducting follow-up; and practicing time management.

The next chapter in this section, *Culturally Competent Helping*, begins by examining the changing demographics in the United States and its impact on being a culturally competent helper. We then review eight reasons why counseling is not working for some clients from diverse cultures. The chapter goes on to identify some definitions of culturally competent helping and then reviews two models of cross-cultural helping: the RESPECTFUL Model and the Multicultural and Social Justice Competencies. The second half of the chapter examines strategies for working with a number of select populations, including: different ethnic and racial groups; people from diverse religious backgrounds; women; men; lesbian, gay, bisexual, and transgender individuals; those who are homeless and the poor; older persons; individuals with mental illness; individuals with disabilities; and substance users and abusers.

Chapter 10, Ethical Issues and Ethical Decision-Making, examines the purpose of ethical guidelines and describes some of their limitations It then highlights four ethical decision-making models (problem-solving, moral, developmental, and social-constructionist) which, in concert with the ethical code, can be used to guide the human service professional toward wise and thoughtful actions. The chapter then presents some of the more important ethical issues that human service professionals face, including those related to informed consent; competence and scope of knowledge; supervision; confidentiality; privileged communication; dual and multiple relationships; sexual relationships with clients; whether the primary obligation of the human service professional is to the client, agency, or society; continuing education; multicultural counseling; and values in the helping relationship. Ethical vignettes associated with each of these areas are examined. The chapter concludes with an examination of how human service professionals have responded to 88 select ethical behaviors.

CHAPTER 8

Case Management

LEARNING OBJECTIVES

1. Review the purpose and importance of case management to the helping process.

2. Understand the importance and ethical obligation of informed consent and professional disclosure statements.

3. Examine how to conduct an assessment for treatment planning in four areas: conducting a clinical interview, administering tests, doing informal assessment, and coming up with a diagnosis.

4. Understand the importance of the development, evaluation, and monitoring of progress toward client goals.

5. Learn about the use of psychotropic medications and their classification in five categories: antipsychotics, mood-stabilizing drugs, antidepressants, anti-anxiety agents, and stimulants.

6. Learn the differences between writing process notes, case notes, and case reports, and learn the basics for writing such reports.

7. Understand the importance of, and legal ramifications to, ensuring the security and confidentiality of records.

8. Learn how to manage and document client contact hours and understand their importance.

9. Understand proper procedures in making referrals.

10. Understand proper procedures in conducting follow-up.

11. Examine the importance of time management.

INTRODUCTION

This chapter examines the broad range of activities known as case management, which has been viewed as the overall process involved in maintaining the optimal functioning of clients (Neukrug, 2017; Woodside & McClam, 2013; Summers, 2016). Thus, case management involves such things as (1) providing informed consent and professional disclosure statements, (2) conducting assessment for treatment planning, (3) developing, evaluating, and monitoring progress toward client goals, (4) monitoring the use of psychotropic medications, (5) writing process notes, case notes and reports, (6) ensuring the security and confidentiality of records, (7) managing and documenting client contact hours, (8) making referrals, (9) conducting follow-up, and (10) practicing time management. With an increased emphasis on accountability within the mental health professions, case management has become critical to the work of the human service professional. Let's take a look at each these activities that make up the broad area of case management.

INFORMED CONSENT AND PROFESSIONAL DISCLOSURE STATEMENTS

As you are aware, human service professionals are bound by their ethics code and when faced with difficult ethical dilemmas, do their utmost to follow such guidelines (see NOHS, 2015). Equipped with their ethics code, and with knowledge of ethical decision-making models, helpers can make wise decisions for their clients and their professional standing in the field (Corey, Corey, Corey, & Callanan, 2015; Neukrug & Milliken, 2011) (see Chapter 10). One aspect of ethical helping is to obtain informed consent from clients, acknowledging that they understand the nature and general limits of the helping relationship:

> Human service professionals obtain informed consent to provide services to clients at the beginning of the helping relationship. Clients should be informed that they may withdraw consent at any time except where denied by court order and should be able to ask questions before agreeing to the services. Clients who are unable to give consent should have those who are legally able to give consent for them review an informed consent statement and provide appropriate consent. (NOHS, 2015, Standard 2)

Informed consent is generally obtained after a client has received and reviewed a *professional disclosure statement*, which summarizes the nature and limits of the professional helping relationship. Such statements are reviewed by clients and then signed, indicating that they understand the many aspects of the helping relationship and that they give consent to such treatment. Professional disclosure statements often include the following (Corey et al., 2105; Remley & Herlihy, 2014):

1. Information about credentials
2. The purpose of the helping relationship
3. A synopsis of the helper's theoretical orientation or way of working with clients
4. A statement about the importance of respecting cross-cultural differences
5. A statement noting that the helper will keep promises made to clients
6. A notation about the fact that the helper is committed to assisting the client
7. Information that underscores the fact that confidentiality will be kept under most, but not all circumstance (e.g., danger to self or others; legal issues; issues unique to the specific agency)
8. An acknowledgement of the importance of the client's self-determination
9. A statement highlighting agency rules and legal issues that need to be adhered to
10. Information about limits to and boundaries of the helping relationship
(see Experiential Exercise 8.1).

Experiential Exercise 8.1: Informed Consent and Professional Disclosure Statements

Revisit the professional disclosure statement you wrote from Chapter 3, Experiential Exercise 3.1. If you no longer have it, or never did it, then do that now. Then find another student in class and role play the process of giving the client your professional disclosure statement. Have the client read it thoroughly, and then sign a statement asserting that he or she gives informed consent for treatment. After you are finished, in small groups or as a class, discuss the positive aspects of a professional disclosure statement and of obtaining informed consent. Finally, discuss any negative aspects of this process you may have found.

CONDUCTING ASSESSMENT FOR TREATMENT PLANNING

Treatment planning assessment involves multiple ways of understanding client concerns and can include (1) conducting a clinical interview, (2) administering tests, (3) doing informal assessment, and (4) coming up with a diagnosis (Neukrug & Fawcett, 2015; Schwitzer & Rubin, 2015). Ultimately, such assessments help clarify the client's needs and will assist in the goal setting process.

The Clinical Interview

Probably the most important area of assessment, the clinical interview allows the helper to gather basic information directly from the client. Often, this interview takes place during the initial contact with the agency and is called an *intake interview*. This interview must be completed in a manner that will allow the client to be open and honest with the helper so that the understanding of client issues is clear and comprehensive. Of course, the helping skills and techniques discussed throughout this text are the basis for the clinical interview.

Testing

Testing involves conducting a formal assessment of the client with a well-researched testing instrument that has been shown to be valid (measures what it's supposed to measure) and reliable (measures accurately). Although human service professionals are able to give some tests, many other tests require additional education and training. Thus, sometimes testing can be provided by the human service professional, whereas other times helpers with advanced training will be asked to provide testing. For instance, whereas a human service professional may be able to provide some kinds of vocational testing to clients, more involved intellectual or personality assessments would need to be provided by a psychologist, or a similarly trained professional. Some of the many different kinds of test categories include career and vocational assessment, intellectual and cognitive assessment, personality testing, achievement testing, and aptitude testing.

Informal Assessment

Informal assessment includes a wide variety of assessment procedures that require little advanced training and are aimed at providing a quick and focused assessment of a client. Although generally not as valid or reliable as tests, they do provide a service in that they can be quickly administered and are focused directly upon the client's presenting issues. Some of the many types of informal assessment include observation; rating scales; classification methods, such as behavior or feeling word checklists (see Appendix B); environmental assessment, such as observing a person at his or her home or workplace; records and personal documents; and performance-based assessment, such as when a person is assessed on a task in a real-life situation. Informal assessments are often helper-made, and the number and types of instruments that one can come up with is only limited by our imaginations. Reflection Exercise 8.1 shows one type of easily developed informal assessment that one can use with a client. Can you come up with others?

Reflection Exercise 8.1: Lifelines

Pair up with a student and develop a lifeline like mine below. Start at your birth, with the midpoint between Happiness and Depression representing Satisfaction. After you have completed your lifeline, discuss your "ups and downs" with your partner. Each student should feel free to not discuss a particular event. In that case, just say to your partner, "I'll pass on that."

After you have completed the first lifeline, do the second lifeline below. In this case, draw a straight line from your birth to your current age, like I have done. Write your current age at the end of that line and then draw a staggered line from your current age to the age at which you think you might die. Then, discuss with your partner how satisfied you are with your life to date and what you want to do to make your life fulfilled.

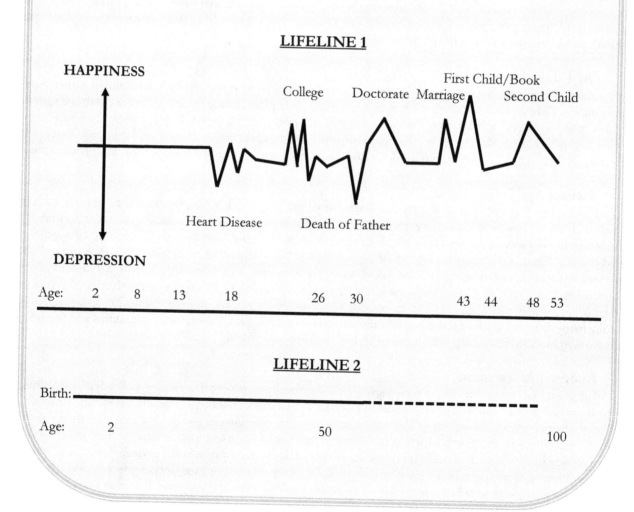

LIFELINE 1

HAPPINESS

College   Doctorate Marriage First Child/Book Second Child

Heart Disease   Death of Father

DEPRESSION

Age: 2   8   13   18   26   30   43   44   48   53

LIFELINE 2

Birth:

Age: 2   50   100

Diagnosis and The DSM-5

Derived from the Greek words *dia* (apart) and *gnosis* (to perceive or to know), the term diagnosis refers to the process of making an assessment of an individual from an outside or objective viewpoint (Hersen & Van Hasselt, 2001). A natural outgrowth of the assessment process, a mental health diagnosis can provide valuable information for clients and helpers and is an important step in treatment planning. Although attempts to classify mental disorders have been made since the turn of the century, it was not until 1952 that the American Psychiatric Association (APA) published the first comprehensive mental health diagnosis system called the *Diagnostic and Statistical Manual of Mental Disorders* (DSM-I).

The DSM has been revised numerous times over the years with the latest edition being the *DSM-5* (APA, 2013). The DSM is the most widespread and accepted diagnostic classification system of emotional disorders, and has become increasingly important for a number of reasons:

- It is a means for human service professionals to communicate with one another, and with related professionals, about a client's situation
- It aids in conceptualizing client problems
- It can be helpful in treatment planning
- It helps clients and helpers understand the client's mental disorder
- It can be helpful in deciding which medications might be an aid in a person's treatment plan
- It is used to provide diagnostic information for insurance companies so that they will reimburse helpers for treatment (Neukrug & Fawcett, 2015; Schwitzer & Rubin, 2015)

Today, anywhere between 20 and 25% of all people have a diagnosable mental disorder and up to 50% of all adults will have a mental disorder in their lifetime (National Alliance on Mental Illness, 2016). With these eye-opening figures, it's not surprising that the DSM has become a critical tool in the diagnostic process by providing hundreds of diagnoses organized into 21 diagnostic categories (see Appendix C). In addition to providing diagnoses for mental disorders, the DSM-5 can also assist helpers in identifying what are called *psychosocial and environmental stressors* through the use of what are called *V Codes* or *Z Codes*—a classification system for these common concerns (e.g., job loss, marital problems, homelessness, relationship issues). The mental disorder codes, and the V and Z Codes, parallel the same codes offered in the *International Classification of Disease* (ICD) manual used by health care providers (e.g., doctors and nurses), albeit the DSM-5 gives more involved definitions than the ICD. When making a diagnosis, in addition to listing a mental disorder diagnosis and a V or Z code, helpers are encouraged to list medical diagnoses when they have an impact on their clients' psychological functioning. Thus, a diagnosis of an individual could look this:

296.22 (F32.1)	Major depression, single episode, moderate
V62.29 (Z56.9)	Problems related to employment
V61.10 (Z63.0)	Relationship distress with spouse
722.0	Displacement cervical intervertebral disc (chronic back pain)

Although human service professionals are sometimes (but not always!) viewed as not having the skill set to diagnose, they frequently see the diagnoses of clients. Thus, it is important that they understand the diagnoses that are made and what their purposes are. It should be noted that the DSM has its critics, including those who question some of the diagnoses, believe its categorization is dehumanizing, suggest it leads to labeling, and argue that it does not account for societal factors that impact their formulation (Jackson, 2012; Miller, 2012; Pickersgill, 2013). Despite these naysayers, the DSM continues to be widely used, and courses are even taught that focus solely on the diagnostic process and the DSM. You are encouraged to learn more about the DSM-5 and make a decision for yourself regarding its efficacy (see Experiential Exercise 8.2).

Experiential Exercise 8.2:
Developing a Diagnosis

After reading this section on the DSM and reviewing the diagnoses in Appendix C, have a student in class volunteer to role-play one of the disorders without the class knowing what disorder it is. Your instructor can also bring in the DSM-5 or Google the diagnosis to get a more involved description of the diagnoses for the role-play student. Then, the rest of the class can sit in a circle around the student and ask him or her questions. See if you can come up with the correct diagnosis and then respond to these questions:

1. Were you able to come up with the correct diagnosis?
2. Were there any V Codes (or Z Codes) that would apply to this individual's situation?
3. Were there competing diagnoses, and, if so, do you think it is necessary to zero in on one diagnosis?
4. What benefit do you think there is to discovering the diagnosis?
5. What stigma might the role-play student live with if he or she was to actually have this diagnosis?
6. How helpful do you think the diagnosis would be in treatment planning?

When you have finished the role play, consider other ones, answering the same questions.

DEVELOPING, MONITORING, AND EVALUATING CLIENT GOALS

The actual development of client goals should be a relatively easy process if the helper has completed a thorough assessment of the client. In developing goals, the following should be considered:

1. *Goal development should be an outgrowth of the assessment process.*

2. *Goal development should be collaborative.* Goals should not be "given" to the client.

3. *Goals should be attainable.* If too lofty, the client will feel like a failure if goals are not met. If too simple, goals are less likely to help the client feel successful.

4. *Progress should be monitored.* Not monitoring progress can lead clients to question their helper's ability or commitment. In addition, it can result in lack of follow through on the part of clients. Lack of progress needs to be reviewed to determine whether goals need to be changed.

5. *Goals can be changed.* If a client is not reaching his or her goals, discuss why. Were they too difficult or too easy? Were they the wrong goals? Were they not attempted due to lack of time or motivation? After determining why they were not reached, rework the goals and try again.

6. *Attainment of goals should be affirmed.* Clients work hard to reach their goals and it is important that they are affirmed for their success. Clients can be affirmed verbally, through small awards (e.g., a certificate), and in other ways.

7. *Develop new goals as former goals are reached.* As clients reach their goals, determine whether they are ready to work on new ones.

8. *Know when to stop.* Although it is important to keep clients moving forward, also know when to encourage a client to stop. Sometimes a client has simply finished!

The documentation of progress toward goals is increasingly being reviewed by funding sources (Woodside & McClam, 2013). In fact, some funding sources today will not renew funding if documentation and progress are not demonstrated. The simplest way to document progress toward goals is to make a note in the client's chart. Innovative human service professionals can create charts and graphs to visually document client progress (see Experiential Exercise 8.3).

Experiential Exercise 8.3:
Assessing Needs and Developing Goals

Part I: Spend 10 to 20 minutes interviewing another student who is role-playing a client or discussing a real situation. While interviewing your client, assess the client's needs. When the interview is near completion, write down the client's needs as you view them. After you have finished, obtain feedback from your client as to the accuracy of your assessment.

Part II: With your role-play client in Part I, spend a minimum of 10 minutes developing your client goals. The goals should be an outgrowth of your client's needs that were formulated in Part I. Make sure that the goal-setting process is collaborative, and the client is comfortable with the ones developed.

MONITORING THE USE OF PSYCHOTROPIC MEDICATIONS

The use of *psychotropic medications*, or *psychopharmacology*, has come a long way since the first time we saw their widespread utilization during the mid-1900s (Preston, O'Neal, & Talaga, 2013; Videbeck, 2014). With an increase in the types of medications available, and the lessening of side effects, medications are now prescribed for almost any kind of psychological problem and despite some challenges (see Fact Sheet 8.1), should often be considered as an adjunct to treatment.

Although human service professionals cannot prescribe medication and should not be making major decisions about medication, today, many, if not most, human service professionals are working with clients who are taking some medication. Therefore, human service professionals should know the basics of such medications so that they can assist clients in adhering to their medication regime, help identify potential side effects, and have a sense of knowing whether or not the medication is working. When concerns about medication usage and efficacy arise, human service professionals should be able to discuss them with clients and refer to psychiatrists, or other medical personnel, who are monitoring clients' usage of such medication. Commonly, psychotropic medications have been classified into five groups known as *antipsychotics, mood-stabilizing drugs, antidepressants, anti-anxiety agents,* and *stimulants* (National Institute of Mental Health, 2016). The following provides a very brief overview of these drug groups to give you a sense of what they can do, along with a few of the possible problems associated with some of them (see Experiential Exercise 8.4).

Fact Sheet 8.1: Advantages and Disadvantages of Psychotropic Medication

Advantages of Medication	*Disadvantages of Medication*
• The effectiveness of medication can be examined easily.	• Only counseling can address the complexity of the human condition.
• Medications can sometimes instill hope as a person quickly begins to feel better.	• Counseling can lead to autonomy, drugs can lead to dependence.
• Medication can help motivate clients to put work into the helping relationship.	• The positive effects of medications can lessen the desire for some clients to work on their problems.
• Sometimes the quick response of medication can reduce the likelihood of a serious mental illness (e.g., schizophrenia) occurring again.	• Targeted medications for certain mental illnesses can increase some clients' beliefs that they embody the illness for which the medicine is prescribed.
• Medication may help some people that psychotherapy won't help.	• Outcome research on some psychotropic medications is mixed and confusing.
• Sometimes, medications are more cost effective than psychotherapy.	• Most psychotropic medications have side effects, and sometimes these can be serious and long-lasting.
• The biological basis of some disorders means treatment by medication is crucial.	• Psychotropic medications do not solve life's problems—only the client can.

Experiential Exercise 8.4:
Has Medication Helped or Hurt?

As you discuss the classifications of psychotropic medications listed below, share with the class your experience of individuals you know who have benefited from or been harmed by the use of medication. If you wish, discuss your own use of medication for a mental health problem.

Antipsychotics

Antipsychotic drugs, sometimes called *neuroleptics*, are used to treat all types of psychoses and occasionally bipolar disorder, depression with psychotic features, paranoid disorder, delirium, and dementia. Today, there are a wide range of these drugs, and sometimes, they can dramatically alter the course of treatment for an individual who is having an acute psychotic episode (see Fact Sheet 8.2). For instance, the quicker an individual can recover due to the use of medication, the greater the likelihood that future psychotic episodes will not occur. Although antipsychotic medications can assist an individual in living a more normal life, they are often not a cure and can have a wide range of side effects, including blood disorders, involuntary movement problems, memory problems, decreased libido, motor issues, and much more (Goldberg & Ernst, 2012).

Fact Sheet 8.2: Some Common Anti-Psychotic Medications

Conventional Antipsychotics		Second-Generation Antipsychotics	
Generic Name	Trade Name	Generic Name	Trade Name
Chlorpromazine	Thorazine	Clozapine	Clozaril
Haloperidol	Haldol	Risperidone	Risperdal
Thioridazine	Mellaril	Olanzapine	Zyprexa
Trifluoperazine	Stelazine	Quetiapine	Seroquel
Fluphenazine	Prolixin	Ziprasidone	Geodon
Perphenazine	Trilafon	Aripiprazole	Abilify
Thiothixene	Navane		
Loxapine	Loxitane		
Molindone	Moban		

Mood-Stabilizing Drugs

As far back as the 1800s, the element lithium was found to be helpful in treating a number of afflictions (Freeman, Wiegand, & Gelenberg, 2009). Then, in the early 1950s, lithium was found to be an effective treatment for bipolar disorder (then called manic-depression). Lithium seems to act particularly well in lessening the effects of manic symptoms. For individuals who take lithium, the level of drug in the system has to be assessed through a blood test. Too much lithium can cause severe side effects and too little will be ineffective in treatment. Like the antipsychotics, lithium can produce a number of undesirable side effects, although they are generally viewed as less serious than those of the antipsychotic medications. For individuals who don't respond well to lithium, a number of anticonvulsant medications, such as Depakote, Tegretol, and some benzodiazepines (anti-anxiety drugs) have been helpful in treating manic episodes (Freeman, et al., 2009; McElroy & Keck, 2009; Patterson, Albala, McCahill, & Edwards, 2010).

Antidepressants

Over the past 100 years, there have been a host of psychotropic drugs to help with the treatment of depression. Starting with the use of *amphetamines* in the early 1900s, and later in the century with *monoamine oxidase inhibitors* (MAOIs) and then *tricyclics*, new and better drugs to treat depression were found. However, in more recent years, the *selective serotonin reuptake inhibitors* (*SSRIs*) have been the drug of choice and have shown more success than past medications. In fact, for some, the SSRIs have been called miracle drugs due to their limited side effects and often dramatic results. Consequently, such drugs as Celexa, Luvox, Paxil, Prozac, and Zoloft have very quickly become commonplace in American society. In addition to being beneficial for depression, SSRIs also show promise in treating obsessive-compulsive disorder, panic disorder, some forms of schizophrenia, eating disorders, alcoholism, obesity, and some sleep disorders. Along with the SSRIs, a number of *atypical antidepressants* have also shown promise in the treatment of depression. Some of these include Serzone, Desyrel, Effexor, Serzone, Remeron, and Wellbutrin. Recent research shows that counseling may be as effective as these drugs, and counseling plus drugs may be slightly more effective (Qaseem, Barry, & Kansagara, 2016).

Anti-anxiety Medications

The use of modern-day anti-anxiety agents started with the discovery of Librium, which came on the market in 1960 (Ballenger, 1996). Today, *benzodiazepines*, such as Valium, Librium, and Xanax, are frequently used in conjunction with psychotherapy for generalized anxiety disorders, as they have a calming effect on the individual. Benzodiazepines have also been shown to be helpful in reducing stress, for insomnia, and in management of alcohol withdrawal (Nishino, Mishina, Mignot, & Dement, 2009). However, tolerance of and dependence on benzodiazepines can occur, and there is a potential for overdose on these medications. In addition to benzodiazepines, *nonbenzodiazepines*, such as Buspar and Gepirone, are an alternative to the benzodiazepines (Robinson, Rickels, & Yocca, 2009).

Stimulants

Over the years, amphetamines were used, mostly unsuccessfully, as a diet aid, as an antidepressant, and to relieve the symptoms of sleepiness. However, during the 1950s amphetamines were found to have a *paradoxical effect* in many children diagnosed with attention deficit disorder with hyperactivity (ADHD); it seemed to calm them down and help them focus. Today, the use of stimulants in the treatment of attention deficit disorder is widespread, with the three most common drugs being Ritalin, Cylert, and Dexedrine (Ballas, Evans, & Dinges, 2009; Fawcett, & Busch, 1998). Stimulants have also been successful in treating narcolepsy and are somewhat successful in treating residual attention deficit disorder in adults.

Managing Psychotropic Medications

Psychopharmacology has come a long way since the 1950s when the first "modern" psychotropic medications were introduced. Today, medications are used for a wide array of disorders, are more effective, and have fewer side effects. As psychological disorders become better understood, new and even more effective medications can be developed. Increasingly, human service professionals will be working with clients who are taking an array of psychotropic medications. Although not experts on their use, human service professionals should know the basics of such drugs, when such drugs are not being effective, and when to refer to medical professionals when a client is in need of a medication review (see Reflection Exercise 8.2).

Reflection Exercise 8.2:
Diagnosis and Medication: Helpful or Problematic?

In small groups, for each of the following vignettes, discuss whether you believe a diagnosis hurts or helps each person. Also, discuss whether you believe medication is part of the problem or the solution to the problem.

- Tenesha is in the fifth grade and has been assessed as having a conduct disorder and attention deficit disorder with hyperactivity (ADHD). Tenesha takes Ritalin to help her with her attention deficit disorder. Tenesha's mother has a panic disorder and is taking anti-anxiety medication. Her father is bipolar and taking lithium. It is written into Tenesha's Individualized Education Plan that she should see Jill, her school counselor, for individual counseling and for group counseling.

- John is intellectually disabled and lives in a group home. He generally has a happy attitude toward life; however, once in a while he "loses it" and has an angry outburst. A few times he almost harmed one of his helpers or one of the other group members. Although behavioral strategies to deal with his outbursts have been tried, they have not been very successful. Thus, he has been placed on medication to assist him in controlling his anger. Everyone, including John, seems more at peace since he started his medication.

Continued on Next Page

Reflection Exercise 8.2:
Diagnosis and Medication: Helpful or Problematic? (Cont'd)

- Eduardo goes daily to the day treatment center at the local mental health center. He seems fairly stable and generally in good spirits. He has been hospitalized for schizophrenia on numerous occasions and now takes Haldol and Cogentin to relieve his symptoms. He admits to Jordana, one of the human service practitioners who works with him, that when he doesn't take his medication he believes that computers have consciousness and are conspiring through the World Wide Web to take over the world. His insurance company pays for his treatment. He will not receive treatment unless the psychiatrist, who periodically consults with Jordana, writes his diagnosis on the insurance form.

WRITING PROCESS NOTES, CASE NOTES, AND CASE REPORTS

The writing of notes and reports has become increasingly important to the helping process in recent years for a number of reasons (Neukrug & Schwitzer, 2006; Summers, 2016). For instance, today, notes and reports may:

- be used in court to show adequate client care took place,
- assist helpers in conceptualizing client problems and making diagnoses,
- help determine whether clients have made progress,
- be useful when obtaining supervision,
- assist the helper in remembering what the client said,
- be mandated by insurance companies and government agencies in order to approve the treatment being given to clients, and
- be used in assessing agency effectiveness for funding agencies.

The kinds of notes or reports that you write will likely depend on the agency in which you work. However, three types of notes and reports typically required at agencies include process notes, case notes, and case reports.

Process Notes

In many, if not most agencies, helpers are asked to write relatively brief notes (often one to three paragraphs long) that highlight important points and summarize every meeting a client has with the helper. These notes are used to jog the memory of the helper the next time he or she meets with the client. With some helpers having dozens of clients, such process notes are useful and often essential.

Although clients generally have the legal right to see any paperwork about them, the one exception tends to be process notes. For instance, although the *Health Insurance Portability and Accountability Act* (*HIPAA*) ensures the privacy of client records, limits sharing of such information, and ensures that clients have rights to view their records (American Psychological Association, 2013; U.S. Department of Health and Human Services, n.d.), process notes are exempt from client access to them. However, if such notes are used for other purposes, they are not exempt. Process notes should be distinguished from other types of case notes or from case reports, which tend to be more involved and are not used for the sole purpose of the helper's memory enhancement.

Case Notes and Case Reports

Although the terms *case notes* and *case reports* are often used interchangeably, some view case reports as more involved and longer than case notes. Both case notes and case reports can include a wide variety of ways of summarizing obtained client information. Some examples include the intake interview, highlights of a client's goals and objectives, periodic summaries of clients' progress, termination summaries, specialized reports for the courts or other agencies, and more. In contrast to process notes, clients almost always have the right to access case notes and case reports.

Today, helpers often use sophisticated software to assist in their writing of case notes and case reports. Whether using such software or writing the report on your own, the minimum information usually includes the name of the client, the date, major facts noted during contact, progress made toward achieving client goals, and the helper's signature. More involved reports may include demographic information (e.g., date of birth, address, phone number, date of interview), reason for report, family background, other pertinent background information (e.g., health information, vocational history, history of adjustment issues/emotional problems/mental illness), mental status, assessment results, diagnosis, and a summary, conclusions, and recommendations section (see example of report in Appendix D). Although all of these headings are important, the mental status deserves special attention as it is often the most misunderstood area of the case report.

Mental Status Exam and Report. The mental status exam is when the helper assesses a client in four areas, including (1) how the client presents himself or herself (appearance and behavior), (2) the client's emotional state (affect), (3) the client's ability to think clearly (thought components), and (4) the client's memory state and orientation to the world (cognition) (Akiskal, 2008; Polanski & Hinkle, 2000; Sommers-Flanagan & Sommers-Flanagan, 2015). Generally, the mental status exam is conducted as part of the clinical interview and is highlighted in a one or two paragraph section of the report called the *mental status* or *mental status report*. Below are abbreviated definitions of the four areas used in developing the wording for the mental status report. Common words used in the mental status report can be found in Appendix E.

Appearance and Behavior. This includes observable appearance and behaviors during the clinical interview, such as manner of dress, hygiene, body posture, tics, significant nonverbal behaviors (eye contact or the lack thereof, wringing of hands, swaying), and manner of speech (e.g., stuttering, tone).

Emotional State. Here, the examiner describes the client's affect and mood. Affect includes the client's current, prevailing feeling state (e.g., happy, sad, joyful, angry, depressed, etc.) and may also be reported as constricted or full, appropriate or inappropriate to content, labile, flat, blunted, exaggerated, and so forth. The client's mood, on the other hand, represents the long-term, underlying emotional well-being of the client and is usually assessed through client self-report. Thus, a client may seem anxious and sad during the session (affect) and report that his or her mood has been depressed.

Thought Components. The manner in which the client thinks, or thought components, are generally broken down into the content and the process of thinking. Content includes such things as whether the client has delusions, distortions of body image, hallucinations, obsessions, suicidal or homicidal ideation, and so forth. A statement about a client's thought process often includes references to circumstantiality, coherence, flight of ideas, logical thinking, intact as opposed to loose associations, organization, and tangentiality.

Cognition. Whether a client is oriented to time, place, and person (knows what time it is, where he or she is, and who he or she is) is one important aspect of cognition and should generally be included in the mental status report. Other aspects include a write-up on the client's short- and long-term memory, an evaluation of the client's knowledge base and intellectual functioning, and a statement about the client's level of insight and ability to make judgments. Experiential Exercise 8.5 gives you the opportunity to write a mental status report.

Experiential Exercise 8.5:
Writing a Mental Status Report

Find a partner and first have one person role-play a seriously impaired client while the other, the helper, tries to assess the client's mental status. Then write a mental status report. After the first role-play, switch roles and have the second helper assess the client and write the mental status report. Use the mental status report section of the case report in Appendix D as a model to write the report and the common terms noted in Appendix E to help you with common language usage. When you have finished, discuss the following issues in class:

1. How difficult was it to assess a client's mental status?
2. What would have helped you in your assessment?
3. What questions might help you in assessing all four areas of the client's mental status? Write them on the board and note them for future use.
4. What value do you see in conducting a mental status report?

Any written information about a client needs to be objective and should be based on observable behavior, not opinion. Remember that whatever a helper writes could be subpoenaed by the courts, and the helper could be held liable for his or her statements. Therefore, writing from an objective, dispassionate point of view is essential when keeping case notes. Generally, only the third person should be used in referring to the client. For example, it would be better to say, "Family information was gathered from Jim," than "I collected family information from Jim." Any subjective information that is gathered from the client should be noted as such. To assist in this, begin subjective statements with phrases such as, "It seems that...," "Jim noted that...," "It appears that...," "Jim reported that...," "Claire related that...," and "Claire recounted that...."

When writing case notes, helpers should not: be biased, portray sexist attitudes, use significant amounts of psychological jargon, or make statements expressing their own values or opinions (unless the helper's opinions are called for, as when a court is asking for it or the helper is making a diagnosis). Also, should write the report so that other mental health professionals can readily understand it. Finally, of course, helpers should use good grammar. See Appendix D for an example of a case report, and then try writing your own using the directions in Experiential Exercise 8.6.

SOAP Reports

One approach to writing case notes that has gained popularity over the years is called the SOAP Note or Report, which stands for Subjective, Objective, Assessment, and Plan (Woodside & McClam, 2013). These notes focus on the client's subjective understanding of what he or she has experienced, the helper's description of what he or she sees, the helper's assessment of the client's situation, and a description of the treatment plan. Column 1 of Table 8.1 defines these four areas, while Column 2 gives examples of how this might be written, and finally, Column 3, offers some pointers of things to watch out for when writing such notes.

Table 8.1

SOAP Notes/Reports

Subjective-Description	Subjective-Examples	Subjective-Pointers
• What the client tells you (feelings, concerns, plans, goals, thoughts) • How the client experiences the world • Client's orientation to time, place, and person	• Client reports… • Client shares… • Client describes… • Client indicates…	• Avoid quotations • Full names of others are generally not needed • Be concise • Limit adjectives
Objective-Description	**Objective-Examples**	**Objective-Pointers**
• Factual: What the helper personally observes and/or witnesses • Quantifiable: What was seen, heard, smelled, counted, or measured (may include outside written materials)	• Appeared____, as evidenced by… • Test results indicate… • Client's hair uncombed; clothes unkempt	• Avoid words like client "appeared" or "seemed" when not supported by objective examples • Avoid labels, personal judgments, or opinionated statements
Assessment-Description	**Assessment-Examples**	**Assessment-Pointers**
• Summarizes the helper's clinical thinking • Includes diagnoses or clinical impressions and reasons for behavior	• Behavior/attitude consistent with individuals who… • *The DSM* diagnosis • Rule out…	• May note themes, or recurring issues • Remain professional • Remember that others may view assessment
Plan-Description	**Plan-Examples**	**Plan-Pointers**
• Describes parameters of treatment • Includes action plan; interventions; progress; prognosis; treatment direction for next session	• Helper established rapport, challenged, etc. • Client progress is indicated by… • Next session, helper will… • Client and helper will continue to…	• Give supporting reasons for progress • Progress is often described as "poor, guarded, fair, good, or excellent"

**Experiential Exercise 8.6:
Writing a Case Report**

Using the guidelines below, interview a student and subsequently write a case report. When complete, share it with others in small groups to gain feedback, or hand it in to your instructor who will review it and give you feedback. Use Appendix D as a model.

Possible Categories for Case Report
1. Demographic Information (e.g., Date of Birth, Address, Phone Number, Date of Interview)
2. Reason for Report
3. Family Background
4. Other Pertinent Background Information (e.g., Health Information, Vocational History, History of Adjustment Issues/Emotional Problems/Mental Illness)
5. Mental Status
6. Assessment Results
7. Diagnosis
8. Summary, Conclusions, and Recommendations

ENSURING THE SECURITY AND CONFIDENTIALITY OF RECORDS

> Human service professionals protect the integrity, safety, and security of client records. Client information in written or electronic form that is shared with other professionals must have the client's prior written consent except in the course of professional supervision or when legally obliged or permitted to share such information. (NOHS, 2015, Standard 8)

Generally, clients have the right to have their mental health records kept confidential. However, there are some exceptions, such as (1) when the helper's employer (e.g. agency administrator) requests information from the helper regarding a client, (2) if a helper shares client information with a supervisor as a means of assisting the helper in his or her work with the client, (3) if the court subpoenas a helper's records, (4) if a client gives permission, in writing, to share information with others, or (5) if a parent requests information about his or her child. Written client records need to be kept in secured places, such as locked file cabinets and password-secured computers. In addition, those who give clerical help need to understand the importance of confidentiality when working with records. In fact, many agencies have clerical staff sign statements, often legally binding, acknowledging that they understand the importance of the confidentiality of records and that they will keep all correspondences and information confidential (see Reflection Exercise 8.3).

Increasingly, clients have been given approval by the courts to obtain copies of records about them that are kept on file in schools, hospitals, and clinics (Remley & Herlihy, 2014). Also, it has generally been assumed that parents have the right to view records of their children (C. Borstein, attorney, personal communication, February 20, 2016).

Reflection Exercise 8.3:
How Secure Are Records?

Unfortunately, helpers sometimes forget how easily client records can be misplaced or the information in them made too readily available to the public. The following true stories highlight the ways that information in records can be mishandled and stress the importance of keeping records secure and confidential.

1. When I worked as an outpatient therapist at a mental health center, a client appropriated his records that had been left "lying around." Because the records were written in "psychologese," using diagnostic language, the client was understandably quite upset by what he found. He would periodically call emergency services and read his records over the phone to the emergency worker while making fun of the language used in the records.

2. While taking a class in my doctoral program, we were reviewing an intellectual test assessment of an adolescent that had been completed a number of years earlier. Suddenly, one of the students in the class yelled out, "That's me!" Apparently, although there was no identifying name on the report, he recognized it as describing him (he had been given a copy of the report previously).

3. In 2014, 4.5 million medical records, including mental health records, were hacked from Community Health Systems (CHS) (Pagliery, 2014). Although CHS thought they had a secure system, they found out otherwise and due to HIPAA, individuals could now sue CHS for breach of information.

The three examples above show how vulnerable we are to the unforeseen release of client information, which can result in clients suing us. What would you do to ensure the safety of client records?

In terms of federal law, the *Freedom of Information Act of 1974* allows individuals access to records maintained by a federal agency that contain personal information about the individual (U.S. Department of Justice, 2014a). Similarly, the *Family Education Rights and Privacy Act (FERPA)* assures parents the right to access their children's educational records (U.S. Department of Education, 2014). Finally, the *Health Insurance Portability and Accountability Act (HIPAA)* ensures the privacy of client records and limits sharing of such information (American Psychological Association, 2013). In general, HIPAA restricts the amount of information that can be shared without client consent and allows clients to have access to their records, except for process notes as noted earlier in the chapter (U.S. Department of Health and Human Services, n.d.).

On a more practical level, a client rarely asks to see his or her records. Nevertheless, if a client did make such a request, I would first attempt to talk with the client about what is written in the records. If this was not satisfactory to him or her, I would then suggest that I might write a summary of the records. However, if a client steadfastly expressed a desire to view his or her records, it is generally his or her legal right to secure access to such records, and I would give that client a copy of the records.

MANAGING AND DOCUMENTING CLIENT CONTACT HOURS

Managing Client Hours

Human service professionals often find themselves with very large caseloads and are expected to meet with all of their clients in a manner that assures sound clinical treatment. Unfortunately, with large numbers of clients, it is sometimes easy to not follow-up when appointments are missed, to arrange shorter meeting times or longer periods between appointments than are clinically appropriate, or to even forget about arranging appointment times at all for some clients. To assure that clients are afforded appropriate treatment, it is essential that human service professionals find mechanisms that result in proper management of client contact hours. This sometimes takes some creative activities, such as running special groups (e.g., medication review groups) or working additional evening or weekend hours to meet with clients who cannot make it in during the day. Ensuring that all of our clients are given their deserved services is a critical ethical practice that human service professionals need to uphold.

Documenting Client Contact Hours

Today, it has become important for helpers to document contact hours, as reimbursement by insurance companies, as well as local, state, and federal funding agencies, is often based on clear recording of these hours (Summers, 2016). Thus, most agencies, today, have some mechanism for recording client meeting times with helpers. This can be done by hand on a simple grid; but increasingly, documentation is completed with the use of computer software specifically developed for this purpose. Experiential exercise 8.7 helps you determine how client hours should be recorded.

> ### Experiential Exercise 8.7:
> ### Ways of Documenting Hours
>
> On your own, or in small groups, develop a sample grid you could use to document client hours. What information do you need to include? When you have finished, share your grid with others in class.

MAKING REFERRALS

There are many reasons to refer a client to another professional (Summers, 2016; Woodside & McClam, 2013). For instance, a client might be referred as a part of the treatment plan, because the professional is leaving the agency, because the professional feels incompetent to work with the client, or because the client has reached his or her goals and is ready to move on to another form of treatment. In any case, the manner in which the referral is made should be seamless. In referrals, professionals should do the following:

1. Discuss the reason for making the referral with the client and obtain his or her approval.

2. Obtain, in writing, permission to discuss anything about the client with another professional, even if this involves simply sharing the client's name with another professional.

3. Monitor the client's transition to the other professional to ensure appropriate continued care.

4. Assure that confidentiality of client information is maintained in the referral process (see Experiential Exercise 8.8).

> ## Experiential Exercise 8.8:
> ## Making Referrals
>
> Find a fellow student and have one role-play a helper while the other role-plays a client. Choose one of the aforementioned reasons why a helper might refer a client, and role-play a situation in which such a referral is to take place. Reflect on how it feels to make a referral of a client. Share your feelings in small groups or with the class.

CONDUCTING FOLLOW-UP

Follow-up, another important function of case management, can be completed by a phone call, by a letter, by an elaborate survey of clients, or in other ways. It can be done a few days to a few weeks after the relationship has ended and serves many purposes (Neukrug & Schwitzer, 2006; Summers, 2016):

1. It functions as a check to see whether clients would like to return for counseling or be referred to a different helper.

2. It allows the helper to assess whether change has been maintained.

3. It gives the helper the opportunity to determine which counseling techniques have been most successful.

4. It offers an opportunity to reinforce client change.

5. It allows the helper to evaluate services provided to the client.

PRACTICING TIME MANAGEMENT

With ever-increasing caseloads and demands placed on the helper, time management has become crucial if the helper is to avoid burnout (Woodside & McClam, 2013). *Time management* strategies serve a number of purposes, including helping human service professionals ensure that all clients are seen within a reasonable period of time and assisting professionals in remembering meetings, appointment times, and other obligations. Today, there are a number of time management systems. Although this text will not delve into these different systems, suffice it to say that addressing time management concerns is paramount in today's world.

SUMMARY

This chapter reviewed ten important areas of case management, or the overall process involved in maintaining the optimal level of functioning for clients. We started by highlighting the importance of obtaining informed consent, in writing, from clients, usually through the practice of giving clients a professional disclosure statement that spells out critical areas related to the nature and limits of the helping relationship.

We next pointed out that conducting an assessment for treatment planning purposes was critical to optimal client care, and we highlighted four areas of assessment: conducting a clinical interview, administering tests, doing informal assessment, and coming up with a diagnosis. Relative to diagnosis, we gave a brief overview of the DSM-5 and presented the purpose of such a classification system.

Noting that goal development was a natural outgrowth of the assessment process, we highlighted some points to consider when developing, monitoring, and evaluating client goals. We then moved on to a discussion about monitoring client use of psychotropic medications. We pointed out advantages and disadvantages of such use and gave a quick overview of the five groups of psychotropic medications: antipsychotics, mood-stabilizing drugs, antidepressants, anti-anxiety agents, and stimulants. We noted that since human service professionals will be working with clients who are taking an array of psychotropic medications, they should know the basics of such drugs, should be aware of when such drugs are not being effective, and should know when to consult with and refer to medical professionals regarding psychotropic medication.

Knowing how to write process notes, case notes, and case reports was next discussed. We stated that process notes are very brief and are used to jog the memory of the helper for the next time he or she sees the client. Although sometimes used interchangeably, we pointed out that case notes are generally viewed as less involved than case reports and that at a minimum, both tend to include the name of the client, the date, major facts noted during contact, progress made toward achieving client goals, and the helper's signature. We also explained the use of the mental status exam and report and showed how the mental status report is sometimes embedded in a case report. Additionally, we highlighted one type of case report, Subjective, Objective, Assessment, and Plan (SOAP), and noted that SOAP reports have become particularly popular in recent years.

Ensuring the security and confidentiality of records was next examined in the chapter. We explained that except for a few exceptions, clients generally have the legal right to have their mental health records kept confidential. We spoke about the importance, and sometimes difficulty, of ensuring the security of client records, whether paper or electronic. We noted that generally, clients have the right to their records, that parents have the right to their children's records, and we highlighted three laws that protect the confidentially of records and clients' rights to access them: the *Freedom of Information Act of 1974*, the *Family Education Rights and Privacy Act (FERPA)*, and the *Health Insurance Portability and Accountability Act (HIPAA)*.

We next spoke of the difficulty, yet responsibility, of human service professionals to properly manage client contact hours, despite often having very large caseloads. We acknowledged that it has become important for helpers to document contact hours, as reimbursement by insurance companies, as well as local, state, and federal funding agencies, is often based on clear records of these hours.

As the chapter neared its conclusion, we emphasized the importance of making seamless referrals to other mental health professionals and pointed out some things the professional should be cognizant of when making such referrals. We also spoke to the importance of follow-up with clients to ensure they are continuing to make progress. Finally, we noted the significance of practicing time management if human service professionals are to avoid burnout.

KEY WORDS AND TERMS

Amphetamines
Anti-anxiety agents
Antidepressants
Antipsychotics
Assessment for treatment planning
Atypical antidepressants
Benzodiazepines
Case note
Case reports
Client contact hours
Conducting follow-up
Confidentiality of records
Diagnostic and Statistical Manual of Mental Disorders
DSM-5
Family Education Rights and Privacy Act
FERPA
Freedom of Information Act of 1974
Health Insurance Portability and Accountability Act
HIPAA
ICD
Informed consent

Intake interview
International classification of disease
Making referrals
Mental status exam
Mental status report
Monoamine oxidase inhibitors
Mood-stabilizing drugs
Nonbenzodiazepines
Neuroleptics
Paradoxical effect
Process notes
Professional disclosure statement
Progress toward client goals
Psychopharmacology
Psychosocial and environmental stressors
Psychotropic medications
Selective serotonin reuptake inhibitors
SOAP notes/reports
Time management
V codes
Z codes

CHAPTER 9

Culturally Competent Helping

LEARNING OBJECTIVES

1. Examine the changing demographics of the United States to highlight how it underscores the need for helpers to be culturally competent.

2. Review eight reasons that explain why counseling is not working for some diverse clients, including the helper (a) believing in the melting pot myth, (b) having incongruent expectations about helping, (c) lacking an understanding of social forces, (d) having an ethnocentric world view, (e) being ignorant of his or her racist attitudes and prejudices, (f) not understanding cultural differences in the expression of symptomatology, (g) using unreliable assessment and research instruments, and (h) not being attuned to institutional discrimination.

3. Review definitions and models of culturally competent helping, including McAuliffe's definition, which views cultural competence as a consistent readiness and ability to integrate culture into one's work; Sue and Torino's definition that examines client identities, collectivism vs. individualism, and types of strategies used; the RESPECTFUL Model; and the Multicultural and Social Justice Competencies.

4. Examine strategies for working with a number of select populations, including:

   a. Different ethnic and racial groups
   b. Individuals from diverse religious backgrounds
   c. Women
   d. Men
   e. Lesbian, gay, bisexual, and transgender individuals
   f. Those who are homeless or poor
   g. Older persons
   h. Individuals with mental illness
   i. Individuals with disabilities
   j. Individuals using and abusing substances

5. Examine our ethical responsibilities to working with diverse clients.

INTRODUCTION

This chapter offers an understanding of how to work with culturally diverse clients and highlights the importance of helpers having appropriate beliefs and attitudes, knowledge, and skills to work successfully with a wide variety of clients. The chapter first focuses on the importance of multicultural counseling and offers definitions and models to use when working with diverse clients. The second part of the chapter suggests ways to work with individuals from different ethnic and racial groups; people from diverse religious backgrounds; women; men; lesbian, gay, bisexual, and transgender individuals; those who are homeless and poor; older persons; individuals with mental illness; individuals with disabilities; and substance users and abusers.

WHY MULTICULTURAL COUNSELING?

The U.S. today is one of the most diverse countries in the world, and is increasingly becoming more so. In fact, by the year 2043, minorities are expected to be the majority of the population (U.S. Census Bureau, 2016). And, by the year 2060, America will look quite differently than it does today (See Figure 9.1).

Figure 9.1: Changes in Ethnic Composition of U.S. Over Time

YEAR	Non-Hispanic White	Hispanics	African-American	Asian	American Indian	Native Hawaiian/Other Pacific Islander	Two or More Races
2012	63%	17%	13%	5.1%	1.2%	0.20%	2.4%
2060	43%	31%	15%	8.2%	1.5%	0.30%	6.4%

These changing demographics are a function of several factors, such as the fact that birth rates are higher within minority populations; most legal immigrants are now Asian, Black, Latino/a, or other minority, as opposed to White; and immigration rates are the highest in American history (Kotkin, 2010; Migration Policy Institute, 2014; Pew Research Center, 2014). Like past immigrants, today, many immigrants claim a strong affiliation to their cultural heritage.

Change in the racial, ethnic, and cultural backgrounds of American society has transformed the religious composition of the country, as well (Newport, 2011). As increased numbers of Asians, Hispanics, and Middle Easterners arrive at our shores, we find religions that were previously rare in America. Diversity in religion, however, is not only brought by immigrants. Although America is largely Christian, diversity in Christianity is greater than ever. From those who identify with a multitude of Protestant faiths, to Roman Catholics who are increasingly varied in their beliefs, to Eastern Orthodox, Mormons, Christian Scientists, Seventh Day Adventists, Amish, Mennonites, and on and on, the Christian religion in America is a religious mosaic in and of itself.

In addition to the increasing ethnic, cultural, and religious diversity, there has been greater acceptance of diversity in regard to gender identity, gender role stereotypes, and same-sex relationships (Szymanski, 2013; Trepal, 2013). For instance, the "macho" male is becoming decreasingly accepted as the optimal model for maleness, while expectations concerning the woman's role in the workplace and as the primary child care provider have changed dramatically. With same sex marriage now legal across the country, and with individuals like Caitlyn Jenner asserting their gender identity, we have seen a dramatic shift in attitudes towards transgender individuals and in acceptance of same sex relationships—albeit, we still have a way to go.

Changes in local, state, and federal laws have precipitated a gradual move toward acceptance of diversity in our culture and have given many Americans a heightened sensitivity to and awareness of a number of special groups, such as those who are homeless and poor, older persons, the mentally ill, and more. Changing demographics in the country make it increasingly important for helpers to make sure that their approach to helping works with a wide variety of clients. Unfortunately, this has not always been the case. Experiential Exercise 9.1 will help you explore your values toward diverse clients.

Experiential Exercise 9.1: A Loving Story?

Read the following story, and then follow the instructions:

While on a business trip, Lovey's significant other, Fine, is called to active duty to fight a war in another part of the world. Fine leaves for base camp before Lovey can get home. Wanting one last night with Fine, Lovey approaches the base commander, March, and begs March to let Lovey spend one last night with Fine. March, who is a national hero for saving POWs, explains that this is against the rules and to break them for one person is not right. March, who silently struggles with constant severe back pain from saving the POWs, goes on to state that "under the right circumstances, rules could be broken." Realizing March is making a pass, Lovey says, "no way," and walks off discouraged.

Lovey next approaches Friend, a long-time college pal, who reminds Lovey that Lovey has "slept around" and then states, "What's the big deal about sleeping with one more person?" Thinking that Friend has a point, Lovey returns to March, flirts, and eventually makes a deal to trade sex for one last night with Fine. After sex, Lovey is allowed to see Fine. Believing in honest relationships, Lovey tells Fine the whole story, at which point Fine becomes enraged and strikes Lovey.

Feeling guilt-ridden and dejected, Fine leaves, later attempts suicide, and ends up in a psychiatric hospital. Accepting blame as the cause of Fine's suicide attempt, Lovey goes to talk with Dr. Jaime, who explains that Fine's suicide attempt was of Fine's own choosing and that Lovey shouldn't have self-blame.

Instructions for scoring: Using the grid that follows, rate each of the five characters in the story. Place an X under number 1, across from the name of the person you like most. Then, place an X under number 2, across from the name you like second most, and so forth. Next, your instructor will count up all of the 1s, 2s, 3s, 4s, and 5s in the class and place them on a master grid on the board.

Final thoughts: When you read the story then rated the individuals, did you make any assumptions about their gender, sexual orientation, ethnic and cultural background, or other demographic factors? If so, consider what impact those assumptions had on your ratings. When you have finished your ratings, discuss how our different values about people impact how we are likely to view others.

Continued on Next Page

Experiential Exercise 9.1: A Loving Story? (Cont'd: The Grid)

	Ratings				
	1	2	3	4	5
Lovey					
Fine					
March					
Friend					
Dr. Jamie					

COUNSELING IS NOT WORKING FOR MANY DIVERSE CLIENTS

If you were distrustful of helpers, confused about the counseling process, or felt worlds apart from the helper you were seeing, would you want to continue in the helping relationship? Assuredly not. Unfortunately, this is the state of affairs for many minority clients. In fact, when compared to Whites, racial minority clients are more likely to be spoken down to, find the helping relationship less helpful, seek mental health services at lower rates, and terminate the helping relationship prematurely (Escobar, 2012; National Alliance of Mental Illness, 2016a, 2016b; Sewell, 2009; U.S. Department of Health and Human Services, 2001; Vogel, Wester, & Larson, 2007; Williams, 2013). It's also not surprising that compared with Whites, racial minority clients tend to be more distrustful and confused about the helping process.

Why is counseling not working for a good segment of our population? Some have suggested the following reasons (Buckley & Franklin-Jackson, 2005; Constantine & Sue, 2005; McAuliffe, Goméz, & Grothaus, 2013; Sue & Sue, 2013; Suzuki, Kugler, & Aguiar, 2005):

1. The melting pot myth. Some helpers see this country as a melting pot or blend of cultural diversity. However, this is not the experience of many minority clients who find themselves on the fringe of American culture and cannot relate to many of the customs and beliefs held by the majority. Probably, viewing America as a *cultural mosaic* that has a myriad of diverse values and customs is a more accurate conceptualization of the country today.

Example: A helper encourages a minority client to become involved with a counseling group. Unfortunately, the group is made up of all Whites, with most of whom she could not particularly relate.

2. Incongruent expectations about the helping relationship. Most counseling theories have developed from a Western, White perspective and emphasize individualism, expression of feelings, cause and effect, self-disclosure, and the importance of insight. Clients from some cultures, however, may not value some of these attributes and would feel uncomfortable with such an approach.

Example: A Vietnamese client is encouraged to talk about her feelings regarding her family's immigration to the U.S. She feels embarrassed, put on the spot, and wronged when she tries to refuse.

3. Lack of Understanding of Social Forces. Helpers often assume that negative feelings are created by the individual. This causes some helpers to overlook the power of social influences, and such helpers may have a difficult time with a client who has been considerably harmed by external factors.

Example: A client who was illegally denied jobs due to his disability may be discouraged when a helper says, "What have you done to prevent yourself from obtaining a job?"

4. Ethnocentric worldview. Many helpers falsely assume that clients view and live in the world in the same way that they do, or believe that when clients present a different worldview, it is an indication of emotional instability or client misunderstanding. In actuality, each of us has a different worldview, and each worldview needs to be respected.

Example: A helper may inadvertently offend a Muslim client when she says to her client, "Have a wonderful Christmas."

5. Ignorance of one's own racist attitudes and prejudices. Helpers who are not in touch with conscious and unconscious prejudices, stereotypes, and racist attitudes, cannot work effectively with clients.

Example: A helper who unconsciously believes being gay or lesbian is not normal but sees himself or herself as accepting of all sexual orientations, may subtly treat a gay client as if there is something wrong with him or her.

6. Inability to understand cultural differences in the expression of symptomatology. The helper's lack of knowledge about cultural differences as they relate to the expression of symptoms can harm the helping relationship, resulting in misdiagnosis, mistreatment, and early termination.

Example: A Puerto Rican client comes in with somatic complaints and is immediately referred to his doctor. Referring to the doctor is fine, except the helper missed the fact that some cultures show grief in this manner. In this case, the helper did not pick up on the fact that the somatic symptoms were in response to the client dearly missing his daughter who is back in Puerto Rico.

7. Unreliability of assessment and research instruments. Over the years, assessment and research instruments have notoriously been culturally biased. Although they have gotten better, an effective helper should assess the effectiveness of such instruments with all populations before using them.

Example: A lesbian client is given a wellness instrument and scores low on a number of factors. The helper assumes she has a number of wellness concerns when, in actuality, the instrument does not measure accurately for gay women.

8. Institutional discrimination. Because racism, heteronormativity, and more are embedded in society, they often go unrecognized and becomes a natural, but unhealthy part of organizations and institutions.

Example: Higher rates of schizophrenia diagnoses have been found in African Americans. However, this is not because they actually have higher rates, but because there is an over-diagnosis of this disorder due to clinicians not being adequately trained to understand responses to questions from diverse clients. This is a function of embedded racism in training programs.

155

Conclusion

These eight examples highlight some of the reasons the helping relationship has not been effective for many clients from diverse backgrounds. They demonstrate the need for helpers to be culturally competent and for greater sensitivity in counseling diverse clients. By attending to these issues, and similar ones, helpers will hopefully obtain an improved understanding of diversity, be able to make better treatment plans, see a decrease in the dropout rate when counseling by minorities, and see an increase in satisfaction with the helping process by minority clients. The following offers some definitions and models for working with culturally diverse clients.

DEFINITIONS AND MODELS OF CULTURALLY COMPETENT HELPING

Every person is like all persons, like some persons, and like no other persons...
(Kluckohn & Murray, 1953, p. 335)

A number of individuals have provided definitions and models to guide helpers in their work with diverse clients. Here, we will take a look at McAuliffe's (2013a) definition, Sue and Torino's (2005) definition, the RESPECTFUL Model, and the recently developed Multicultural and Social Justice Competencies. All of these definitions and models can help us become more effective when working with clients from diverse backgrounds.

McAuliffe's Definition

McAuliffe (2013a) suggests that culturally competent helping is "a consistent readiness to identify the cultural dimensions of clients' lives and a subsequent integration of culture into counseling work" (p. 6). This definition suits me, as it implies that helpers should always be concerned about cultural issues and constantly thinking about how their work with clients is impacted by such issues.

Sue and Torino's Definition

A somewhat more involved definition, by Sue and Torino (2005), suggest that culturally competent helping is a state that "can be defined as both a helping role and process that uses modalities and defines goals consistent with the life experiences and cultural values of clients, utilizes universal and culture-specific helping strategies and roles, recognizes client identities to include individual, group, and universal dimensions, and balances the importance of individualism and collectivism in the assessment, diagnosis and treatment of client and client systems." (p. 6)

This approach highlights the client's *individual identity*, which is the client's unique issues and concerns; the client's *group identity*, which is the client's shared cultural background with others (e.g., gender, sexual orientation, ethnicity, race); and the client's *universal identity*, or shared common experiences that we all have as human beings. The culturally competent helper, suggests Sue and Torino, also examines whether the client views the world from an *individualistic perspective* or *collectivist perspective* (see Figure 9.2).

The above definition, along with McAuliffe's understanding, reminds us to be constantly cognizant of a wide range of client experiences (individual, group, universal), to know what culture specific or universal skills will work best, and to take into account whether the client has an individual or collectivist focus when developing treatment plans and working toward client goals. The following models of culturally competent helping take us one step closer to being effective when working with diverse clients.

Figure 9.2: Sue and Torino's Understanding of Cultural Competent Helping

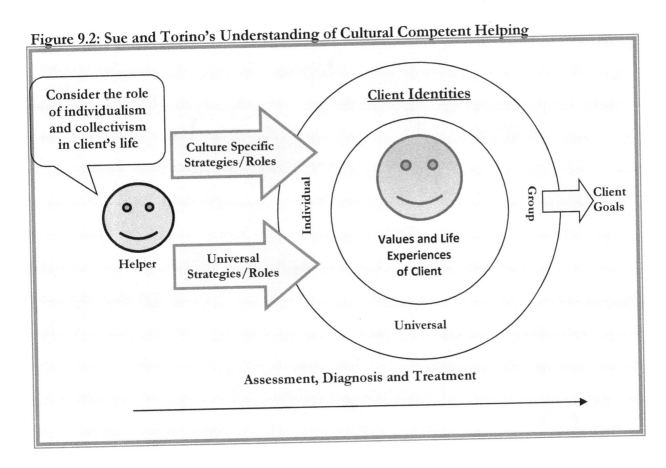

The RESPECTFUL Model

Touched on in Chapter 1 when discussing cultural sensitivity as one of the eight characteristics of the effective helper, this model offers a pragmatic approach when working with all clients and reminds us to consider a number of personal dimensions:

R: religious/spiritual identity
E: economic class/background
S: sexual identity
P: level of psychological development
E: ethnic/racial identity
C: chronological/developmental challenges
T: various forms of trauma and other threats to one's sense of well-being
F: family background and history
U: unique physical characteristics
L: location of residence and language differences (Lewis, Lewis, Daniels, & D'Andrea, 2011, p. 54)

The RESPECTFUL Model offers us one way to get inside the client's world quickly and view some of the ways that his or her situation and outlook have been impacted by these various attributes (see Experiential Exercise 9.2).

> ### Experiential Exercise 9.2:
> ### Using the RESPECTFUL Model
>
> Pair up with another student in class, or if completed after class, with a person you would like to learn more about. Then, using your foundational skills and your information gathering questions, ask the individual about the 10 dimensions of the RESPECTFUL model. When you have finished, reflect on what you have learned about the person that you didn't know before. How might the information you gathered impact your work with this person if he or she was a client? If possible, share some of your thoughts with the class.

The Multicultural and Social Justice Counseling Competencies[1]

As cross-cultural issues became increasingly important to the helping relationship, it quickly became apparent that social justice concerns, often seen as a subset of multicultural counseling, were an integral aspect of what the helper should be doing. Originally, multicultural counseling competencies and separate social justice counseling competencies were created to assist helpers when working with diverse clients. However, knowing the intimate relationship between multicultural helping and social justice work, it was decided to combine the two into one set of competencies: The Multicultural and Social Justice Counseling Competencies (Ratts, Singh, Nassar-McMillan, Butler, & McCullough, 2015). A brief version of these competencies is presented here.

The Multicultural and Social Justice Counseling Competencies are sectioned off into four domains: (1) counselor [helper] self-awareness, (2) client worldview, (3) counseling [helping] relationship, and (4) counseling and advocacy interventions. Each of the first three domains are defined by attitudes and beliefs, knowledge, skills, and action. The last domain focuses on social justice work in the following areas: intrapersonal, interpersonal, institutional, community, public policy, and international and global affairs.

Domain I: Counselor [Helper] Self-Awareness

Attitudes and Beliefs: Helpers "are aware of their social identities, social group statuses, power, privilege, oppression, strengths, limitations, assumptions, attitudes, values, beliefs, and biases."

Knowledge: Helpers "possess an understanding of their social identities, social group statuses, power, privilege, oppression, strengths, limitations, assumptions, attitudes, values, beliefs, and biases."

Skills: Helpers "possess skills that enrich their understanding of their social identities, social group statuses, power, privilege, oppression, limitations, assumptions, attitudes, values, beliefs, and biases."

Action: Helpers "take action to increase self-awareness of their social identities, social group statuses, power, privilege, oppression, strengths, limitations, assumptions, attitudes, values, beliefs, and biases." (See Experiential Exercise 9.3).

---

[1] Quotes in this section are excerpts from Manivong J. Ratts, Anneliese A. Singh, Sylvia Nassar-McMillan, S. Kent Butler, and Julian Rafferty McCullough, Multicultural and Social Justice Counseling Competencies. Copyright © 2014 by American Counseling Association. Reprinted with permission.

Experiential Exercise 9.3:
Helper's Awareness About Privilege

Awareness of the kinds of privilege that some of us do and do not have is important when working with clients. It allows us to realize that as a result of their life circumstances, some clients have a much more difficult time than others. This exercise helps us examine the kinds of privilege we have had in our lives.

This exercise can be done in two ways. Students in a classroom will stand in a line about 10 feet away from the instructor and face him or her. The instructor will then read each of the statements found in Appendix F, and each student should simply follow the instructions (take a step back or forward for each statement). This will visually show you who has grown up with more privilege.

Students not in a classroom can read each statement and place a "plus" sign next to each statement if the student were to take a step forward and a 'minus" sign next to each statement if the student were to take a step back. Students can then count all of their plusses and minuses and add them up (7 plusses and 5 minuses result in 2 plusses overall). Then, the instructor can obtain the average score from the class and each student can compare his or her score to the average score.

Discussion: After the exercise is complete, students can discuss the following questions:
1. How advantageous is it to have privilege in our society?
2. How disadvantageous is it to not have privilege?
3. If you have had a lot of privilege, what would your life be like if you hadn't?
4. If you have not had much privilege, what would your life look like if you did have privilege?

Domain II: Client World View

Attitudes and Beliefs: Helpers "are aware of clients' worldview, assumptions, attitudes, values, beliefs, biases, social identities, social group statuses, and experiences with power, privilege, and oppression."

Knowledge: Helpers "possess knowledge of clients' worldview, assumptions, attitudes, values, beliefs, biases, social identities, social group statuses, and experiences with power, privilege, and oppression."

Skills: Helpers "possess skills that enrich their understanding of clients' worldview, assumptions, attitudes, values, beliefs, biases, social identities, social group statuses, and experiences with power, privilege, and oppression."

Action: Helpers "take action to increase self-awareness of clients' worldview, assumptions, attitudes, values, beliefs, biases, social identities, social group statuses, and experiences with power, privilege, and oppression" (see Reflection Exercise 9.2).

Reflection Exercise 9.2:
Helper's Knowledge About Client Assumptions

A White female elementary school teacher in the United States posed a math problem to her class one day: "Suppose there are four blackbirds sitting in a tree. You take a slingshot and shoot one of them. How many are left?" A White student answered quickly, "That's easy. One subtracted from four is three." An African immigrant youth then answered with equal confidence, "Zero." The teacher chuckled at the latter response and stated that the first student was right and that, perhaps, the second student should study more math. From that day forth, the African student seemed to withdraw from class activities and seldom spoke to other students or the teacher. ...

If the teacher had pursued the African student's reasons for arriving at the answer zero, she might have heard the following: "If you shoot one bird, the others will fly away." Nigerian educators often use this story to illustrate differences in world views between United States and African cultures. The Nigerians contend that the group is more important than the individual; that the survival of all members depends on the interrelationships among various parts. (Sue, 1992, pp. 7–8)

Lacking knowledge of a client's world view can limit our understanding of the client, as is evidenced in the above example. Have you ever been misunderstood because your knowledge or understanding of the world was different than another person's? What was that like for you?

Domain III: Counseling [Helping] Relationship

Attitudes and Beliefs: Helpers "are aware of how client and counselor worldviews, assumptions, attitudes, values, beliefs, biases, social identities, social group statuses, and experiences with power, privilege, and oppression influence the counseling relationship."

Knowledge: Helpers "possess knowledge of how client and counselor worldviews, assumptions, attitudes, values, beliefs, biases, social identities, social group statuses, and experiences with power, privilege, and oppression influence the counseling relationship."

Skills: Helpers "possess skills to engage in discussions with clients about how client and counselor worldviews, assumptions, attitudes, values, beliefs, biases, social identities, social group statuses, power, privilege, and oppression influence the counseling relationship."

Action: Helpers "take action to increase their understanding of how client and counselor worldviews, assumptions, attitudes, values, beliefs, biases, social identities, social group statuses, and experiences with power, privilege, and oppression influence the counseling relationship" (see Experiential Exercise 9.4).

Experiential Exercise 9.4:
Talking About Cultural Differences in the Helping Relationship

Sometimes, no one wants to acknowledge the elephant in the room. For instance, when a client is culturally different than the helper, the helper and the client will often think about their differences, but never acknowledge them. Sometimes this is fine, but in ongoing helping relationships it is often important to acknowledge differences and talk about how the client's identity has impacted his or her life, including the relationship with the helper. Do you possess the skills to "talk race" or other diversity issues with clients in a positive way?

Find a person, in our out of class, who in some way identifies as a minority. As a helper, broach any class, gender, race, sexual orientation, and cultural differences with the person you found. Using the following questions, or others, see if you can get the person to talk about the following issues. In class, discuss the ease you had in doing this exercise.

1. Have you experienced any prejudice in your life?
2. When you have faced bias or prejudice in your life, how did you react?
3. What kind of privileges do you think you were denied due to your class, gender, race, sexual orientation, cultural identity, or other differences?
4. What is it like to be… (female, Black, gay, lesbian, poor, disabled, etc.,)?
5. Do you think that cultural differences between the two of us influences our helping relationship?
6. What can I do to ensure a good helping relationship between the two of us?

Domain IV: Counseling and Advocacy Interventions

A. *Intrapersonal:* "The individual characteristics of a person such as knowledge, attitudes, behavior, self-concept, skills, and developmental history."

   Intrapersonal Interventions: Helpers "address the intrapersonal processes that impact privileged and marginalized clients."

B. *Interpersonal:* "The interpersonal processes and/or groups that provide individuals with identity and support (i.e. family, friends, and peers)."

   Interpersonal Interventions: Helpers "address the interpersonal processes that affect privileged and marginalized clients."

C. *Institutional:* "Represents the social institutions in society such as schools, churches, community organizations."

   Institutional Interventions: Helpers "address inequities at the institutional level."

D. *Community:* "The community as a whole represents the spoken and unspoken norms, values, and regulations that are embedded in society. The norms, values, and regulations of a community may either be empowering or oppressive to human growth and development."

Community Interventions: Helpers "address community norms, values, and regulations that impede the development of individuals, groups, and communities."

E. *Public Policy:* "Public policy reflects the local, state, and federal laws and policies that regulate or influence client human growth and development."

Public Policy Interventions: Helpers "address public policy issues that impede on client development with, and on behalf of clients."

F. *International and Global Affairs:* "International and global concerns reflect the events, affairs, and policies that influence psychological health and well-being."

International and Global Affairs Interventions: Helpers "address international and global events, affairs and polices that impede on client development with, and on behalf of, clients" (see Experiential Exercise 9.5).

Experiential Exercise 9.5:
Advocating Locally and Globally

I'm pretty confident that the vast majority of students enter the helping professions to be of service to the downtrodden and those struggling with life problems. Although the helping relationship can assist a client in raising his or her self-esteem and in helping clients learn how to advocate for themselves, another way to help our clients is through institutional, community, public policy, and global advocacy interventions. In small groups, brainstorm ways that your group could advocate for individuals. Make a list, and then share it with the larger class. If the energy and will is felt in the class, pick one or two of the items on the list and follow through with them.

CONSIDERATIONS WHEN WORKING WITH SELECT POPULATIONS

If you consider the fact that the United States is a conglomerate of people from hundreds of countries, dozens of religions, multiple racial groups, multitudes of ability/disability categories, numerous sexual orientations and gender identifications, and more, you can see that dozens of books can be written on how to build a successful helping relationship with the many different kinds of people that inhabit this country. In this section of the chapter, we have chosen just a limited few of these many groups and have highlighted some suggestions when working with individuals from them. We hope that these groups typify the backgrounds of a large number of clients you might work with. However, remember that you can gain additional knowledge about other individuals who are not listed here and keep in mind that the suggestions listed here will not work with all individuals from the specific group highlighted—they are generalizations (see Reflection Exercise 9.3).

Reflection Exercise 9.3:
Is This You?

As you read about the following populations, consider whether you are, or have ever been, one of these individuals. If so, see if the suggestions for working with these groups make sense to you. If they don't seem to ring true, do you have other suggestion to add to those that are listed? Are there some that should be removed? Send them to me through the publisher's address or email me. I'll consider them for the next addition.

Working with Individuals from Different Ethnic and Racial Groups

Although cultural differences are great among African Americans, Asians, Latinos/as, and Native Americans, there are some broad suggestions that can be followed for working with individuals from these and other ethnic and racial groups. Some suggestions include the following (McAuliffe, 2013b; Sue & Sue, 2013):

1. *Embrace the Multicultural Counseling and Social Justice Competencies.* Be aware of your own biases, have knowledge about your client's cultural background, gain the skills to work with your client based on his or her cultural background, help the client advocate for himself or herself, and be prepared to advocate for your client.

2. *Encourage clients to speak their own language.* A helper is not necessarily expected to be bilingual, although that would often be beneficial. However, clients will often feel respected if you know meaningful expressions from the client's primary language.

3. *Assess the client's cultural identify.* Using a model, like the RESPECTFUL Model and/or Sue and Torino's model, assess the client's cultural identity.

4. *Check accuracy of the client's nonverbal expression.* Don't assume that nonverbal communication is consistent across cultures. Helpers should ask their clients about their nonverbal expression when in doubt.

5. *Make use of alternate communication modes.* Because of cross-cultural differences, some clients will be reticent to talk, and for others, English may be a second language that they are hesitant to use for fear of making mistakes. When reasonable, use acting, drawing, music-sharing, storytelling, or collage making, to enhance communication.

6. *Encourage clients to bring in culturally significant and personally relevant items.* Helpers should have clients bring in items that will assist the helper in understanding them and their culture (e.g., books, photographs, articles of significance, culturally meaningful items).

7. *Vary the helping environment.* The helping relationship may be unfamiliar territory to a client, and sitting in a small, private room might be anxiety provoking. Thus, it may be important to explore alternative helping environments to ease clients into the helping relationship (e.g., take a walk, have a cup of coffee at a quiet restaurant, initially meet a client at his or her home).

8. *Don't jump to conclusions about clients.* Don't fall into the trap of assuming that clients will act in stereotypical ways. Many clients won't match a stereotype.

9. *Assess sociopolitical issues.* Ask the client about his or her life and sociological and/or political issues that are impacting the client.

Working with Individuals from Diverse Religious Backgrounds

When working with any individual, it is important to understand his or her religious background and how it might impact the helping relationship. Some pointers to keep in mind concerning religion and the helping relationship include the following (Fowler, 1981/1995; See Association for Spiritual, Ethical, and Religious Values in Counseling's Spiritual Competencies, 2009):

1. *Embrace the Multicultural Counseling and Social Justice Competencies.* Be aware of your own biases, have knowledge about your client's cultural background, gain the skills to work with your client based on his or her cultural background, help the client advocate for himself or herself, and be prepared to advocate for your client.

2. *Determine the client's religious background early in the helping relationship.* As a basis for future treatment planning, helpers should know the client's religious affiliation and how it might impact the helping relationship (e.g., holidays, times for prayer, how to address individuals, issues of touch, etc.). This information can be acquired at the initial interview; however, a helper should also be sensitive to any client who may initially resist a discussion of religion.

3. *Ask the client how important religion is in his or her life.* For some clients, religion holds little influence; for others, it is a driving force. In either case, some clients have only a rudimentary understanding of their religious tradition, and helpers should not assume that clients know much about the intricacies of their religion (even if they present themselves as deeply religious). Assessment of the role religion plays in a client's life can assist in goal setting and treatment planning.

4. *Assess the client's level of faith development. Low stage faith development clients* will tend to be more dualistic and concrete. This client works better with a fair amount of structure and firm goals. *High stage faith development clients* see the world in complex ways and value many kinds of faith experiences. This client would likely feel more comfortable in a helping relationship that values abstract thinking and self-reflection.

5. *Don't make false assumptions about clients.* Be careful not to stereotype (e.g., a helper who might falsely believe that all Jews keep a kosher home). Also, don't project your faith onto others (e.g., a Christian helper who assumes that all people of faiths are born with original sin).

6. *Educate yourself concerning your client's religious beliefs.* Helpers should know about the religious affiliation of clients. They can learn by taking a course or workshop, by reading, by attending a client's place of worship, and if appropriate, by asking the client.

7. *Educate yourself about your client's religious beliefs and become familiar with holidays and traditions.* Clients are more likely to feel a sense of closeness with a helper if they see that the helper has gone out of his or her way to learn about the client's religion. This knowledge also helps to avoid making embarrassing errors (e.g., a Muslim would not want to be offered food during the month of Ramadan).

8. *Remember that religion can deeply affect a client on many levels, including unconscious ones.* Some clients who deny any religious affiliation may continue to be unconsciously driven by the basic values they were originally taught. Look at clients' actions; don't just listen to their words. For instance, a "lapsed Catholic" may continue to feel guilty over certain issues related to the religious beliefs he or she was taught.

Working with Women

Several authors have suggested that due to the oppression that women face in society and as a result of their unique identity development, specific guidelines should be applied when working with them (American Psychological Association [APA], 2007, Brown & Bryan, 2007; Brown, Weber, & Ali, 2008; Pusateri & Headly, 2015). The following addresses some of these guidelines:

1. *Embrace the Multicultural Counseling and Social Justice Competencies.* Be aware of your own biases, have knowledge about your client's cultural background, gain the skills to work with your client based on his or her cultural background, help the client advocate for herself, and be prepared to advocate for your client.

2. *Use a helping model that has been adapted for women.* Many helping theories have been based on a so-called male model of behavior. Therefore, ensure that whatever model you use, it is adapted to or amenable for women.

3. *Build an equal relationship, give up power, and demystify the helping relationship.* Downplay the "expert" role and encourage women to trust themselves. Female helpers may want to use self-disclosure with female clients, but male helpers should be much more tentative about this technique. In either case, the helper should not be seen as omnipotent. Instead, the helper should be seen as an equal who is there to help.

4. *Identify ways in which client problems may be a function of sociopolitical forces.* Women are often rendered powerless through abusive men, institutional sexism (e.g., salary inequities), and gender-role expectations (e.g., women must look a certain way to be considered "beautiful"). Help female clients see how their lives may have been impacted by these forces.

5. *Validate and legitimize angry feelings toward their predicament.* As women come to see how they have been victimized, helpers can assist them in combating feelings of powerlessness, helplessness, and low self-esteem. This can be facilitated by encouraging women to participate in consciousness-raising activities about women's issues (reading books, attending seminars, taking part in women's groups, etc.).

6. *Provide a safe environment to express feelings as clients begin to form connections with other women.* Helpers can validate feelings of fear and competition with other women that result from society's objectification of women. As these feelings dissipate, clients can move toward having a strong and special connection to other women. Helpers can assist clients in understanding the difference between anger at a man and anger at a male-dominated system.

7. *Promote healing through learning about women's issues.* Encourage clients to learn about women's issues, oppression of women, societal stereotypes of women, etc. This can help women understand the many barriers they have faced. Such knowledge can be soothing as the women moves to develop a new sense of self.

8. *Help clients with conflicting feelings between traditional and newly found values.* Clients may feel torn between newfound feminist beliefs and values that they may not see as congruent with those beliefs (e.g., wanting to be independent versus wanting to stay home to raise the children). Helpers should validate these contradictory feelings, acknowledge the confusion, and assist clients to fully explore their belief systems.

9. *Facilitate an integration of client's new identity.* After women have explored their traditional and newly found values, helpers can assist them in integrating those personal or feminist beliefs which they choose to embrace. This helps women feel empowered, as they come to realize that they, alone, decide which beliefs and ways of living they want to live out.

10. *Say goodbye.* Help women move on with their newfound identity by encouraging them to try being in the world without counseling. Counseling can always be resumed in the future if needed.

Working with Men

"You're not allowed to have issues; you're just a male." (Kristina Williams-Neukrug)

When I was writing this section, my wife said the above profound statement to me. You see, men in today's society are sometimes seen as not having issues because they have occupied, and continue to occupy, many positions of power. Thus, they are often viewed as holding a certain amount of privilege, which is accurate. However, helpers must be aware that having power can have its own unique problems, that there are many men who are not in such positions, and that there are unique men's issues that need to be understood within the helping relationship. A number of authors have offered ideas that can be incorporated into a set of guidelines when working with male clients (Englar-Carlson & Kiselica, 2013; Evans, Duffey, & Englar-Carlson, 2013; Good & Brooks, 2005; Greer, 2005; Neukrug, Britton, & Crews, 2013; Wexler, 2009):

1. *Embrace the Multicultural Counseling and Social Justice Competencies.* Be aware of your own biases, have knowledge about your client's cultural background, gain the skills to work with your client based on his or her cultural background, help the client advocate for himself, and be prepared to advocate for your client.

2. *Accept men where they are.* Men can often be on guard when initially entering the helping relationship. Thus, the helper should accept men as they are in an effort to build trust. Once men feel safe, they tend to work hard on their issues.

3. *Don't push men to express what may be considered "softer feelings."* Some have suggested that the helping relationship has resulted in the expectation that men should express what are typically considered "female feelings" when entering a helping relationship (e.g., deep sadness, feelings of incompetence, feelings of inadequacy, and feelings of closeness). However, men can often feel uncomfortable with the expression of certain feelings and more at ease with "thinking things through," problem solving, goal setting, and the expression of some other feelings, such as anger and pride. Push a man too quickly, and he may be pushed out of the helping relationship.

4. *Validate men's feelings.* To protect their egos, men will sometimes initially blame others or society for their problems. Men need to feel validated in these feelings if they are to continue in the helping relationship.

5. *Validate men's view of how they have been constrained by male gender-role stereotypes.* Early on in the helping relationship, note how the man is constrained by gender-role stereotypes and pressure in society (e.g., he must work particularly hard for his family). Validation of these views helps to build trust and establish the relationship.

6. *Have a plan.* Men often like structure and a sense of goal directedness, even if goals are changed later on. Thus, the helper should be willing to collaborate with men on a plan for the helping relationship.

7. *Discuss developmental issues.* Although each man has his own unique issues, he will also likely be struggling with common male developmental issues. The helper should be aware of and willing to discuss these issues (e.g., mid-life crises).

8. *Slowly encourage the expression of new feelings.* As trust is formed, men may begin to express what are typically considered softer, sometimes labeled "feminine" feelings (e.g., tears, caring, feelings of intimacy). The helper should reinforce the expression of these newfound feelings.

9. *Explore underlying issues and reinforce new ways of understanding the world.* Expression of new feelings will lead to the emergence of underlying issues (e.g., unresolved childhood issues, feelings of inadequacy). One important, critical, yet sometimes painful issue for men is their relationship with their fathers. How fathers modeled, distanced themselves, and showed love can become a template for men's relationships.

10. *Explore behavioral change.* As men gain new insights into self, they may wish to try new ways of acting in the world. The client, in collaboration with the helper, can identify new potential behaviors and "try them out."

11. *Encourage the integration of new feelings, new ways of thinking about the world, and new behaviors into the man's lifestyle.* The expression of new feelings, newly gained insights, and new ways of thinking and acting will slowly take on a life of its own and be integrated into the client's way of living. Helpers can actively reinforce these new ways of being.

12. *Encourage new male relationships.* As male clients grow, new male friendships that allow the man to freely express his feelings with another man can be encouraged. Men's groups can allow men to develop more intimate relationships with other men, feel supported, and be challenged to change.

13. *Say goodbye.* Although some men may want to continue in the helping relationship, others will see it as time limited—a means to a goal. Thus, the helper should be able to say goodbye and end the relationship. Doing this sets the groundwork for the client to come back, if he so desires.

Working with Lesbian, Gay, Bisexual, and Transgender (LGBT) Individuals

Helpers should always consider one's gender identification (being "male" or "female") when working with all clients. In addition, those who are lesbian, gay, bisexual, and transgender individuals have unique concerns that helpers should consider. Thus, general guidelines have been developed for counseling individuals who are lesbian, gay, bisexual, and transgender (e.g., Pope, 2008; Ritter, 2015; Sue & Sue, 2013; Szymanski, 2013):

1. *Embrace the Multicultural Counseling and Social Justice Competencies.* Be aware of your own biases, have knowledge about your client's cultural background, gain the skills to work with your client based on his or her cultural background, help the client advocate for himself or herself, and be prepared to advocate for your client.

2. *Know identity issues.* Be familiar with the identity development of lesbian, gay, bisexual, or transgender individuals, especially as it relates to the coming out process.

3. *Understand the differences among people who are lesbian, gay, bisexual, or transgender.* Although lumped together here, great differences exist among LGBT individuals. For instance, identity development for gays, lesbians, bisexuals, and transgender individuals is often considerably different.

4. *Promote an LGBT-friendly agency atmosphere.* Make sure that the agency atmosphere and your office is inviting to all individuals. This can be done by not having heteronormative or heterosexist materials in the office and ensuring that all forms are lesbian, gay, bisexual, and transgender friendly. Of course, staff and helpers should be nonjudgmental and accepting of all individuals who come into the agency.

5. *Understand how societal oppression impacts LGBT clients.* Be cognizant that various forms of prejudice continue to be prevalent in society and be sensitive to how such prejudice may impact your clients.

6. *Adopt an affirming and strength-based approach.* Affirm your clients' sexual orientation and gender identity and view all sexual identities and orientations as equally healthy.

7. *Don't jump to conclusions about lifestyle.* Don't assume that a lesbian, gay, bisexual, or transgender client is comfortable living in what the dominant culture understands to be a lesbian, gay, bisexual, or transgender lifestyle. This lifestyle, often portrayed in movies and on TV, is not how most lesbian, gay, bisexual, or transgender individuals live.

8. *Know the unique issues of LGBT clients.* By reading professional literature about LGBT individuals, and by becoming involved with LGBT groups, helpers can gain an understanding of some of the unique issues of lesbian, gay, bisexual, and transgender individuals.

9. *Know community resources.* Be aware of community resources that might be useful to LGBT individuals.

10. *Understand the idiosyncrasies of religion toward being LGBT.* Be familiar with particular religious and spiritual concerns unique to those of the LGBT community.

Working with Homeless and the Poor

Although legislation, like the *McKinney-Vento Homeless Act*, was developed to assist those who are homeless with a variety of services, this population is still particularly in need of services ("History of the McKinney Act," 2015). And, with as many as 3.5 million Americans experiencing homelessness each year (U.S. Department of Housing and Urban Development, 2014), it is essential that human service professionals know how to help them. Here are some general guidelines (APA, 2015; Barrett-Rivera, Lindstrom, & Kerewsky, 2013; Dykeman, 2011; McBride, 2012; Sun 2012):

1. *Embrace the Multicultural Counseling and Social Justice Competencies.* Be aware of your own biases, have knowledge about your client's cultural background, gain the skills to work with your client based on his or her cultural background, help the client advocate for himself or herself, and be prepared to advocate for your client.

2. *Focus on social issues.* When working with individuals struggling to have their basic needs met, it is important for the helper to focus on social issues, such as helping a person obtain food and housing, as opposed to spending an inordinate amount of time on intrapersonal issues. Although intrapersonal concerns are important, they are often not as pressing for those who are homeless and those dealing with poverty.

3. *Know the client's racial/ethnic/cultural background.* Because a disproportionate number of homeless and poor people come from minority racial/ethnic/cultural groups, if helpers are to connect with those who are homeless and poor, they need to educate themselves about and feel comfortable working with clients who may be different from themselves.

4. *Be knowledgeable about health risks.* The homeless and the poor are at greater risk of developing AIDS, tuberculosis, and other diseases. The helper should have basic knowledge of such diseases, be able to do a basic medical screening, and have referral sources available.

5. *Be prepared to deal with multiple issues.* Because as many as 50% of those who are homeless are struggling with mental illness and/or substance abuse, helpers must often deal with the multiple issues of homelessness, poverty, mental illness, and chemical dependence.

6. *Know about developmental delays and be prepared to refer.* Homeless and poor children are more likely to have delayed language and social skills, be abused, and have delayed motor development compared with other children. Helpers should know how to identify developmental delays.

7. *Know psychological effects.* Helpers should know how to respond to clients' psychological and emotional reactions to homelessness and poverty, which can include despair, depression, and a sense of hopelessness.

8. *Know resources.* Helpers should be aware of the vast number of resources available in the community and make referrals when appropriate.

Working with Older Persons

Older persons present a different set of issues to the helper than younger persons. And with those over the age of 65 quickly becoming 20% of the U.S. population, it is likely that the human service professional will increasingly be working with older individuals (U.S. Census Bureau, 2014). To ensure that their concerns are addressed, helpers should consider the following (Anderson, Goodman, & Schlossberg, 2012; Barstow & Lum, 2011; Chatters & Zalaquett, 2013):

1. *Embrace the Multicultural Counseling and Social Justice Competencies.* Be aware of your own biases, have knowledge about your client's cultural background, gain the skills to work with your client based on his or her cultural background, help the client advocate for himself or herself, and be prepared to advocate for your client.

2. *Adapt your counseling style.* The helper may need to adapt the helping relationship to fit the older client's needs. For instance, use journal writing or art therapy for older persons who have difficulty hearing. For non-ambulatory clients, have a session in the client's home.

3. *Build a trusting relationship.* Older persons seek counseling at lower rates than other clients, and those who do may be less trustful, having been raised during a time when counseling was much less common. Thus, helpers need to pay particular attention to building a sound relationship based on trust.

4. *Know potential sources of depression.* Depression can have many origins for an older person, including the loss of loved ones, lifestyle changes, identity confusion, and changes in health. Helpers should be capable of identifying the many potential sources of depression.

5. *Know about identity issues.* Many older persons may have previously based their identities on their career, family, or roles in the community. Changes in these roles can lead to feelings of depression, anxiety, or despair. Some older persons may need to redefine themselves as they no longer function in their previous roles. Helpers can assist clients in finding a new sense of meaning in their lives.

6. *Know about possible and probable health changes.* Predictable health changes can yield depression and concern for the future. Unpredictable changes can lead to loss of income and emotional problems. Helpers should be alert to potential health problems and their emotional counterparts in older persons.

7. *Have empathy for changes in interpersonal relations.* Aging brings changes in significant relationships as a result of such things as the death of a spouse, partners, and friends; changes in health status; and relocation. Helpers should be knowledgeable about such changes and have empathy toward their clients concerning these changes.

8. *Know about physical and psychological causes of sexual dysfunction.* Helpers should be aware of the possible physical and psychological causes of sexual dysfunction in older persons and should always be cognizant that regardless of age, people are always sexual beings.

Working with People with Mental Illnesses

Helpers who work with those who are chronically mentally ill need to understand psychiatric disorders, psychotropic medications, and the unique needs of chronically mentally ill clients, such as homelessness, continual transitions, difficulty with employment, and dependent family relationships (Barstow & Lum, 2011; Crowe & Averett, 2015; Garske, 2009; Wong, 2006). Specific steps that helpers can take when working with this population include the following:

1. *Embrace the Multicultural Counseling and Social Justice Competencies.* Be aware of your own biases, have knowledge about your client's cultural background, gain the skills to work with your client based on his or her cultural background, help the client advocate for himself or herself, and be prepared to advocate for your client.

2. *Help your client understand his or her mental illness.* Many clients do not have an understanding of their illness, the usual course of the illness, and best methods of treatment. Clients should be fully informed, with up-to-date knowledge, about their mental illness.

3. *Help your client work through feelings concerning his or her mental illness.* Mental illness continues to be stigmatized in society, and many clients can be embarrassed about their disorder. Support groups, and a nonjudgmental attitude, can help to normalize clients' views of themselves.

4. *Ensure attendance to counseling.* Clients may miss appointments because they are in denial about their illness, embarrassed, or simply do not care. Helpers can call clients the day before their appointment, have a relative or close friend help the client get to the helper's office, work on specific strategies to help clients remember to come in for their appointments, or find innovative ways of contacting their clients (e.g., online, home visits).

5. *Assure compliance with medication.* Clients may discontinue medication out of forgetfulness, denial about the illness, uncomfortable side effects, because they believe they won't have a relapse, or because they believe medication is not helpful. Helpers need to ensure that clients continue to take their medication, and when doubts arise about the effectiveness of medication, they must make a referral for a medication review.

6. *Assure accurate diagnosis.* Accurate diagnosis is crucial for treatment planning and the appropriate use of medication. Helpers can assure accurate diagnosis through testing, clinical interviews, interviews with others close to the client, and through appropriate use of supervision.

7. *Reevaluate the client's treatment plan and do not give up.* The mentally ill are some of the most difficult clients to work with and it is easy for helpers to become discouraged. Helpers need to continue to be vigilant about their work with the mentally ill, be committed to them, and continually reevaluate treatment plans.

8. *Involve the client's family.* Some families can offer great support to clients, and they can be a window into the client's psyche. Thus, it is important to assure adequate family involvement and to help families understand the implications of the client's diagnosis.

9. *Know resources.* The mentally ill are often involved with many other resources in the community (e.g., Social Security office, housing authority, support groups). It is therefore crucial that the helper have a working knowledge of these resources.

Working with Individuals with Disabilities

With nearly 20% of Americans having a disability (U.S. Census Bureau, 2012), human service professionals will undoubtedly be working with this population. As federal laws have increasingly supported the rights to services for individuals with disabilities, the helper has taken a more active role in their treatment and rehabilitation. Observing the following treatment issues can assist helpers in providing positive services for this group (Kelsey & Smart, 2012; Martin, 2007; Smart, 2012):

1. *Embrace the Multicultural Counseling and Social Justice Competencies.* Be aware of your own biases, have knowledge about your client's cultural background, gain the skills to work with your client based on his or her cultural background, help the client advocate for himself or herself, and be prepared to advocate for your client.

2. *Have knowledge of the many disabling conditions.* Obviously, a helper cannot adequately work with an individual who has a disability if he or she does not understand the emotional and physical consequences of that disability.

3. *Help the client know his or her disability.* Clients should be fully informed of their disability, the probable course of treatment, and their prognosis. Knowledge of their disability will allow them to be fully involved in any emotional healing that needs to take place.

4. *Assist the client through the grieving process.* Clients who become disabled often go through stages as they grieve their loss and accept their condition. Similar to people going through stages of death bereavement (Kubler-Ross & Kessler, 2005/2014), clients can be expected to experience denial, anger, negotiation, resignation, and acceptance. The helper can facilitate the client's progression through these stages.

5. *Know referral resources.* Individuals with disabilities often have diverse needs. Thus, it is important that helpers are aware of community resources (e.g., physicians, social services, physical therapists, special education teachers, experts on pain management, vocational rehabilitation).

6. *Know the law and inform clients of the law.* By knowing the law, the helper can assure that the client is receiving all necessary services and not being discriminated against. Helping clients understand the law empowers them by giving them the ability to protect their rights.

7. *Be prepared for vocational/career counseling.* When faced with a disability, many people are also faced with making a career transition. Helpers should be ready to do career/vocational counseling or refer a client to a career/vocational helper.

8. *Include the family.* Families can offer support, assist in long-term treatment planning, and help with the emotional needs of the client. Whenever reasonable, include the family.

9. *Be an advocate.* Individuals with disabilities are faced with prejudice and discrimination. Helpers can be client advocates by knowing the law, fighting for client rights, and assisting the client in fighting for his or her rights. A client who knows his or her rights and who acts as an advocate for himself or herself will likely feel empowered.

Working with Individuals Who Use and Abuse Substances

With alarming numbers of individuals in the inner city and in middle class America abusing illicit and prescription drugs, there is little question that human service professionals today need to be mindful of how to work with clients who may be dependent or addicted to substances. The following guidelines offer a map of how you might work with such individuals (Fisher & Harrison, 2013; Lewis, Dana, & Blevins, 2015; Substance Abuse and Mental Health Services Administration, 2016):

1. *Embrace the Multicultural Counseling and Social Justice Competencies.* Be aware of your own biases, have knowledge about your client's cultural background, gain the skills to work with your client based on his or her cultural background, help the client advocate for himself or herself, and be prepared to advocate for your client.

2. *Assess for substance dependency and abuse.* Since substance users and abusers can be particularly private about their use, you may want to conduct a structured interview that specifically asks about a wide range of substance use or abuse issues or provide an assessment instrument that can assess for use or abuse. It can be useful to catch substance use or abuse early, because the longer one uses or abuses, the more embedded such use becomes.

3. *Gain knowledge about substance abuse.* Because substances can vary greatly, it is important to have basic knowledge about theories of substance abuse as well as specific knowledge about different substances to help you understand the appropriate course of treatment.

4. *Build a relationship and stay committed.* Individuals who abuse substances may want to stop their abuse, but also may have a difficult time doing so. It is common for substance abusers to have a "slip," and when this happens, they need to see the helper as a "rock"—a person who is always there for them.

5. *Be prepared to refer to a therapist.* Individuals who abuse substances often need more in-depth counseling than a human service professional can provide, so have a referral base of counselors and therapists who specifically work with substance abuse clients.

6. *Be prepared to refer to rehabilitation facilities or hospitals.* Sometimes, hospitalization is critical to save the life of a substance abuser. Other times, rehabilitation facilities may be the only mechanism to help the abuser. Know these resources and how to refer to them.

7. *Refer to self-help groups.* Alcoholics Anonymous, Alanon, Narcotics Anonymous, and other self-help groups have become an important part of treatment for many substance abusers. Be aware of these resources and have them available for your clients.

8. *Focus on family support.* Interventions with families in an effort to help the substance abuser seek treatment, or to offer support when in treatment, can be particularly helpful for clients.

9. *Stay in touch and stay committed.* Substance abuse can be a lifelong problem, and it is important the abuser know that you are committed to him or her as long as he or she needs you—even if it is over the span of several years (see Experiential Exercise 9.6).

Experiential Exercise 9.6:
Interviewing Diverse Clients

Pick one of the diverse clients we discussed in the chapter and find a person to interview who matches that description. Then, using as a guide the descriptions outlined in this chapter, ask the individual questions about his or her life. Add other questions as needed to obtain a full picture of the individual. For instance, if I was interviewing a person struggling with substance use or abuse, I might ask the following questions:

1. What kind of substances have you abused over your lifetime?
2. Are you still using?
3. If you ever stopped, or are currently not using, what most helped you stop?
4. How has your substance use or abuse impacted your life?
5. Have you ever sought counseling for your substance use and/or abuse?
6. Have you ever been hospitalized or in a rehabilitation facility for your substance use and/or abuse?
7. Have you ever been to a self-help group, like AA, for your substance use and/or abuse?
8. What kind of support have you received from your family and friends for you substance use or abuse?
9. What kind of help and commitment from a helper would you find worthwhile if you were seeking such assistance?
10. What resources do you think would be most helpful for you in stopping your substance use or abuse?
11. Any other thoughts about your substance use or abuse that might be helpful to a helper?

ETHICAL CONCERNS RELATED TO CULTURALLY COMPETENT HELPING

As you might expect, the ethics code of human service professionals speaks to the importance of practicing responsible cross-cultural counseling (NOHS, 2015, Standards 10 through 18). This includes being knowledgeable about cultures and communities; knowing local, state, and federal laws and when one should advocate to change such laws because they are harmful to our clients; staying informed about current social issues; being aware of how social and political issues affect our clients; advocating for client needs and assets at the individual, community, and societal levels; advocating for social justice issues in an effort to fight oppression; and helping to raise awareness of underserved clients.

Being an effective cross-cultural helper is more than giving lip service to the above cross-cultural concerns. It means protesting a law when it is clearly hurting our clients. It means taking the time to learn about your clients.

It takes active work to help members of the community and others to learn about clients with whom they might feel uncomfortable. It takes collaboration, consultation, and cooperation with all those in the community who can impact the lives of our diverse clients.

SUMMARY

In this chapter, we examined the reasons that knowledge of culturally competent helping is important in today's world. We began by highlighting the fact that the face of America is rapidly changing, with minorities becoming an increasingly larger share of the population. We noted that changing demographics make it increasingly pertinent for helpers to make sure that their approach to helping works with a wide variety of clients. Unfortunately, we identified a number of reasons that helpers are not always helpful to clients from diverse cultures. Eight reasons to explain why the helping relationship does not seem to be working for minorities were explored, and included that (1) many helpers still believe in the melting pot myth; (2) clients and helpers often have incongruent expectations about the helping relationship; (3) some helpers lack understanding of the impact of social forces on minorities; (4) some helpers have an ethnocentric worldview; (5) most helpers are ignorant, at least to some degree, of their own racist attitudes and prejudices; (6) many helpers do not understand cultural differences in the expression of symptoms; (7) helpers sometimes have to work with assessment and research instruments that are not as reliable with minorities as they are with White clients; and (8) helpers often have to work within institutions that continue to harbor embedded racist or prejudicial attitudes.

The chapter went on to identify some definitions and models of culturally competent helping. We highlighted McAuliffe's definition, which views cultural competence as a consistent readiness and ability to integrate culture into one's work. We also reviewed Sue and Torino's definition which examines client identities, collectivism vs. individualism, and types of strategies used when working with clients from diverse cultures. We reminded readers of the RESPECTFUL Model that was first noted in Chapter 1, and then we described the recent Multicultural and Social Justice Competencies. The Multicultural and Social Justice Counseling Competencies are sectioned off into four domains: (1) counselor [helper] self-awareness, (2) client worldview, (3) counseling relationship, and (4) counseling and advocacy interventions. We noted that each of the first three domains are defined by attitudes and beliefs, knowledge, skills, and action. The last domain focuses on social justice work in the following areas: intrapersonal, interpersonal, institutional, community, public policy, and international and global affairs.

The last part of the chapter examined a number of groups of individuals with whom human service professionals often work. For each group, we identified guidelines which may be useful to the helper when working with these populations. The populations included (a) different ethnic and racial groups, (b) individuals from diverse religious backgrounds, (c) women, (d) men, (e) lesbian, gay, bisexual, and transgender individuals, (f) individuals who are homeless and poor, (g) older persons, (h) individuals with mental illness, (i) individuals with disabilities, and (j) individuals using and abusing substances. The chapter concluded with a short section that examined our ethical responsibilities to working with diverse clients.

KEY WORDS AND TERMS

Attitudes and beliefs, knowledge, skills, and actions
Collectivist perspective
Cultural differences in the expression of symptoms
Cultural mosaic
Different ethnic and racial groups
Ethnocentric worldview
Group identity
Homeless and poor individuals
Incongruent expectations about the helping
   relationship
Individual identity
Individualistic perspective
Individuals from diverse religious backgrounds
Individuals using and abusing substances
Individuals with disabilities
Individuals with mental illness

Institutional Discrimination
Lack of understanding of the impact of social forces
Lesbian, gay, bisexual, and transgender individuals
McAuliffe's definition of culturally competent helping
Melting pot myth
Men
Multicultural and Social Justice Counseling
   Competencies
Older persons
Racist attitudes and prejudices
Sue and Torino's definition of culturally competent
   helping
Universal identity
Unreliable assessment and research instruments
Women

CHAPTER 10

Ethical Issues and Ethical Decision Making

LEARNING OBJECTIVES

1. Understand the purpose of ethical codes.

2. Learn about and apply four different ethical decision-making models, including: problem–solving, moral, developmental, and social constructionist models.

3. Examine the following ethical issues important in the work of the human service professional and apply the knowledge to related vignettes.

    a. Informed consent
    b. Competence and scope of knowledge
    c. Supervision
    d. Confidentiality
    e. Privileged communication
    f. Dual and multiple relationships
    g. Sexual relationships with clients
    h. Primary obligation: client, agency, or society?
    i. Continuing education
    j. Multicultural counseling
    k. Values in the helping relationship

4. To enhance your knowledge of what is ethical, review a study of 88 ethical situations to which human service professionals responded.

177

INTRODUCTION

Human service professionals are regularly faced with thorny ethical situations to which they must respond, and it is our ethical codes, as well as thoughtful decision making, that help professionals respond wisely. To help you in your ethical decision-making process, this chapter will begin by examining the purpose of ethical guidelines and then describe some of their limitations. Next, it will go on to describe four ethical decision-making models (problem-solving, moral, developmental, and social-constructionist) which, in concert with the ethical code, can be used to guide the human service professional toward wise and thoughtful actions. It then presents some of the more important ethical issues that human service professionals face, such as informed consent; competence and scope of knowledge; supervision; confidentiality; privileged communication; dual and multiple relationships; sexual relationships with clients; whether the primary obligation of human service professionals is to the client, agency, or society; continuing education; multicultural counseling; and values in the helping relationship. Ethical vignettes associated with each of these areas are examined. The chapter concludes with an examination of 88 behaviors of human service professionals which you are asked to review, reflect upon, and determine if you think they are ethical.

PURPOSE OF ETHICAL CODES

In 1995, the National Organization for Human Services (NOHS) adopted its first ethics code: the *Ethical Standards for Human Service Professionals* (NOHS, 1996). Although similar codes had been adopted years earlier by related social service associations (e.g., American Counseling Association, American Psychological Association, National Association of Social Workers), with human services not coming of age until the latter part of the twentieth century, this was a solid accomplishment. In 2015 the code was revised, and today, the new code helps guide the behavior of human service professionals. Today, ethics codes are critical to the practice of human services and serve a number of purposes (Corey, Corey, Corey, & Callanan, 2015; Dolgoff, Harrington, & Loewenberg, 2012; Remley & Herlihy, 2014). For instance, they:

- Protect consumers
- Further the professional stance of the organization
- Show that a profession has a particular body of knowledge and skills
- Assert the identity of the profession
- Reflect values of a profession
- Offer a framework for the ethical decision-making process
- If adhered to, offer some measure of defense in case one is sued

Although ethical guidelines serve all of the above purposes, they do have limitations (Corey et al., 2015; Dolgoff et al., 2012; Remley & Herlihy, 2014). For instance, they:

- Do not address all issues one will face
- Cannot always be enforced
- Often do not bring the consumer into the code construction process
- Can be at odds with other methods of addressing the issue (e.g., laws)
- Sometimes conflict with other codes, or even with the same code
- Sometimes conflict with the values of the professional

Ethical guidelines delineate the values of a professional organization, but they are not legal documents, and as such, professional associations expect us to be bound by them. Sometimes, when a person violates the codes of ethics, actions against the professional will occur, such as a letter of reprimand, requiring continuing education, or dismissal from the professional association. In some instances, states have incorporated part or all of a code of ethics into their law to which professionals must adhere. In these cases, stiffer penalties such as fines or even imprisonment could result from an infraction.

ETHICAL DECISION-MAKING

Since ethical codes are just guides, they are limited in how much they can help when making an ethical decision. For instance, suppose you had a client who seemed suicidal. Your responsibility under the code is to:

> [act] in an appropriate and professional manner to protect the safety of those individuals. This may involve, but is not limited to, seeking consultation, supervision, and/or breaking the confidentiality of the relationship. (NOHS, 2015, Standard 4)

You can see that you may have to consult with others, seek supervision, and even break confidentiality. But, which should you do and what specific actions should you take? Sometimes, the answer is not clear cut. Thus, ethical decision-making models have been devised to help us determine what to do, while using the ethical code as a guide (Cottone & Tarvydas, 2007; Levitt & Moorhead, 2013; Welfel, 2013). Four ethical decision-making models that have been identified include problem-solving models, moral models, developmental models, and the social constructionist perspective.

Problem-Solving Models

This pragmatic, hands on model has been described by Corey et al. (2015), and it includes eight steps. By carefully going through these steps, you can move toward a well thought out decision, instead of haphazardly deciding which direction to take.

1. Identifying the problem or dilemma
2. Identifying the potential issues involved
3. Reviewing the relevant ethical guidelines
4. Knowing the applicable laws and regulations
5. Obtaining consultation
6. Considering possible and probable courses of action
7. Enumerating the consequences of various decisions
8. Deciding on the best course of action

You can see how going through these eights steps can help a professional gain some clarity into an ethical dilemma while offering a clear cut method of dealing with a thorny ethical issue.

Moral Models

While the problem-solving model emphasizes the pragmatic aspects of ethical decision making, other theorists stress the role of moral principles in this process. For instance, Kitchener (1984, 1986; Urofsky, Engels, & Engebretson, 2008) describes the role of six moral principles in making ethical decisions. In her view, mental health professionals should consider the following when working with clients: (1) *autonomy,* the client's self-determination, (2) *beneficence,* protecting the good of others and society, (3) *nonmaleficence,* avoiding doing harm to clients and others, (4) *justice,* treating clients fairly and equally, (5) *fidelity,* maintaining clients' trust and being committed to them, and (6) *veracity,* being truthful and genuine within the helping relationship. Other moral models suggest that helpers should be cognizant of their character or virtues and strive to make decisions by being self-aware, compassionate, understanding of cultural differences, doing good, and having a vision for the future (e.g., Kleist & Bitter, 2009).

Developmental Models

Instead of focusing on how one makes ethical decisions, this model zeroes in on one's cognitive ability at making decisions and how it specifically impacts ethical decision-making (Lambie, Hagedor, & Ieva, 2010; Levitt & Moorhead, 2013). Those who are at lower levels of cognitive development tend to be black and white in their thinking, believe there is a "right" and "wrong" when making decisions, and tend to look for the "truthful" or "correct" response. In contrast, those who are at higher levels of cognitive development view ethical decision-making as a more complex process that is deeply self-reflective. They can see multiple ways of viewing the problem, are more flexible, and are adept at considering differing points of view.

For instance, let's examine two human service professionals: Jason, who is at a lower developmental level, and Jawanda, who is at a higher level. Both are faced with the same dilemma: A client of theirs is smoking crack cocaine, and the agency at which they work requires that such individuals be reported to the administration who will then contact the police. Jason examines the ethical guidelines, reads the agency policy guidelines, and decides that the "right thing to do" and the only choice he has is to report his client to an administrator. Jawanda, however, views ethical decision making differently. She also reads the agency policy and reviews the ethical guidelines. In addition, she is likely to use a model such as that of Corey et al. or Kitchener to help her decide what to do. She consults with others to gain other points of view, and only then carefully deliberates about what would be best for her client, the agency, society, and herself. After careful deliberation, she comes to a conclusion.

The conclusion in this case is really less important than the process, as Jawanda has dealt with the situation in a complex and thoughtful manner, as opposed to Jason's somewhat hasty decision making. In fact, although both may come to the same conclusion, I would rather work with someone like Jawanda because she shows thoughtfulness and the ability to self-reflect—qualities I would want in a colleague (and a friend!). Thus, one can see that ethical decision making can, and perhaps should be a complex process (see Reflection Exercise 10.1).

Reflection Exercise 10.1:
Ethical Decision Making—Considering Alternatives

Although many human service professionals would feel obligated to report the client just described, there may be situations when doing so might not make sense. In small groups, brainstorm reasons why you might not want to report a client to an administrator in this case. Have your small groups share their responses in class.

Social Constructionist Perspective

Those who take a social constructionist perspective believe that solutions to problems occur through dialogue between clients, helpers, and others (e.g., supervisors and others in the client's world) (Van Rooyen, Durrheim, & Lindegger, 2011). They don't expect answers to necessarily be the result of reading an ethics code or from some solo decision-making process. These individuals are humble with their clients, collaborators, supervisors, and others involved in the dilemma, approach them with curiosity and wonder, and treat them as equals and collaborators in the decision-making process as they jointly try to find the best solution to the ethical dilemma being faced. They believe solutions come out of dialogue and conversation. This approach is not for the faint-hearted, as it requires including people in the decision-making process that are often left out (e.g., clients and people close to the clients) (see Reflection Exercise 10.2).

Reflection Exercise 10.2:
Using Ethical Decision-Making Models

Using the various ethical decision-making models just described, reflect on the following vignette and then share your thoughts in small groups or with the class. Show how each model can be used to help guide your decision-making process.

As a human service professional for the local department of human services, you have been assisting Becky, a single mother of a four-year-old daughter, for the past few years as she has attempted to remove herself from the welfare rolls, obtain employment, and secure child care. Today, Becky tells you that she has been HIV-positive for the past eight years and that two years ago she developed AIDS. She has not responded well to her recent regime of medication. She is clearly despondent, very concerned for the well-being of her child, and confides in you that she is considering killing herself. She reports having few significant people in her life, realizes that it may only be a matter of time before she dies, and is concerned that in the time she has left she will not be able to adequately care for her daughter. She therefore would like your help in finding a good home for her child and in "getting her affairs in order" before she commits suicide. You are one of her few confidantes, and she is someone you care about. As a helper, what should you do?

SELECT ETHICAL ISSUES AND ETHICAL DILEMMAS

Following are descriptions of prevalent ethical issues faced by today's human service professionals. These issues are followed by related ethical vignettes. In reviewing these issues and responding to the vignettes, consider the points made earlier in the chapter and refer to the Ethical Standards of Human Service Professionals (see www.national humanservices.org/ethical-standards-for-hs-professionals).

Informed Consent

Already discussed in Chapter 8, informed consent involves the client's right to know the purpose and nature of all aspects of client involvement with the helper (Remley & Herlihy, 2014). Today, it is common for clients to be handed, at the beginning of the helping relationship, a *professional disclosure statement* that describes its parameters. Such statements are read and signed by clients, indicating they give their informed consent. If you remember from Chapter 8, such statements usually include information about (1) fees for services, (2) relevant legal issues, (3) length of the interview, (4) purpose of the interview, (5) limits of confidentiality, (6) professional's credentials, (7) professional's theoretical orientation, (8) limits to and boundaries of the relationship, and (8) agency rules that might affect the client (e.g., reporting a client's use of illegal drugs).

Obtaining informed consent from a client used to be something that was given lip service. Today, however, ethical guidelines highlight the importance to all human service professionals of having obtained this consent:

> Human service professionals obtain informed consent to provide services to clients at the beginning of the helping relationship. Clients should be informed that they may withdraw consent at any time except where denied by court order and should be able to ask questions before agreeing to the services. Clients who are unable to give consent should have those who are legally able to give consent for them review an informed consent statement and provide appropriate consent. (NOHS, 2015, Standard 2)

Ethical Vignettes Related to Informed Consent

1. You decide to refer a client because you have not worked with a situation like hers before and feel that it's out of your area of expertise. She becomes livid, stating that you did not warn her of this possibility (such as in your informed consent statement). Does she have a point? Can everything be explained in an informed consent statement?

2. A human service professional gives a written document to a family explaining the limitations of confidentiality and the general direction the family sessions will take. After reading the informed consent document, the parents sign it and bring in the family. The informed consent document is not given to or described to the children. Has the helper acted ethically? Professionally? Should children be involved in reading and/or signing informed consent statements?

3. In the course of a conversation with a client, you discover that she has been smoking marijuana, which is illegal in your state. An agency rule is that any client suspected of using illegal drugs must be immediately referred to rehabilitation, and if he or she refuses, you can no longer see the client at your agency. You explain this to her, she gets angry, walks out, and says she's going to sue you because you did not previously explain this to her. Does she have a point?

Competence and Scope of Knowledge

Helper competence is consistently acknowledged as a crucial ethical concern by most professional associations (Corey, et al., 2015). Knowing one's limits of professional knowledge and level of competence is essential for the human service professional and highlighted in its code of ethics (Milliken & Neukrug, 2009):

> Human service workers know the limit and scope of their professional knowledge and offer services only within their knowledge, skill base, and scope of practice. (NOHS, 2015, Statement 27)

In addition to knowing one's limits and level of competence, helpers must continually seek out new professional opportunities to enhance their work:

> Human service professionals continually seek out new and effective approaches to enhance their professional abilities and use techniques that are conceptually or evidence based. When practicing techniques that are experimental or new, they inform clients of the status of such techniques as well as the possible risks. (NOHS, 2015, Standard 31)

Ethical Vignettes Related to Competence and Scope of Practice

1. A human service professional attends a number of workshops in Gestalt therapy, an advanced therapeutic approach. He feels assured about his skills and decides to run a Gestalt therapy group. The state in which he works licenses counselors, psychologists, and social workers as therapists, but not human service professionals. Is it ethical and legal for him to run such a group?

2. A human service professional with a bachelor's level degree has just been accepted to a master's degree program in human series. She tells her colleagues that she is a "master's degree candidate." Is this person misrepresenting herself? Might clients be confused by the term "master's degree candidate?" Is this ethical? Professional? Legal?

3. You are working with a client who begins to share bizarre thoughts concerning the end of the world. You decide that this individual needs special attention, so you spend extra time with him. Is this appropriate? Ethical? Professional? Legal?

4. A client tells a human service professional that she is taking Prozac, an antidepressant, and it isn't having any effect. She asks advice on increasing the dosage, and the human service professional states, "If the current dosage isn't working, consider taking a higher dosage." Is this response appropriate? Ethical? Professional? Legal? How do you think the human service professional should respond?

5. A human service professional who has received specialized training in directing parenting workshops on communication skills decides to run a workshop at the local Hampton Inn. She pays the Hampton Inn for workshop space and runs an ad in a local newspaper that reads, "Learn How to Talk to Your Kid-Rid Your Family of All Communication Problems." Should she do the workshop? Is this ad ethical? Professional? Legal?

Supervision

One method of seeking new and effective approaches to the helping relationship is through supervision. Supervision allows the helper to examine his or her view of human nature, theoretical approach, ability at implementing techniques, and effectiveness with clients. Supervision should start during a helper's training program and continue as long as a person is working with clients. There is nothing better than a good supervisory relationship that is based on trust, mutual respect, and understanding to assist helpers in taking a good look at what they are doing at their work (Borders & Brown, 2005; Corey et al., 2015).

The supervisor has a number of roles and responsibilities that include assuring the welfare of the client; making sure that ethical, legal, and professional standards are being upheld; overseeing the clinical and professional development of the supervisee; and evaluating the supervisee (American Counseling Association [ACA], 2014, Section F). It is the responsibility of the human service professional to seek out supervision when questions and concerns about the helping relationship arise:

> Human service professionals seek appropriate consultation and supervision to assist in decision-making when there are legal, ethical or other dilemmas. (NOHS, 2015, Statement 28)

Like the effective helper, the "good" supervisor is empathic, flexible, genuine, and open (Borders & Brown, 2005; Corey et al., 2015). In addition, the good supervisor is comfortable evaluating the supervisee and being an authority figure, understands the helping relationship, has good client conceptualization skills, and is a good problem solver.

Unfortunately, all too often I have seen professionals avoid supervision because of fears about their own adequacy. These fears can create an atmosphere of isolation for the human service professional, an isolation that leads to rigidity and an inability to examine varying methods of working with clients. Professionals must face their vulnerable spots in an effort to examine what they do well and what they don't do well.

Ethical Vignettes Related to Supervision

1. A human service professional decides to pay lip service to her supervisor because she does not like him. She tells her co-workers that her supervisor is "stupid" and does not know what he's talking about. What, if anything, is unethical about this behavior? What should the human service professional do? What should her colleagues do?

2. Your supervisor tells you that he is going to have to report your client to social services for possible child abuse. You believe that he would be breaking the confidentiality of your relationship with your client. Is what he's doing ethical? Professional? Legal?

3. After meeting with a supervisee, the supervisor believes the supervisee's client is in danger of harming herself. The supervisee believes the client is not a risk and decides not to take action despite requests by the supervisor. The supervisor decides to contact the client herself and arranges to have her committed to a psychiatric unit. Has the supervisee acted ethically? Professionally? Has the supervisor acted ethically? Professionally?

4. In offering a professional disclosure statement to clients, a helper fails to tell the clients that she is being supervised. Is this ethical? Professional?

5. A supervisor believes that a helper is doing harm to a client and insists the helper change his approach. The helper argues that he believes he is helping the client. The supervisor tells the helper either to change his approach or be fired. Has the supervisee acted ethically? Professionally? Has the supervisor acted ethically? Professionally?

6. A supervisee believes that her supervisor is incompetent and giving her poor supervision. She decides to report him to his superior. Has she acted ethically? Professionally? Is there anything else she could have done?

Confidentiality

Keeping client information confidential is one of the most important ingredients in building a trusting relationship (Milliken & Neukrug, 2009; Neukrug & Milliken, 2011). However, is confidentiality always guaranteed or warranted? For instance, suppose you encounter the following situation:

A 17-year-old client tells you that she is pregnant. Do you need to tell her parents? What if the client was 15 or 12? What if she was drinking or using cocaine while pregnant? What if she tells you she wants an abortion? What if she tells you she is suicidal because of the pregnancy?

Although most of us would agree that confidentiality is a key part of the helping relationship, it may not always be the best course. All ethical decisions are to some degree a judgment call, but some general guidelines can be followed when you are making a decision to break confidentiality (always check local laws, however, to see if there are variations). Generally, confidentiality can be broken for the following reasons:

- If a client is in danger of harming himself or herself or someone else (see Reflection Exercise 10.3). This is known as *duty-to-warn* or *foreseeable danger*.

- If a child is a minor, and the law states that parents have a right to information about their child (usually, they do have such a right).

- If a client asks the helper to break confidentiality (e.g., the helper's testimony is needed in court).

- If a helper is bound by the law to break confidentiality (e.g., calling child protective services for suspected child abuse).

- To reveal information about a client to the helper's supervisor in order to get help with processing the helping relationship and benefit the client.

- When a helper has a written agreement from his or her client to reveal information to specified sources (e.g., other mental health professionals that are working with the same client).

There are also times when breaking confidentiality is not permissible. Generally, it is not appropriate under the following conditions:

- If the helper is frustrated with a client and he or she talks to a friend or colleague about the case just to "let off steam" (note: even if names and identifying information is not given, this is unethical).

- When a human service professional has a request from another helping professional about information on the client, but the other helping professional has not obtained a signed request form from the client.

- When a friend asks a helper to tell him or her something interesting about a client with whom the helper is working.

- When breaking confidentiality will clearly cause harm to a client and does not fall into one of the categories listed earlier.

Reflection Exercise 10.3:
The Tarasoff Case

The case of *Tarasoff v. Board of Regents of University of California* (1976) set a precedent for the responsibility that mental health professionals have regarding maintaining confidentiality and acting to prevent a client from harming self or others. This case involved a client who was seeing a psychologist at the University of California at Berkeley health services. The client told the psychologist that he intended to kill Tatiana Tarasoff, his former girlfriend. After the psychologist consulted with his supervisor, the supervisor suggested that he call the campus police. Campus security subsequently questioned the client and released him. The client refused to see the psychologist any longer, and two months later, he killed Tatiana. The parents of Tatiana sued and won, with the California Supreme Court stating that the psychologist did not do all that he could to protect Tatiana. Although state laws vary on how to handle confidentiality, this case is generally seen as signifying to mental health professionals they have a "duty-to-warn" individuals and must break confidentiality when the public's safety is at risk. Generally, they must do all that is reasonably possible to assure that a person is not harmed. In this case, contacting Tatiana Tarasoff may have been the prudent thing to do.

If you were faced with a situation in which you thought a client was in danger of harming self or someone else, what do you believe is your responsibility? Is it enough to consult with your supervisor? What if you disagree with your supervisor's decision?

Not surprisingly, the Ethical Standards of Human Service Professionals offers guidelines in how to respond to situations when there is potential harm to self or others:

> Human service professionals protect the client's right to privacy and confidentiality except when such confidentiality would cause serious harm to the client or others, when agency guidelines state otherwise, or under other stated conditions (e.g., local, state, or federal laws). Human service professionals inform clients of the limits of confidentiality prior to the onset of the helping relationship. (NOHS, 2015, Standard 3)

and

> If it is suspected that danger or harm may occur to the client or to others as a result of a client's behavior, the human service professional acts in an appropriate and professional manner to protect the safety of those individuals. This may involve, but is not limited to, seeking consultation, supervision, and/or breaking the confidentiality of the relationship. (NOHS, 2015, Standard 4)

Ethical Vignettes Related to Confidentiality

1. After working at an agency for a few months, you realize that employees are committing many breaches of confidentiality. What, if anything, should you do?

2. After working at an agency for a few months, you realize that many of your co-workers tend to make fun of their clients during break. What, if anything should you do?

3. In your conversation with a client at the homeless shelter, you discover that he is drinking and taking Percocet in amounts that you believe could kill him. You mention this to him, but he tells you to mind your own business. What do you do?

4. While working with a client, she expresses her concern about her grandmother who, she states, lives by herself, is depressed, has stopped eating, and has lost a considerable amount of weight. You contact the grandmother, but she refuses services. What do you do?

5. While you are talking with a 15-year-old male client, he informs you that on a recent vacation he was sexually molested by an uncle. He asks you not to tell his parents. What do you do?

6. A 15-year-old client tells you he is having sexual relations with his 14- year-old stepsister. What do you do?

7. A client of yours tells you that from time to time, usually when she's drinking, she gets severely depressed and thinks about killing herself. You ask her if she has a plan, and she says, "Well, sometimes I think about just doing it with that gun my husband has." One day, she calls you; she's been drinking, and she tells you she's depressed. She hangs up saying, "I don't know what I might do." What do you do?

8. While you are helping a client find preparation classes for the GED exam, she reveals that sometimes, when she's drinking, she takes the belt out and "whacks my kids good 'cause they just won't shut up." Do you break confidentiality and tell child protective services?

9. A client who is receiving services in your agency demands to see her case notes. In them, you have noted that you suspect she may be lying about her Social Security eligibility and that you also suspect she might be paranoid. What do you do?

10. A client you have been seeing at a crisis center comes in and asks to see records pertaining to him. These include crisis logs that have information in them about other clients, as well as case notes you have made concerning his situation. How do you respond?

Privileged Communication

Whereas confidentiality is generally described in one's ethical standards and speaks to the importance of keeping client information in confidence, privileged communication is decreed by state legislatures and refers to information that can legally be held in confidence (remember: ethical guidelines are not legal documents!) (Remley & Herlihy, 2014). The client decides what is privileged. For the most part, human service professionals are *not* legislated as professionals who hold privileged communication. Generally, licensed therapists, priests and ministers, lawyers, and doctors are afforded the right of privilege communication.

The 1996 court ruling, *Jaffee v. Redmond*, upheld the right to privileged communication for licensed social workers (Remley, Herlihy, & Herlihy, 1997). In this case, a police officer, Mary Lu Redmond, shot and killed a man she believed was about to stab another man. The family of the man she killed sued Redmond, the police department, and the village, alleging that officer Redmond had used excessive force. When the plaintiff's lawyers learned that Redmond had received counseling from a licensed social worker, they sought to compel the social worker to turn over her records and testify at the trial. Redmond and the social worker claimed their communications were privileged, and both refused to reveal the substance of their counseling. The judge then instructed jurors to assume that the information withheld would have been unfavorable to Redmond, and the jury awarded the plaintiffs $545,000. After a series of appeals, the U.S. Supreme Court decided that the licensed therapist did indeed hold privileged communication and that the judge's instruction to the jury was unwarranted. Since the decision described the social worker as a "therapist" and "psychotherapist," the ruling likely protects all licensed therapists in federal courts.

Although it's heartening that this case upheld the right to confidentiality of a licensed professional, it almost assuredly does not apply to the vast majority of human service professionals. Thus, despite the fact that the ethics code for human service professionals states we should protect the confidentiality of our clients, courts probably have the right to order the human service professional to break confidentiality. This is because human service professionals are not licensed therapists and are thus, not legally protected by privileged communication. However, just knowing that our ethics codes protect confidentiality might dissuade some courts from asking for confidential information.

Ethical Vignettes Related to Privileged Communication

1. You are working with a woman who is divorcing her husband. Suddenly, you receive a subpoena to go to court to discuss information about your client for a child custody battle the couple is having. You decide to go to court but do not reveal any information, stating, "This is confidential information; I refuse to reveal anything." Are you acting ethically? Legally?

2. A licensed social worker tells you that she was recently asked to reveal information about her client who was being sued for injuring a person while driving intoxicated. The social worker refused to reveal any information and was cited by the judge for contempt of court. The social worker is appealing the case, stating she has privileged communication and does not have to reveal such information. Does she have a point? What if this was a human service professional?

3. A client's husband shows up at your office, demanding information about his wife. You refuse to let him know if his wife has been in a helping relationship with you and note that, in either case, all information at your office is confidential and privileged. He tells you that he'll sue you and the rest of

this "flea bag" operation and that you do not hold privileged communication. Is what you stated accurate? Does he have a point?

4. Referring to item 3 above: Even though you do not hold privileged communication, must you share information about your client with the husband? If the husband came to you with a letter from his lawyer asking for such information, how would you respond?

Dual and Multiple Relationships

Dual, sometimes called multiple relationships, are those professional helping relationships in which there exist multiple roles between the helper and the client (Dewane, 2010). For instance, is it alright to have a client as an acquaintance, friend, colleague, or relative? Most professional groups have taken clear stands that these kinds of dual or multiple relationships should be avoided when possible. For instance, the Ethical Standards of Human Service Professionals strongly discourages dual relationships and multiple relationships:

> Human service professionals recognize that multiple relationships may increase the risk of harm to or exploitation of clients and may impair their professional judgment. When it is not feasible to avoid dual or multiple relationships, human service professionals should consider whether the professional relationship should be avoided or curtailed. (NOHS, 2015, Standard 5)

Human service professionals recognize that in their relationships with clients, power and status are unequal. Given this disparity, dual or multiple relationships may increase the risk of harm to, or exploitation of, clients and may impair the professional's judgment. With this potential for harm, the human service professional must decide if it is prudent to see a person in a professional relationship who may also be an acquaintance, friend, or colleague (Milliken & Neukrug, 2009). Some factors to consider when deciding whether to have a dual or multiple relationship include the following:

1. *The nature of the helping relationship.* The more akin the relationship is to counseling or therapy (as opposed to coaching, support, or information giving) the more the helper should avoid dual or multiple relationships.

2. *The length of the relationship.* When the helper and the client have a very short, time-limited relationship, the risk tends to be lower (although it still may exist).

3. *The nature of the existing relationship with the potential client.* The more intimately you know the potential client, the greater the possibility there is for problems related to power, control, and embarrassment.

4. *The possibility of finding another helper.* If another helper is available to see the potential client, there is no logical argument for the helper to have a dual or multiple relationship with that client.

If one reviews the risks above and still decides it makes sense to see the potential client, then the helper can likely see the client in a helping relationship. However, given the potential risks involved, when such a relationship does take place, the helper should take a periodic inventory of the relationship to ensure issues of power and control are not hindering the relationship and should periodically check in with the client to make sure he or she feels comfortable with the relationship.

Ethical Vignettes Related to Dual Relationships

1. While driving to work one day, your car breaks down. A client of yours sees you and says, "I'm good with mechanical things; let me help for a small fee. Besides, I could use a little money for buying

188

my motorcycle." You want to get your car fixed, and you want your client to have his bike. Do you let him help you?

2. For months you have been encouraging a client to get involved in more social activities. One day, your client shows up at your art class saying that she signed up for the same class. What do you do?

3. You work for social services and are assigned to see Mr. Jones who is requesting Temporary Assistance for Needy Families (TANF) (welfare). As soon as Mr. Jones walks into your office, you realize that he is your neighbor from down the street. You don't know him that well and decide to meet with him. Is this ethical? Why or why not?

4. Using the vignette in number 3: In this case, when Mr. Jones walks into your office, you realize he is your next-door neighbor, with whom you are fairly friendly. What do you do?

5. One of the secretaries in your office asks to see you "informally" to discuss a problem she is having with her child. After meeting with her for a few minutes, you realize that your "informal" meeting is becoming pretty "heavy" and "therapeutic." What do you do? Is this a dual relationship?

Sexual Relationships with Clients

A particular kind of dual relationship, sexual relationships with clients, has consistently been one of the most egregious complaints made against mental health professionals (Neukrug, Milliken, & Walden, 2001). Because a sexual relationship with a client is among the most damaging of all ethical violations (Kaplan et al., 2009), virtually all helping professions have issued prohibitions against them. Thus, according to NOHS (2015):

> Sexual or romantic relationships with current clients are prohibited. Before engaging in sexual or romantic relationships with former clients, friends, or family members of former clients, human service professionals carefully evaluate potential exploitation or harm and refrain from entering into such a relationship. (Standards 6)

Human service professionals must understand the inherent problems with having sexual relationships with clients, former clients, and individuals close to clients (Corey et al., 2015). These include power and control issues, self-esteem issues, dependency concerns, damage to a client's sense of self, and much more. In some situations, having sex with a client may have legal ramifications and could lead to a misdemeanor or felony violation and/or a civil law suit. Human service professionals should realize the legal implications this violation carries and the ways in which helpers can manage their sexual feelings toward clients without acting on them.

Ethical Vignettes Related to Sexual Relationships with Clients

1. You are becoming increasingly attracted to one of your clients, and even though you have no intention of acting on your feelings, you realize that you cannot concentrate as fully as you would like. Is this a dual relationship? What should you do?

2. Because you are becoming increasingly attracted to one of your clients, you decide to be honest with him and share your feelings. Is this appropriate? Why or why not?

3. You suspect that a colleague of yours is having a sexual relationship with one of his clients. What should you do?

4. You are working at a crisis center that has a number of volunteer workers. You become attracted to a volunteer who used to be one of your clients but is no longer seeing you professionally. You decide

to pursue a relationship with the former client. Is this appropriate? Is this ethical? Are there any safeguards you should adhere to?

Primary Obligation: Client, Agency, or Society?

Although our ethical code generally asserts our client's right to confidentiality, right to be respected, and right for self-determination (NOHS, 2015, Preamble, Standard 3), human service professionals also recognize, and sometimes favor, the right of other individuals and of society to be protected from harm. Take, for instance, the following scenario:

> In building your relationship with a 17-year-old client, you discover that she is taking the drug ecstasy, possibly selling drugs to friends, and involved in gang violence including looting and possible physical harm to others. Your agency has a policy to report any illegal acts to the "proper authorities."

Does the client have the right to sell drugs, be involved in gang violence, and loot? What is your responsibility to this client? What are the limits of confidentiality with her? If you are primarily responsible to your client, what are the implications of you being required to report her to the proper authorities? If you do not report her, what implications might this have on your employment? What responsibility do you have to protect society from the illegal activities in which she is involved? What liability concerns do you have if you do not report the illegal acts in which she is participating? Are there ethical and legal ramifications if you do report her?

After examining the above scenario, you probably would agree that there may be times when a client's right to self-determination and respect is superseded by a helper's ethical obligation to protect others and to protect society. Along these lines, the Ethical Standards of Human Service Professionals suggests that the human service professional should seek out consultation and/or supervision and even break confidentiality if anyone is at risk of being harmed.

> If it is suspected that danger or harm may occur to the client or to others as a result of a client's behavior, the human service professional acts in an appropriate and professional manner to protect the safety of those individuals. This may involve, but is not limited to, seeking consultation, supervision, and/or breaking the confidentiality of the relationship. (NOHS, 2015, Standard 4)

The same standards also require that the human service professional follow agency guidelines, whenever reasonable, as well as local, state, and federal law.

> Human service professionals protect the client's right to privacy and confidentiality except when such confidentiality would cause serious harm to the client or others, when agency guidelines state otherwise, or under other stated conditions (e.g., local, state, or federal laws). Human service professionals inform clients of the limits of confidentiality prior to the onset of the helping relationship. (NOHS, 2015, Standard 3)

As you can see, sometimes our ethical obligation of confidentiality may be superseded by other concerns. Thus, deciding what information should be kept confidential is not always clear cut and may involve some thoughtfulness on the part of the human service professional, as well as consultation with supervisors. Look at the following vignettes and see how you would make sense of these concerns.

Ethical Vignettes Related to Obligation to Client, Agency, or Society

1. Your agency has implemented a new policy that all clients who are using illegal drugs will be reported to the police. You vigorously oppose such a policy and decide to ignore it. Are you acting ethically? Professionally? Legally?

2. An adult client informs you that he wants to kill his ex-girlfriend and her new boyfriend. He denies that he actually will act on these feelings but that he just "thinks about it a lot." What do you do?

3. You're working for social services, and in the course of a conversation with a client you discover that she has been using heroin. An agency rule states that any client suspected of using illegal drugs must be immediately referred to rehabilitation, and if he or she refuses, you can no longer see the client at your agency. You explain this to her, she gets angry, walks out, and states she'll "blow this place up." What do you do?

4. The director of the agency in which you work tells all employees to report any client who is using illegal substances to the police. Can the director do this? Is this ethical? Professional? What, if anything, should you do?

5. A client of yours, who has stopped taking his medication, stops by your office and seems pretty angry. He says, "That cheating Harley-Davidson dealer, he's trying to rip me off. He told me I could have that bike at discount and went back on his word." You try to talk with your client, but he storms out of your office saying, "I'm going to get that man!" What do you do?

6. A married client of yours tells you she is pregnant by her neighbor. She's going to have an abortion. Your state has a law requiring women to tell their spouses if they're to have an abortion. She refuses. What do you do?

Continuing Education

Education never ends. Although you obtain a degree and work hard for it, to be effective throughout your career as a human service professional, you must never stop learning. Today, credentialing boards are increasingly requiring continuing education for professionals to maintain their credentials. This requirement ensures that the professional is continuing to learn and that he or she can offer the best services possible to his or her clients. Continuing education is both our professional and ethical obligation and is highlighted in our ethical code:

> Human service professionals promote the continuing development of their profession. They encourage membership in professional associations, support research endeavors, foster educational advancement, advocate for appropriate legislative actions, and participate in other related professional activities. (NOHS, 2015, Standard 30)

and

> Human service professionals continually seek out new and effective approaches to enhance their professional abilities and use techniques that are conceptually or evidence based. When practicing techniques that are experimental or new, they inform clients of the status of such techniques as well as the possible risks. (NOHS, 2015, Standard 31)

Continuing education occurs by joining professional associations and participating in workshops they sponsor, participating in staff development workshops where you work, and taking additional coursework, perhaps to earn an advanced degree. It occurs by reading your journals, by being involved in your local and national associations, and by being "present" to new ways of working with clients. It is a never-ending process that continues throughout your professional life.

Ethical Vignettes Related to Continuing Education

1. After obtaining your first job, you discover that many of your human service colleagues have forgotten the theories they once learned in school and do not feel obligated to engage in continuing education. What is your ethical responsibility in this situation to yourself and to your colleagues?

2. A new colleague of yours who is fresh out of school, seems to have rigid views about his clients and refuses to participate in continuing education activities. He says, "I'm just out of school, I know all that's new. Besides, I'm tired of learning." Is he acting ethically? Professionally? Legally? What, if anything, should you do?

3. A colleague tells you that she has learned some new, "experimental" ways of working with clients. These new methods have not been fully researched and you question their efficacy. What, if any, ethical responsibility do you have toward this colleague and toward his clients?

4. A colleague of yours works mostly with female clients who have been abused. She encourages all her clients to leave their husbands and claims that this is the "right thing to do" from a feminist perspective. Does she have a point? Is what she's doing ethical? Professional? Legal?

5. A human service professional, who has worked in the field for twenty years, is your colleague. He does not belong to his professional associations. He never attends any continuing education workshops. He is not abreast of new information in the field. Is this ethical? Is this professional? Is there anything you can do?

6. A human service professional you know has attended a number of workshops on substance abuse, obtained "certificates of attendance," and now advertises that he is certified in substance abuse counseling. Is this ethical? Professional? Legal? What, if anything, should you do?

Multicultural Counseling

The identity of mental health professionals has long been based on a Western/European model that tends to embrace the values and beliefs of White clients while negating the values and beliefs of some minority clients (Sue & Sue, 2013). If the human service professional is to be effective with all clients, helpers must graduate from training programs with more than just a desire to help all people. As a profession, we will have achieved competence in working with diverse clients only when each graduate of a training program has learned helping strategies that can work for a wide range of clients, has worked with clients from diverse backgrounds, and has an appreciation for diversity and an identity as a helper that includes a multicultural perspective (McAuliffe, 2013b).

As highlighted in Chapter 9, working with diverse clients means having the attitudes and beliefs, knowledge, and skills in a number of domains if one is to be effective. It also means empowering clients to advocate for themselves, being advocates for our clients, as well as being advocates for broad social justice issues that impact our clients' lives. Our ethics code reinforces this notion in no less than six standards that specifically address multicultural issues, as well as other standards that also raise related concerns (NOHS, 2015, Standards 11 through 16):

STANDARD 11 Human service professionals are knowledgeable about their cultures and communities within which they practice. They are aware of multiculturalism in society and its impact on the community as well as individuals within the community. They respect the cultures and beliefs of individuals and groups.

STANDARD 12 Human service professionals are aware of local, state, and federal laws. They advocate for change in regulations and statutes when such legislation conflicts with ethical guidelines and/or client rights. Where laws are harmful to individuals, groups, or communities, human service professionals consider the conflict between the values of obeying the law and the values of serving people and may decide to initiate social action.

STANDARD 13 Human service professionals stay informed about current social issues as they affect clients and communities. If appropriate to the helping relationship, they share this information with clients, groups and communities as part of their work.

STANDARD 14 Human service professionals are aware of social and political issues that differentially affect clients from diverse backgrounds.

STANDARD 15 Human service professionals provide a mechanism for identifying client needs and assets, calling attention to these needs and assets, and assisting in planning and mobilizing to advocate for those needs at the individual, community, and societal level when appropriate to the goals of the relationship.

STANDARD 16 Human service professionals advocate for social justice and seek to eliminate oppression. They raise awareness of underserved populations in their communities and with the legislative system.

Ethical Vignettes Related to Multicultural Counseling

1. Because of cross-cultural differences, you believe that your work with a Pakistani client has not been successful. Rather than referring the client, you decide to read more about your client's culture to gain a better understanding of him. Is this ethical? Is this professional?

2. You discover some fellow human services students are making sexist jokes. What should you do? Have you encountered such behavior before? Do you have any ethical, professional, and or moral responsibility in this situation?

3. You find some members of your family making ethnic/cultural slurs. What should you do? Have you encountered such behavior before? Do you have any ethical, professional, and or moral responsibility in this situation?

4. A colleague of yours refuses to admit that some external forces, such as racism, prejudice and bias, can impact some minority clients' ability to obtain a job. What is your responsibility to this helper's clients and to the helper?

5. You discover that a colleague of yours is telling a gay client that he is acting immorally due to his sexual orientation. What should you do? Is this ethical? Professional? Legal?

6. A friend of yours advertises that she is a Christian counselor. You discover that when clients come to see her, she encourages them to read parts of the Bible during sessions and tells clients they need to ask for repentance for their sins. Is this ethical? Is this professional? Is this legal?

7. When working with a Korean client who is not expressive of her feelings, a colleague pressures the client to express feelings. The helper tells the client, "You can only get better if you express yourself." Is this helper acting ethically? Professionally? Do you have any responsibility in this case?

8. When offering a parenting workshop to individuals who are poor, you are challenged by some of the parents when you tell them that "hitting a child is never okay." They tell you that you are crazy, and that sometimes a good spanking is the only thing that will get the child's attention. Do they have a point? How should you respond?

Values in the Helping Relationship

Human service professionals ensure that their values or biases are not imposed upon their clients. (NOHS, 2015, Standard 7)

Human service professionals are asked to not impose their values on their clients, and the implications of such an ethical guideline are far reaching. Although almost all mental health professionals consider pushing one's basic values onto a client is unethical (e.g., religious beliefs, political ideas, etc.) (Neukrug & Milliken, 2011; Milliken & Neukrug, 2009), in recent years, some professional associations have decided that their professionals should always be able to work with clients regardless of values clashes; that is, differences in values is not a reason to refer a client to someone else. In fact, a situation highlighting this opinion occurred at Eastern Michigan University's (EMU) counseling program (Kaplan, 2014; Rudow, 2013).

At EMU, Julea Ward, a graduate student in counseling, discovered she would be counseling a client who had been in a same-sex relationship. Believing she could not counsel him due to her religious beliefs regarding same-sex relationships, she asked her supervisor to refer him to another counselor. After considering this request, the supervisor decided that Ms. Ward should still be able to counsel this man and scheduled an informal review of Ms. Ward. The result of this review was a statement by the program that Ms. Ward needed to learn how to set aside her religious beliefs and be open to counseling a man in a same-sex relationship. She was thus asked to complete a remediation program or have a formal hearing with the faculty. She asked for a formal hearing and was eventually dismissed from the program. She ended up suing EMU, and the courts initially upheld the school's decision. However, after appeal, the suit was settled out of court. This lawsuit, and others, had the result of changing the ACA ethics code so that it now more strongly states that helpers should not refer clients do to value differences. Instead, it states that referrals should occur if one is not competent to handle the client's issues. What are your thoughts about referring clients as a result of value differences? Consider the following vignettes and see if you could work with each of the following clients.

Ethical Vignettes Based on Values

1. Your client is from Tanzania where partial clitoridectomy, the partial removal of the clitoris, is sometimes practiced. Your client has an eleven-year-old daughter and tells you that it's time for the child to have her partial clitoridectomy. She sees this as an important coming of age ceremony for her child, and family and friends will be at the ceremony. What do you do?

2. You are working with a couple whose 12-year-old child was born a biological boy but now identifies as a girl. The parents want their child to "be a son." They therefore insist that she not wear clothes

identified as "female" and that she partake in what are considered to traditionally be male activities (e.g., being involved in sports and dating girls). What do you do?

3. You are working with a client who states he is a member of a Satanic cult. Their practices, although not physically harmful, involve symbolic killing of others, encouragement of hedonistic activities, and activities that suggest they are against a number of traditional cultural practices (traditional marriage, ways of parenting, immunizations, etc.). What do you do?

4. A client who sees you periodically tells you that he supports some of the major terrorist groups around the world. He lists them for you and says, "If I could join them, I would—but I know that I really don't want to hurt anybody, so I won't." What is your reaction to this person? Would you be able to work with him?

SURVEYING ETHICAL BEHAVIORS OF HUMAN SERVICE PROFESSIONALS

A survey of human service professionals (Milliken & Neukrug, 2009) examined 88 ethical situations and asked human service professionals if they thought they were ethical. The results are listed in Appendix G. Take a look at the items and consider whether you think each is ethical. Make a list of the top 10 items which intrigue you and see if you can find standards that address the issues in the Ethical Standards of Human Service Professionals. In class, discuss any items which are most interesting to a large number of students.

SUMMARY

This chapter reviewed important ethical issues related to the helping relationship. We began by listing a number of purposes that ethics codes serve, such as protecting consumers, furthering professionalism, denoting a body of knowledge, asserting a professional identity, reflecting a profession's underlying values and suggested behavior, offering a framework for ethical decision-making, and providing a measure of defense in case one is sued. Some limitations of ethical guidelines that we then identified included: some issues cannot be handled within a code, there are some difficulties in enforcing codes, the public is often not included in the code construction process, issues addressed by codes are sometimes handled in other ways (e.g., by the law), there are possible conflicts within a code and/or between different related codes, and codes sometimes conflict with the values of the professional.

We next examined four ethical decision-making models. We identified eight steps of problem-solving models, reviewed six moral principles of Kitchener's moral model (i.e., autonomy, beneficence, nonmaleficence, justice, fidelity, and veracity) and spoke of the importance of character or virtue moral models, reviewed the difference between lower level and higher level cognitive development models, and discussed the social constructionist model, which examines the importance of dialoguing with everyone involved in the ethical decision-making process.

Most of the rest of the chapter focused on some of the more important ethical issues that human service professionals face related to: informed consent; competence and scope of knowledge; supervision; confidentiality; privileged communication; dual and multiple relationships; sexual relationships with clients; whether the primary obligation of the human service professional is to the client, the agency, or to society; continuing education; multicultural counseling; and values in the helping relationship. Ethical vignettes associated with each of these areas helped you apply knowledge that was learned. The chapter concluded with an examination of 88 behaviors of human service professionals and you were asked to make a list of the top 10 behaviors that intrigued you and review the Ethical Code of Human Service Professionals to see if there was a standard that spoke to these 10 behaviors.

KEY WORDS AND TERMS

Autonomy

Beneficence

Competence and scope of knowledge

Confidentiality

Continuing education

Developmental models of ethical decision-making

Dual and multiple relationships

Duty-to-warn

Ethical decision-making models

Foreseeable danger

Fidelity

Informed consent

Jaffee v. Redmond

Julea Ward

Justice

Limitations of ethical codes

Moral models of ethical decision-making

Multicultural counseling

Nonmaleficence

Primary obligation: client, agency, or society?

Privileged communication

Problem-solving models of ethical decision-making

Professional disclosure statement

Purpose of ethical codes

Sexual relationships with clients

Social constructionist models of ethical decision-making

Supervision

Tarasoff case

Values in the helping relationship

Veracity

APPENDIX A

Competency Areas for Skill Standards

Competency Areas for Skill Standards

Competency 1: Participant Empowerment
The competent community support human service practitioner (CSHSP) enhances the ability of the participant to lead a self-determining life by providing the support and information necessary to build self-esteem and assertiveness and to make decisions. (p. 21)

Competency 2: Communication
The community support human service practitioner should be knowledgeable about the range of effective communication strategies and skills necessary to establish a collaborative relationship with the participant. (p. 26)

Competency 3: Assessment
The community support human service practitioner should be knowledgeable about formal and informal assessment practices to respond to the needs, desires and interests of the participants. (p. 29)

Competency 4: Community and Service Networking
The community support human service practitioner should be knowledgeable about the formal and informal supports available in his or her community and skilled in assisting the participant to identify and gain access to such supports. (p. 35)

Competency 5: Facilitation of Services
The community support human service practitioner is knowledgeable about a range of participatory planning techniques and is skilled in implementing plans in a collaborative and expeditious manner. (p. 40)

Competency 6: Community and Living Skills and Supports
The community support human service practitioner has the ability to match specific supports and interventions to the unique needs of individual participants and recognizes the importance of friends, family, and community relationships. (p. 45)

Competency 7: Education Training and Self-Development
The community support human service practitioner should be able to identify areas for self- improvement, pursue necessary educational/training resources, and share knowledge with others. (p. 51)

Competency 8: Advocacy
The community support human service practitioner should be knowledgeable about the diverse challenges facing participants (e.g. human rights, legal, administrative, and financial) and should be able to identify and use effective advocacy strategies to overcome such challenges. (p. 54)

Competency 9: Vocational, Educational, and Career Support

The community support human service practitioner should be knowledgeable about the career and education related concerns of the participant and should be able to mobilize the resources and support necessary to assist the participant to reach his or her goals. (p. 57)

Competency 10: Crisis Intervention

The community support human service practitioner should be knowledgeable about crisis prevention, intervention, and resolution techniques and should match such techniques to particular circumstances and individuals. (p. 60)

Competency 11: Organizational Participation

The community-based support worker is familiar with the mission and practices of the support organization and participates in the life of the organization. (p. 63)

Competency 12: Documentation

The community-based support worker is aware of the requirements for documentation in his or her organization and is able to manage these requirements efficiently. (p. 67)

APPENDIX B

Feeling Word Checklist

Abandoned	Disrespected	Hurt	Panicked	Stupid
Adored	Distressed	Impatient	Paranoid	Teased
Aggravated	Doubtful	Impossible	Passionate	Tender
Aggressive	Drained	Inadequate	Peaceful	Terrific
Angry	Dynamic	Incapable	Pitiful	Terrified
Anxious	Eager	Indecisive	Playful	Thoughtful
Appreciated	Elated	Insecure	Pleased	Thoughtless
Apprehensive	Embarrassed	Inspired	Pleasant	Thrilled
Argumentative	Empowered	Interested	Positive	Tormented
Ashamed	Empty	Intolerant	Powerless	Tranquil
Assertive	Energized	Invigorated	Precious	Traumatized
Assured	Enlightened	Invincible	Pressured	Troubled
Awe	Enthusiastic	Irresistible	Proud	Trusting
Awesome	Envious	Irresponsible	Provoked	Unaccepted
Awful	Exasperated	Irritated	Punished	Unconcerned
Betrayed	Excited	Jealous	Quiet	Undesirable
Bitter	Exhilarated	Joyful	Ready	Understood
Bliss	Extraordinary	Joyous	Receptive	Uneasy
Bold	Exuberant	Jubilant	Recognized	Unfriendly
Bored	Failure	Kind	Rejected	Unfulfilled
Brilliant	Fantastic	Let down	Relaxed	Unhappy
Broken-hearted	Fearful	Limitless	Renewed	Unhelpful
Burdened	Fearless	Lonely	Repulsive	Unloved
Calm	Focused	Lost	Resentful	Unsuccessful
Capable	Forced	Lovable	Resilient	Unwanted
Caring	Free	Loving	Respected	Unworthy
Cheerful	Frigid	Lucky	Restless	Uplifted
Comfortable	Frustrated	Lying	Sad	Upset
Concerned	Fulfilled	Magical	Satisfied	Useless
Confident	Fun	Mean	Scared	Valued
Confused	Glad	Mindful	Selfish	Valuable
Content	Glowing	Miraculous	Serene	Victimized
Criticized	Gracious	Miserable	Shameful	Vindictive
Decisive	Grateful	Misunderstood	Shocked	Warm
Dejected	Grieving	Motivated	Shy	Wary
Depressed	Guilty	Neglected	Skeptical	Weary
Difficult	Happy	Nervous	Sorrowful	Whole
Dirty	Helpless	Obligated	Sour	Wise
Disappointed	Hopeful	Open	Spectacular	Worried
Discontented	Hopeless	Oppressed	Stifled	Worthless
Discouraged	Honored	Overwhelmed	Strong	Worthy
Disgusted	Humiliated	Pained	Stubborn	Wrong

APPENDIX C

Overview of DSM-5 Diagnostic Categories

The following offers a brief description of the DSM diagnostic categories and is summarized from DSM-5 (APA, 2013a). Please refer to the DSM-5 for an in-depth review of each disorder:

Neurodevelopmental Disorders. This group of disorders typically refers to those that manifest during early development, although diagnoses are sometimes not assigned until adulthood. Examples of neurodevelopmental disorders include intellectual disabilities, communication disorders, autism spectrum disorders (incorporating the former categories of autistic disorder, Asperger's disorder, childhood disintegrative disorder, and pervasive developmental disorder), ADHD, specific learning disorders, motor disorders, and other neurodevelopmental disorders.

Schizophrenia Spectrum and Other Psychotic Disorders. The disorders that belong to this section all have one feature in common: psychotic symptoms; that is, delusions, hallucinations, grossly disorganized or abnormal motor behavior, and/or negative symptoms. The disorders include schizotypal personality disorder (which is listed again, and explained more comprehensively, in the category of Personality Disorders in the DSM-5), delusional disorder, brief psychotic disorder, schizophreniform disorder, schizophrenia, schizoaffective disorder, substance/medication-induced psychotic disorder, psychotic disorder due to another medical condition, and catatonic disorder.

Bipolar and Related Disorders. The disorders in this category refer to disturbances in mood in which the client cycles through stages of mania or mania and depression. Both children and adults can be diagnosed with bipolar disorder, and the clinician can work to identify the pattern of mood presentation, such as rapid-cycling, which is more often observed in children. These disorders include bipolar I, bipolar II, cyclothymic disorder, substance/medication-induced, bipolar and related disorder due to another medical condition, and other specified or unspecified bipolar and related disorders.

Depressive Disorders. Previously grouped into the broader category of "mood disorders" in the DSM-IV-TR, these disorders describe conditions where depressed mood is the overarching concern. They include disruptive mood dysregulation disorder, major depressive disorder, persistent depressive disorder (also known as dysthymia), and premenstrual dysphoric disorder.

Anxiety Disorders. There are a wide range of anxiety disorders, which can be diagnosed by identifying a general or specific cause of unease or fear. This anxiety or fear is considered clinically significant when it is excessive and persistent over time. Examples of anxiety disorders that typically manifest earlier in development include separation anxiety and selective mutism. Other examples of anxiety disorders are specific phobia, social anxiety disorder (also known as social phobia), panic disorder, and generalized anxiety disorder.

Obsessive-Compulsive and Related Disorders. Disorders in this category all involve obsessive thoughts and compulsive behaviors that are uncontrollable, and the client feels compelled to perform them. Diagnoses in this category include obsessive-compulsive disorder, body dysmorphic disorder, hoarding disorder, trichotillomania (or hair-pulling disorder), and excoriation (or skin-picking) disorder.

Trauma- and Stressor-Related Disorders. A new category for DSM-5, trauma and stress disorders emphasize the pervasive impact that life events can have on an individual's emotional and physical well-being. Diagnoses include reactive attachment disorder, disinhibited social engagement disorder, posttraumatic stress disorder, acute stress disorder, and adjustment disorders.

Dissociative Disorders. These disorders indicate a temporary or prolonged disruption to consciousness that can cause an individual to misinterpret identity, surroundings, and memories. Diagnoses include dissociative identity disorder (formerly known as multiple personality disorder), dissociative amnesia, depersonalization/derealization disorder, and other specified and unspecified dissociative disorders.

Somatic Symptom and Related Disorders. Somatic symptom disorders were previously referred to as "somatoform disorders" and are characterized by the experiencing of a physical symptom without evidence of a physical cause, thus suggesting a psychological cause. Somatic symptom disorders include somatic symptom disorder, illness anxiety disorder (formerly hypochondriasis), conversion (or functional neurological symptom) disorder, psychological factors affecting other medical conditions, and factitious disorder.

Feeding and Eating Disorders. This group of disorders describes clients who have severe concerns about the amount or type of food they eat to the point that serious health problems, or even death, can result from their eating behaviors. Examples include avoidant/restrictive food intake disorder, anorexia nervosa, bulimia nervosa, binge eating disorder, pica, and rumination disorder.

Elimination Disorders. These disorders can manifest at any point in a person's life, although they are typically diagnosed in early childhood or adolescence. They include enuresis, which is the inappropriate elimination of urine, and encopresis, which is the inappropriate elimination of feces. These behaviors may or may not be intentional.

Sleep-Wake Disorders. This category refers to disorders where one's sleep patterns are severely impacted, and they often co-occur with other disorders (e.g., depression or anxiety). Some examples include insomnia disorder, hypersomnolence disorder, restless legs syndrome, narcolepsy, and nightmare disorder. A number of sleep-wake disorders involve variations in breathing, such as sleep-related hypoventilation, obstructive sleep apnea hypopnea, or central sleep apnea. See the DSM-5 for the full listing and descriptions of these disorders.

Sexual Dysfunctions. These disorders are related to problems that disrupt sexual functioning or one's ability to experience sexual pleasure. They occur across sexes and include delayed ejaculation, erectile disorder, female orgasmic disorder, and premature (or early) ejaculation disorder, among others.

Gender Dysphoria. Formerly termed, "gender identity disorder," this category includes those individuals who experience significant distress with the sex they were born and with associated gender roles. This diagnosis has been separated from the category of sexual disorders, as it is now accepted that gender dysphoria does not relate to a person's sexual attractions.

Disruptive, Impulse Control, and Conduct Disorders. These disorders are characterized by socially unacceptable or otherwise disruptive and harmful behaviors that are outside of the individual's control. Generally, more common in males than in females, and often first seen in childhood, they include oppositional defiant disorder, conduct disorder, intermittent explosive disorder, antisocial personality disorder (which is also coded in the category of personality disorders), kleptomania, and pyromania.

Substance-Related and Addictive Disorders. Substance use disorders include disruptions in functioning as the result of a craving or strong urge. Often caused by prescribed and illicit drugs or the exposure to toxins, with these disorders the brain's reward system pathways are activated when the substance is taken (or in the case of gambling disorder, when the behavior is being performed). Some common substances include alcohol, caffeine, nicotine, cannabis, opioids, inhalants, amphetamine, phencyclidine (PCP), sedatives, hypnotics or anxiolytics. Substance use disorders are further designated with the following terms: intoxication, withdrawal, induced, or unspecified.

Neurocognitive Disorders. These disorders are diagnosed when one's decline in cognitive functioning is significantly different from the past and is usually the result of a medical condition (e.g., Parkinson's or Alzheimer's disease), the use of a substance/medication, or traumatic brain injury, among other phenomena. Examples of neurocognitive disorders (NCD) include delirium, and several types of major and mild NCDs such as frontotemporal NCD, NCD due to Parkinson's disease, NCD due to HIV infection, NCD due to Alzheimer's disease, substance- or medication-induced NCD, and vascular NCD, among others.

Personality Disorders. The 10 personality disorders in DSM-5 all involve a pattern of experiences and behaviors that are persistent, inflexible, and deviate from one's cultural expectations. Usually, this pattern emerges in adolescence or early adulthood and causes severe distress in one's interpersonal relationships. The personality disorders are grouped into the three following clusters which are based on similar behaviors:
- Cluster A: Paranoid, schizoid, and schizotypal. These individuals seem bizarre or unusual in their behaviors and interpersonal relations.
- Cluster B: Antisocial, borderline, histrionic, and narcissistic. These individuals seem overly emotional, are melodramatic, or unpredictable in their behaviors and interpersonal relations.
- Cluster C: Avoidant, dependent, and obsessive-compulsive (not to be confused with obsessive-compulsive disorder). These individuals tend to appear anxious, worried, or fretful in their behaviors.

Paraphilic Disorders. These disorders are diagnosed when the client is sexually aroused to circumstances that deviate from traditional sexual stimuli *and* when such behaviors result in harm or significant emotional distress. The disorders include exhibitionistic disorder, voyeuristic disorder, frotteurisitc disorder, sexual sadism and sexual masochism disorders, fetishistic disorder, transvestic disorder, pedophilic disorder, and other specified and unspecified paraphilic disorders.

Other Mental Disorders. This diagnostic category includes mental disorders that did not fall within one of the previously mentioned groups and do not have unifying characteristics. Examples include other specified mental disorder due to another medical condition, unspecified mental disorder due to another medical condition, other specified mental disorder, and unspecified mental disorder.

Medication-Induced Movement Disorders and Other Adverse Effects of Medications. These disorders are the result of adverse and severe side effects to medications, although a causal link cannot always be shown. Some of these disorders include neuroleptic-induced parkinsonism, neuroleptic malignant syndrome, medication-induced dystonia, medication-induced acute akathisia, tardive dyskinesia, tardive akathisia, medication-induced postural tremor, other medication-induced movement disorder, antidepressant discontinuation syndrome, and other adverse effect of medication.

Other Conditions That May Be a Focus of Clinical Assessment. Reminiscent of Axis IV of the previous edition of the DSM, this last part of Section II ends with a description of concerns that could be clinically significant, such as abuse/neglect, relational problems, psychosocial, personal, and environmental concerns, educational/occupational problems, housing and economic problems, and problems related to the legal system. These conditions, which are not considered mental disorders, are generally listed as V codes, which correspond to ICD-9, or Z codes, which correspond to ICD-10.

In addition to the above categories, the DSM offers other *specified* and *unspecified disorders* that can be used when a provider believes an individual's impairment to functioning or distress is clinically significant; however, it does not meet the specific diagnostic criteria in that category. The "other specified" should be used when the clinician wants to communicate specifically why the criteria do not fit. The "unspecified disorder" should be used when he or she does not wish, or is unable to, communicate specifics. For example, if someone appeared to have significant panic attacks but only had three of the four required criteria, the diagnosis could be "Other Specified Panic Disorder—due to insufficient symptoms." Otherwise, the clinician would report "Unspecified Panic Disorder."

APPENDIX D

Case Report

Demographic Information

Name: Jim Needhelp
Address: Nowhere Land
Date of Birth: November 23, 1987

Phone: 555-5353
Date of Interview: June 06, 2016
Clinician: Ed Neukrug

Reason for Report

Jim is a 25-year-old single male who was referred to this agency by his mother. She reports that Jim has been "acting kind of odd" and believes that people can read his mind and that he could read other people's minds. Jim reports social isolation, fears about the world, and concern about the future. He states he hopes a helping relationship would make him a better person and that it would help "rid me of the voices-maybe."

Background Information

Jim is the youngest of three boys of Jane and Bill. His brother, William Jr., is five years older, married, and has two children. His brother, Wally, is two years older, single, and living in another state, and working in construction. Jim stated that he does not work but "does a lot of chores around the house." He reported that his mother works part-time at the local convenience store and his dad works at the power plant, doing general "cleanup." He states that his parents have high school educations and that he "almost finished high school but the teachers were mean to me." He states that he wants to get his G.E.D. so that he could obtain a good job. He states that he loves his mother and father, although notes that his father is a "little too strict" at times.

His mother states that Jim has always been a little "odd" and never really had any friends. Jim and his mother state that he was in counseling once before when he was in high school. His mother reports that it was at this time that she realized Jim first believed he was clairvoyant. Jim states that he did have "odd thoughts" at times. He states he always knew that he could sometimes predict the future and that he could read others' thoughts. When asked specifically if he could give some examples, he refused. Jim stated that he discontinued counseling after he realized his counselor was out to get him, just like everyone else. When asked how, he stated his counselor wanted to put him in the hospital. His mother states that Jim was taking a small dosage of some type of "think right" medication.

Jim states that he thinks it's "weird" that he is 25 years old and still living at home but notes that he does not think he is capable of living on his own. He spends most of his day watching T.V. and reports that he sometimes thinks his thoughts can change the ending to the soap operas he watches. When exploring this further, Jim stated that he realizes he is a little odd and is afraid that if he left his home he would get even odder, and "maybe even hurt someone."

Educational and Vocational History

Jim stated that he did not finish high school because he found his teachers to be mean. His mother states he was a "slow student" and was tested for a learning disability in reading but was not coded as disabled. He has a sparse vocational history, and he and his mother both note that he has held jobs for a few months "here and there." Most of his jobs have been working part-time at convenience stores or in retail at the local mall. He stated that he usually likes to work, at first, but then people with whom he works slowly "begin to turn on me." He states that he has interest in working, but that for now, he likes being at home alone.

Medical and Psychiatric History

Jim reports no significant medical history. His mother states that he was six weeks premature and that his doctors were concerned about possible brain damage. However, she reports that he was "perfectly fine." Jim was in counseling for one year with Dr. Shrink and was medicated with what his mother states was a "think right" medication. When asked if this might have been an antipsychotic, she stated that she thought so, but was not sure. His mother stated that Dr. Shrink did discuss with her the possibility of hospitalizing Jim to observe him and monitor his medication. However, she noted that "nobody was going to put my little Jimmy in the hospital."

Mental Status

Jim was dressed in jeans with his shirt hanging out. He looked somewhat disheveled and there was a strong smell of body odor. He avoided eye contact but was pleasant during the interview. He was oriented to time, place, and person. He responded to questions directly and somewhat concretely. He showed evidence of loose associations and circumstantial thinking, as he would occasionally ramble about unrelated topics and jump from topic to topic, but eventually come back to point. He often alluded to the idea that he and others were clairvoyant and could read people's minds, and there was evidence of paranoia when he noted that because others could read his mind, they would know how to "get him" if they wanted to. His affect seemed constricted and he noted he had few if any friends, little social contact with people, and was anxious about talking or confiding in others. He denied having auditory or visual hallucinations. He denies suicidal and homicidal ideation, but states that if people don't leave him alone, "I will get them." He would not clarify what this means.

Diagnostic Impressions

Rule Out Schizophrenia (295.90; F20.9)
Schizotypal Personality Disorder (301.22; F21)
Other Problem Related to Psychosocial Circumstances (V62.9; Z65.9)

Summary and Recommendations

This 25-year-old single male was referred by his mother who reports that her son has been acting odd lately and insists he is clairvoyant. Jim states that he can read other people's minds, that they can read his mind, and that he can sometimes change the future, such as when he changes the ends of soap operas.

Jim is the youngest of three boys. He reports that he gets along well with his parents, although he reports that his father is "a little strict at times." He has worked sporadically since high school and appears to have difficulty keeping a job. Jim has personal hygiene problems; apparently, he does not bathe regularly. He is oriented to time, place, and person; however, there is evidence of loose associations, circumstantiality, suspiciousness, and possible paranoia. His affect during the session was constricted and he admitted being fearful of talking with others and of being socially isolated. He denies being suicidal or homicidal but states that if people don't leave him alone, "I will get them." He was in counseling for one year during high school and may have been prescribed antipsychotic medication at that time. The following is recommended:

1. Possible testing for further psychiatric assessment
2. Review for possible medication
3. Further exploration of family dynamics
4. Individual counseling, 1 time weekly
5. Possible day treatment
6. Possible assessment for learning disability
7. Explore possibility of attainment of G.E.D.

Ed Neukrug, Ed.D., HS—BCP

APPENDIX E

Common Terms Used in the Mental Status Report

Category	Term	Definition or Description
Appearance and Behavior	Appearance	Appropriate or baseline, eccentric or odd, abnormal movement or gait, good or poor grooming, or hygiene
	Eye contact	Good or poor
	Speech	Within normal limits, loud, soft, pressured, hesitant
	Appropriate or inappropriate	Appropriate or inappropriate to mood (e.g., laughing while talking of recent death)
Emotional State—Affect	Full and reactive	Full range of emotions correctly associated with the conversation
	Labile	Uncontrollable crying or laughing
	Blunted	Reduced expression of emotional intensity
	Flat	No or very little expression of emotional intensity
	Euthymic	Normal mood
Emotional State—Mood	Depressed	Sad, dysphoric, discontent
	Euphoric	Extreme happiness or joy
	Anxious	Worried
	Anhedonic	Unable to derive pleasure from previously enjoyable activities
	Angry/hostile	Annoyed, irritated, irate, etc.
	Alexithymic	Unable to describe mood
	Hallucinations	False perception of reality: may be auditory, visual, tactile (touch), olfactory (smell), or taste
Thought Components—Content	Ideas of reference	Misinterpreting casual and external events as being related to self (e.g., newspaper headlines, TV stories, or song lyrics are about the client)
	Delusions	False belief (e.g., "satellites are tracking me"); may be grandiose, persecutory (to be harmed), somatic (physical symptom with no medical condition), erotic
	Derealization	External world seems unreal (e.g., watching it like a movie)
	Depersonlization	Feeling detached from self often with no control (e.g., "I feel like I'm living a dream")
	Suicidality and homicidality	Ranges from none, ideation, plan, means, preparation, rehearsal, and intent

Thought Components— Process	Logical and organized	Normal state where one's thoughts are rational and structured
	Poverty	Lack of verbal content or brief responses
	Blocking	Difficulty or unable to complete statements
	Clang	Emphasis on using words that rhyme together rather than on meaning
	Echolalia	"Echoing" clients own speech or your speech; repeating
	Flight of ideas	Rapid thoughts almost incoherent
	Perseveration	Thoughts keep returning to the same idea
	Circumstantial	Explanations are long and often irrelevant but eventually get to the point
	Tangential	Responses never get to the point of the question
	Loose	Thoughts have little or no association to the conversation or to each other
	Redirectable	Responses may get off track, but you can direct them back to the topic
	Orientation	Knows who they are, where they are, and date
Cognition	Memory	Ability to remember events from recent, immediate, and long-term
	Insight	Ability to recognize his or her mental illness; good, limited, or none
	Judgment	Ability to make sound decisions; good, fair, or poor

APPENDIX F

Privilege Exercise

1. If your ancestors were forced to come to the USA not by choice, take one step back.

2. If your primary ethnic identity is American, take one step forward.

3. If you were ever called names because of your race, class, ethnicity, gender, or sexual orientation, take one step back.

4. If there were people of color who worked in your childhood household as housekeepers, gardeners, etc., take one step forward.

5. If you were ever ashamed or embarrassed of your clothes, house, car, etc., take one step back.

6. If your parents were professionals: doctors, lawyers, etc., take one step forward.

7. If you were raised in an area where there was prostitution, drug activity, etc., take one stop back.

8. If you ever tried to change your appearance, mannerisms, or behavior to avoid being judged or ridiculed, take one step back.

9. If you studied the culture of your ancestors in elementary school, take one step forward.

10. If you went to school speaking a language other than English, take one step back.

11. If there were more than 50 books in your house when you grew up, take one step forward.

12. If you ever had to skip a meal or were hungry because there was not enough money to buy food when you were growing up, take one step back.

13. If you were taken to art galleries or plays by your parents, during childhood, take one step forward.

14. If one of your parents was unemployed or laid off, not by choice, take one step back.

15. If you attended private school or summer camp, take one step forward.

16. If your family ever had to move because they could not afford the rent, take one step back.

17. If you were told that you were beautiful, smart and capable by your parents, take one step forward.

18. If you were ever discouraged from academics or jobs because of race, class, ethnicity, gender or sexual orientation, take one step back.

19. If you were encouraged to attend college by your parents, take one step forward.

20. If you were raised in a single parent household, take one step back.

21. If your family owned the house where you grew up, take one step forward.

22. If you saw members of your race, ethnic group, gender or sexual orientation portrayed on television in degrading roles, take one step back.

23. If you were ever offered a good job because of your association with a friend or family member, take one step forward.

24. If you were ever denied employment because of your race, ethnicity, gender or sexual orientation, take one step back.

25. If you were paid less, treated unfairly because of race, ethnicity, gender or sexual orientation, take one step back.

26. If you were ever accused of cheating or lying because of your race, ethnicity, gender, or sexual orientation, take one step back.

27. If you ever inherited money or property, take one step forward.

28. If you had to rely primarily on public transportation, take one step back.

29. If you were ever stopped or questioned by the police because of your race, ethnicity, gender or sexual orientation, take one step back.

30. If you were ever afraid of violence because of your race, ethnicity, gender or sexual orientation, take one step back.

31. If you were generally able to avoid places that were dangerous, take one step forward.

32. If you were ever uncomfortable about a joke related to your race, ethnicity, gender or sexual orientation but felt unsafe to confront the situation, take one step back.

33. If you were ever the victim of violence related to your race, ethnicity, gender or sexual orientation, take one step back.

34. If your parents did not grow up in the United States, take one step back.

35. If your parents told you that you could be anything you wanted to be, take one step forward.

APPENDIX G

Survey of NOHS Members Regarding Ethical Behavior

Percent Ethical By NOHS Members

100	Informing clients of the purpose of the helping relationship
100	Keeping information confidential
99.2	Respecting client self-determination
98.4	Breaking confidentiality if the client is threatening harm to others
98	Breaking confidentiality if the client is threatening harm to self
97.6	Being an advocate for clients
91.8	Referring a client due to interpersonal conflicts between you and your client
91.4	Using an interpreter when a client's primary language is different from yours
90.2	Addressing your client by his or her first name
90.2	Having clients address you by your first name
88.6	Sharing confidential client information with your supervisor
86.6	Engaging in two helping relationships with a client at the same time (e.g., individual counseling and group counseling)
85.8	Showing unconditional acceptance even when opposed to a client's behaviors or values
85.8	Consoling your client by touching her or him (e.g., placing hand on shoulder)
85	Publicly advocating for a controversial cause
81.1	Providing services to an undocumented worker (sometimes called an "illegal immigrant")
80.9	Keeping client records on your office computer
70.9	Self-disclosing to a client
67.2	Counseling a pregnant teenager without parental consent
66.7	Hugging a client
64.8	Attending a client's wedding, graduation ceremony, other formal ceremony
63.8	Not being a member of a human services professional association
62.7	In a professional manner, telling your client you like him or her
61.1	Making a diagnosis (e.g., based on DSM-5 or on client symptomology)
58.6	Counseling a terminally ill client about end-of-life decisions including suicide
57.4	Guaranteeing confidentiality for couples and families
54.9	Guaranteeing confidentiality for group members
54.7	Referring a client who is unhappy with his or her homosexuality for reparative therapy (therapy focused on converting sexual identity from homosexual to heterosexual)
51.2	Sharing confidential client information with your employer
51.2	Sending holiday and/or birthday cards to clients
50.8	Providing counseling over the Internet
49	Withholding information about a minor client despite the parents' request for information
48.4	Sharing confidential client information with your colleagues
47.2	Accepting a gift from a client that is worth less than $25
46.7	Not allowing clients to view your case notes about them
46.3	Viewing your client's personal web page (e.g., Facebook, blog, Twitter) without informing client
45.9	Telling your client you are angry with him or her
36.9	Bartering (accepting goods or services) for helping services
36.2	Giving a gift worth $25 or less to a client
34.6	Breaking the law to protect your client's rights
33.6	Selling a product to your client related to the helping relationship
32.5	Pressuring a client to receive needed services
32.1	Reporting a colleague's unethical conduct without first consulting with the colleague
29.3	Counseling clients from a different culture with little or no cross-cultural training

24.4	Based on personal preference, accepting clients who are only male or only female
23.4	Seeing a minor client without parental consent
23	Not having malpractice coverage (on your own or by your agency)
23	Not reporting suspected spousal abuse
21.5	Engaging in a dual helping relationship (a client working with you and another helper) without contacting the other helper
21.1	Becoming sexually involved with a person whom your client knows well
20.7	Engaging in a professional helping relationship with a family member
19.9	Becoming sexually involved with a former client (five years since helping relationship)
19.9	Kissing a client as a friendly gesture (e.g., in greeting)
19.5	Based on personal preference, accepting clients only from specific cultural groups
18.3	Engaging in a professional helping relationship with a friend
18	Accepting a client's decision to commit suicide
15	Engaging in a dual relationship (e.g., your client is also your child's teacher)
15	Not participating in continuing education (e.g., conferences, workshops, trainings) after obtaining your degree
13.9	Trying to change your client's values
13.1	Not allowing clients to view their records (excluding process notes)
12.7	Accepting a client when you have not had training in his or her presenting problem
8.9	Giving a gift worth more than $25 to a client
8.6	Telling your client you are attracted to him or her
8.5	Accepting a gift from a client that is worth more than $25
6.5	Keeping client records in an unlocked file cabinet
6.5	Treating homosexuality as a pathology
6.1	Referring a client who is satisfied with his or her homosexuality for reparative therapy
4.9	Lending money to your client
4.9	Attempting to have your client not have an abortion even though she wants one
4.5	Terminating the helping relationship without warning
4.1	Counseling while you are emotionally impaired
3.7	Releasing records to a third party (e.g., another agency) without client consent
3.3	Making grandiose statements about your expertise
2.5	Not reporting suspected elder abuse
2	Recording your client without his or her permission
1.6	Not revealing the limits of confidentiality to your client
1.6	Selling a product to your client that is not related to the helping relationship
1.6	Not informing clients of their legal rights (e.g., HIPPA, FERPA, confidentiality)
1.2	Attempting to have your client have an abortion even though she does not want one
0.8	Sharing confidential client information with your friends
0.8	Not reporting suspected child abuse
0.4	Becoming sexually involved with a client
0.4	Stating you are credentialed without having a credential
0.4	Sharing confidential client information with your family members
0.4	Counseling while you are impaired by a substance (e.g., drugs or alcohol)
0.4	Attempting to persuade your client to adopt a religious conviction you hold
0	Revealing client records to the spouse of a client without the client 's permission

Source: Tammi Milliken and Edward Neukrug, "Perceptions of Ethical Behaviors of Human Service Professionals," *Human Service Education*, vol. 29, no. 1. Copyright © 2009 by National Organization for Human Services. Reprinted with permission.

GLOSSARY†

Developed by Mike Kalkbrenner

A, B, and Cs. Based on Rational –Emotive Behavior Therapy (REBT), a *cognitive theory* to helping developed by *Albert Ellis* where A is the *activating event*, B is the *belief about the event*, and C is the *consequential feelings and behaviors*.

Acceptance. Respecting people's ideals, thoughts, and emotions unconditionally. Also called *unconditional positive regard* and *unconditional acceptance*. One of the eight *characteristics of the effective helper*.

Activating Event. A stimulus or incident that leads to one's *belief about an event*. *Irrational thoughts* or beliefs result in negative consequences (feelings and/or behavior) while rational beliefs result in positive feelings and functional behaviors. See also, *A, B, and Cs*. A component of *Albert Ellis's cognitive theory*.

Active Listening. A deliberate and focused process where the helper attempts to establish *empathy* with a client by *reflecting feelings* and *reflecting content* of a client's statements.

Advanced Empathic Responses. Empathic responses that help clients gain self-awareness by reflecting *deeper feelings* that were not directly stated by the client or by helping a person see a situation in a new way. Includes *reflecting deeper feelings*, *pointing out conflicting feelings or thoughts*, use of *metaphors and analogies*, *self-disclosure*, and *tactile responses*.

Advice Giving. The process by which the helper offers his or her expert opinion in hopes that the client will follow up on the suggestions. Advice giving should be used sparingly, as there is the potential that the client will develop a dependent relationship on the helper and could end up relying on the helper for problem-solving. Contrast with *information giving* and *offering alternatives*.

Advocacy. One aspect of *social justice* work which involves a helper directly or indirectly taking active steps to heal a societal wound and promote the welfare of his or her client. See *Multicultural Counseling and Social Justice Competencies*, *advocating directly for clients*, *advocating for societal change*, *advocating for community change*, and *empowering clients to advocate for themselves*.

Advocating Directly for Clients. When the helper engages in behaviors that promote and support a client.

Advocating for Community Change. When the helper engages in behaviors that promote making positive community change for the benefit of his or her clients.

Advocating for Societal Change. When the helper engages in behaviors that promote broader social issues for the benefit of his or her clients.

Affirmation. The process by which a helper reinforces a client's actions, feelings, or behaviors by giving a *genuine* positive response to a client's way of being in the world. Contrast with *encouragement*.

Agency Atmosphere. The permeating mood or feel of an agency or institution, including but not limited to: lighting, comfort of furniture, arrangement of the waiting room, and placement of the furniture.

Amphetamines. A classification of *stimulant medication* that used to be primarily prescribed to treat individuals living with Attention Deficit Disorder with Hyperactivity (ADHD).

Anti-Anxiety Agents. A classification of medications used primarily to treat individuals living with Generalized Anxiety Disorder (GAD).

Antidepressants. A classification of medications used primarily to treat individuals living with depressive and anxiety disorders. See also *selective serotonin reuptake inhibitors (SSRIs)*.

Antipsychotics. Sometimes referred to as *neuroleptics*, they are generally used to treat psychoses, bipolar disorder, depression with psychotic features, paranoid disorder, delirium, and dementia.

Assessing for Lethality: Suicidality and Homicidality. The process for evaluating if clients are posing an eminent danger to themselves or to others, including but not limited to the degree to which the client has developed a plan, has the means to carry out the plan, is prepared to implement the plan, has rehearsed the plan, and has acted on the plan.

Italicized words within definitions can be found in the glossary.

Assessment for Treatment Planning. A type of client assessment that involves multiple ways of understanding client concerns which can include (1) conducting a clinical interview, (2) administering tests, (3) doing informal assessment, and (4) coming up with a diagnosis.

Attire or Dress. The overt and covert norms within an agency regarding the style of dress for helpers and for other employees.

Attitude and Beliefs, Knowledge, Skills, and Actions. See the *multicultural and social justice competencies*.

Atypical Antidepressants. *Antidepressant medications* that do not fit within the existing categories.

Automatic Thoughts. Fleeting thoughts that we have all day long about how we are interacting in the world.

Autonomy. Based on *Kitchener's* moral model of *ethical decision-making*, this involves empowering the client's sense of self-determination, independence, and self-sufficiency.

Basic Empathic Responses. Any of a number of responses that reflect back the obvious feelings and content that a person is saying. A "level 3" on the *Carkhuff scale*.

Beck, Aaron. Individual who developed *cognitive therapy*.

Behavioral Rehearsal. See *modeling*.

Being Curious. Helpers who have a genuine interest in getting to know their clients and are comfortable inquiring about a client's life while simultaneously honoring and respecting the person.

Belief About the Event. The patterns of cognitions (rational or irrational beliefs) that one has about an *activating event*.

Beneficence. Based on *Kitchener's* moral model of *ethical decision-making*, this involves protecting the good of others and of society.

Benzodiazepines. A type of *anti-anxiety medication* that has an elevated risk for tolerance, dependence, and overdose if not taken properly.

Board Certified Coach. A credential that is offered through the *Center for Credentialing and Education for coaching*.

Body Positioning. How the helper situates his or her body while working with a client. One of the most important *nonverbal behaviors* that clients initially observe.

Caring Habits. Helpers who develop tendencies of interacting with their clients that involve using language that is supportive, encouraging, accepting, trusting, and respectful and does not use language that is *toxic* and will pathologize, diagnose, blame, or criticize the client.

Carkhuff, Robert. Developed a 5-point scale to measure the ability to make an empathic response. See *Carkhuff Scale*.

Carkhuff Scale. A 5-point scale developed by *Robert Carkhuff* and based on *Carl Rogers's* definition of empathy. The scale has been used in the training of helpers to assist them in learning empathy. Level 3 responses are seen as accurately reflecting the client's affect and content. Responses below Level 3 are seen as detracting, while responses above Level 3 are seen as additive.

Case Notes. A wide variety of ways of documenting and summarizing clients' information, including the *intake interview*, periodic summaries of clients' progress, termination summaries, specialized reports for the courts or other agencies, and more. Also referred to as *case reports*. Generally, clients have the right to see such notes. Contrast with *process notes*. See *SOAP Notes/Reports*.

Case Reports. See *case notes*.

Center for Credentialing and Education. The professional organization that offers a certification for *coaching* and to become a *Human Services—Board Certified Professional*.

Characteristics of the Effective Helper. Eight characteristics important for helpers to embody if they are to be effective. They include *acceptance, cognitive complexity, competence, cultural sensitivity, empathy, genuineness*, the *it factor*, and *wellness*.

Client-Centered. A *non-directive* approach to helping in which helpers allow clients to take the lead in the direction of their session. Contrast with the *helper-centered* approach.

Client Contact Hours. A measure of time, in hours, that helpers provide treatment to their clients.

Closed Questions. Questions that can be answered with a "yes" or "no" response or with a response that tends to limit the number of choices being offered to them. Three types of closed questions include those that delimit affect, those that delimit content, and direct closed questions.

Closed Questions that Delimit Affect. See *closed questions*.

Closed Questions that Delimit Content. See *closed questions*.

Coaching. An approach to helping that relies on a short-term focused helping relationship in which the coach uses solution-focused questions to identify one or more issues to focus upon. The coach collaboratively sets goals, affirms and encourages the client to work on goals, and helps to ensure continued follow-up after goals have been reached to ensure maintenance of goals. In coaching little time is devoted to examining the past or focusing on problems.

Cognitive-Behavioral Responses. Clients' active reactions to their thoughts and feelings.

Cognitive Therapy. An approach to helping that explores a person's *core beliefs* and *irrational thoughts* and how they impact one's feelings, behaviors, and physiology. Developed by *Aaron Beck*, although a related therapy *Rational Emotive Behavior Therapy*, was developed by *Albert Ellis*.

Cognitively Complex. The ability to understand the world (and for helpers, to understand clients) in complex and multifaceted ways. One of the eight *characteristics of the effective helper*.

Collaboration. The purposeful practice of making time to talk with your client about progress being made thus far in the helping relationship.

Collectivistic Perspective. Clients who tend to focus more on a *universal identity* or *group identity* and the impact that the community has on them in the helping relationship as opposed to a focus on self. See also *individualistic perspective*.

Compassion Fatigue. The process by which a helper becomes emotionally exhausted from the process of hearing client concerns. Can result in ineffective work and an inability to feel *empathy* with clients. Also called *vicarious traumatization*.

Competence. Being knowledgeable of the most recent professional research and trends and being able to apply it with clients. Having a thirst for knowledge. Knowing the limits of one's professional capabilities. One of the eight *characteristics of the effective helper*.

Competence and Scope of Knowledge. A crucial ethical concern that involves knowing and practicing within the limits of one's professional knowledge and his or her level of competence.

Conducting Follow-Up. The process by which a helper contacts a client after the helping relationship has ended. An aspect of *case management* which can be completed by a phone call, by a letter, by an elaborate survey of clients, or in other ways.

Confidentiality. The ethical guideline that emphasizes discretion regarding the release of client information. It is driven by knowledge of ethical, professional, and legal issues regarding when such information can be breached.

Confidentiality of Records. Keeping clients' information in secured places, such as locked file cabinets and password secured computers.

Confrontation: Challenge with Support. The process by which a helper assists a client in gaining self-awareness about a discrepancy between a client's values and behaviors, feelings and behaviors, idealized self and real self, and expressed feelings and underlying feelings. Includes *you/but statements, inviting the client to justify the discrepancy, reframing, using satire,* and *using higher level empathy*.

Congruence/Congruent. See *genuineness*.

Consequential Feelings and Behaviors. A concept from *cognitive therapy* approaches to helping that involve the emotions and actions that are influenced by one's *automatic thoughts* or *irrational thoughts or beliefs* about an *activating event*.

Content Self-disclosure. The helper's revelation of some personal information in an effort to enhance the helping relationship. See *self-disclosure*.

Continuing Education. One's career long ethical and professional obligation to pursue knowledge by joining professional associations, participating in workshops, reading journal articles, taking additional coursework, and related activities.

Coping Questions. Questions that identify behaviors which the client has successfully used in the past to deal with his or her problems. One type of *solution-focused questions*.

Coping Self. One of the five factors of the *indivisible self model*. It is composed of developing leisure activities (leisure), successfully coping with stress (stress management), valuing ourselves and having good self-esteem despite problems (self-worth), and having the capacity to be imperfect and to realize that it is unrealistic to think we can be loved by all (realistic beliefs).

Core Beliefs. Deep rooted opinions, values, and judgments that one has about the world and about oneself. A concept from *Aaron Beck's cognitive therapy*.

Countertransference. The process in which the helper's own issues interfere with effectively helping his or her clients. The unconscious transferring of thoughts, feelings, and attitudes onto the client.

Creative Self. One of the five factors of the *indivisible self model*. It is highlighted by our ability to be mentally sharp and open minded (thinking), being in touch with our feelings (emotions), being intentional and planful and knowing how to express our needs (control), being effective at work and using our skills successfully (work), and being able to deal with life as it comes at us (positive humor).

Crisis, Disaster, and Trauma Helping. An approach to helping that focuses on immediate assistance of clients who have recently experienced a crisis, disaster, or traumatic event. This approach is short-term, built on client strengths, non-diagnostic oriented, and provided at agencies or where the crisis has occurred.

Cross-Cultural Issues and Nonverbal Behavior. A helper's awareness and sensitivity in recognizing the cultural context *of nonverbal behaviors*.

Cultural Competent Helping. See *Multicultural Counseling*.

Cultural Differences in the Expression of Symptoms. The impact that a client's cultural background has on his or her presentation of symptoms.

Cultural Mosaic. A society that has many diverse values and customs. Contrast with the *melting pot myth*.

Cultural Sensitivity. The ability and readiness of a helper to understand the cultural identity of a client and to be cognizant of how the client's cultural heritage, as well as the helper's attitudes and beliefs, knowledge, and skills, may impact the helping relationship. One of the eight *characteristics of the effective helper*.

Delimiting Power and Developing an Equal Relationship. The process by which a professional helper shows his or her client respect and joins with the client to form an equitable relationship.

Demonstrating the 3 C's. A helper who is committed (follows-up on promises made to clients), courteous, (continually treats clients respectfully, politely, and is aware of clients' customs), and caring (shows concern for others, has regard for others, and is there for them in times of need).

Developmental Models of Ethical Decision-Making. Approaches to making ethical decisions that emphasize how one's cognitive ability impacts a human service professional's ethical decision-making process. See also *dualistic* and *relativistic*.

Diagnostic and Statistical Manual-5th edition. A manual that details the different types of mental disorders and is used for diagnostic purposes.

Different Ethnic and Racial Groups. See *diverse populations human service professionals work with*.

Direct Closed Questions. See *closed questions*.

Discrepancy Between Client's Expressed and Underlying Feelings. When a client's expressed feelings do not match his or her underlying feelings.

Discrepancy Between Clients Feelings and Behaviors. When a client's expressed feelings do not match his or her behaviors.

Discrepancy Between Client's Values and Behaviors. When a client's expressed values do not match his or her behaviors.

Discrepancy Between Idealized Self and Real Self. When a client's thoughts and fantasies about how he or she want to act (idealized self) does not match who the client actually is (real self).

Diverse Populations Human Service Professionals Work With. Human service professionals work with a variety of different populations, a portion of which include *different ethnic and racial groups, individuals from diverse religious backgrounds, individuals using and abusing substances, individuals with disabilities, individuals with mental illness, lesbian, gay, bisexual, transgender individuals, men, women, older persons, the homeless, and the poor.* See also *multicultural and social justice counseling competencies.*

DSM-5. See *diagnostic and statistical manual-5th edition*

Dual and Multiple Relationships. A professional helping relationship in which there exists potential ethical conflicts because there are multiple roles between the helper and the client, such as when a potential or actual client is also a neighbor, colleague, or when a helper goes to a personal celebration or activity sponsored by a client (wedding, funeral, etc.).

Dualistic. A perspective in which one views the world in terms of black-and-white thinking, concreteness, rigidity, oversimplification, stereotyping, self-protectiveness, and authoritarianism.

Duty-to-Warn. Sometimes referred to as *foreseeable danger*, the ethical and sometimes legal obligation for a professional to take action and breach *confidentiality* if a client is in danger of harming himself or herself or someone else.

Ellis, Albert. Developed a cognitive approach to therapy called Rational Emotive Behavior Therapy (REBT) highlighting the impact that thoughts have on behaviors, feelings, and physiology. See *A, B, and C's* and *irrational thoughts.*

Emotional Intelligence. The ability to monitor one's emotions and knowing the appropriate time to share one's feelings and thoughts.

Empathy. Derived from the German word Einfühlung, empathy has become a core counseling skill. Popularized by Carl Rogers, empathy is viewed as the ability to understand another person's feelings and situation in the world. High-level empathic responses are seen as helping a client see hidden parts of himself or herself. The *Carkhuff Scale* operationalized this important concept. One of the eight *characteristics of the effective helper.*

Empowering Clients to Advocate for Themselves. The process by which a helper supports and encourages a client to advocate for self.

Encouragement. Similar to *affirmations*, this skill focuses on supporting and inspiring a client toward reaching specific goals.

Essential Self. One of the five factors of the *indivisible self model*. It includes recognizing the part of us that is beyond our mind and body (spirituality), feeling comfortable in the way we identify with our gender (gender identity) and with our culture (cultural identity), and being able to care for self and minimizing harm in our environment (self-care).

Ethical Decision-Making Models. Any of a number of models that assists helpers in making difficult ethical decisions. Includes *developmental models, moral models, problem-solving models,* and the *social constructionist perspective.*

Ethnocentric Worldview. When one views the world through the lens of his or her own culture and falsely assumes that clients view the world in a similar manner or believe that when clients present a differing view, they are emotionally disturbed, culturally brainwashed, or just simply wrong.

Evaluative Questions. Questions that are intended to assess whether clients' behaviors have been productive toward reaching their goals. One type of *solution-focused questions.*

Exception-Seeking Questions. Questions that identify times in the client's life when he or she has not had the problem and focuses on what the client was doing during those times. One type of *solution-focused questions.*

Eye Contact. A *nonverbal behavior* related to the ability of the helper to appropriately engage a person through direct contact with their eyes.

Facial Expressions. A *nonverbal behavior* related to a wide range of facial gestures made by a helper and intended to foster the helping relationship.

Family Education Rights and Privacy Act. A federal law, which in part, assures parents the right to access their children's educational records.

FERPA. See *Family Education Rights and Privacy Act.*

Fidelity. Based on *Kitchener's* moral model of *ethical decision-making*, this involves maintaining clients' trust and being committed to them.

Forced Choice Closed Question. Questions that give the client a minimum of two options when responding.

Foreseeable Danger. See *duty-to-warn.*

Formula Responses. Structured empathic responses that are typically made by beginning helpers and use a "You feel (enter feeling word) because (enter content)" structure.

Freedom of Information Act of 1974. Allows individuals access to records maintained by a federal agency that contain personal information about the individual. Most states have similar laws.

Genuineness. The quality of expressing one's true feelings. Being congruent or "in sync" with one's feelings, thoughts, and behaviors. Popularized by "Carl Rogers" and listed as one of his three core conditions of helping along with empathy and unconditional positive regard. One of the eight *characteristics of the effective helper.* Sometimes called *congruence, realness,* or *transparency.*

Glasser, William. Founder of *reality therapy.*

Good Listening. An active process, where the helper talks minimally, concentrates on what is being said, does not interrupt or gives advice, hears the speaker's content and affect, and uses good non-verbal behaviors to show that he or she is understanding the client.

Group Identity. Along with individual and universal identities, one of three identities that make up the person. This identity has to do with shared values and customs that individuals have with specific cultural groups with which they identify.

Health Insurance Portability and Accountability Act (HIPAA). A federal law, which in part ensures the privacy of client records by restricting the amount of information that can be shared without the client's consent and allows clients to have access to their records.

Helper-Centered. In contrast to being *client-centered,* when the helper directs the session.

Higher-level Empathy. See *advanced empathic responses.*

Hindrances to Effective Listening. Factors that prevent or interfere with one's ability to listen effectively such as preconceived notions, anticipatory reaction, cognitive distractions, personal issues, emotional responses, and distractions.

HIPAA. See *Health Insurance Portability and Accountability Act.*

Homeless and the Poor. See *diverse populations human service professionals work with.*

ICD. See *International Classification of Disease (ICD).*

Imitation. See *Modeling*

Inadvertent Modeling. A type of *modeling* in which new behaviors are learned from the helper in a passive way as the helper demonstrates basic counseling skills toward the client. See *modeling.*

Incongruent Expectations About the Helping Relationship. A potential cross-cultural impediment to the helping relationship related to disparities between the helper's and client's expectations about the purpose and goals of the helping relationship.

Individual Identity. Along with group and universal identities, one of three identities that make up the person. This identity has to do with an individual's unique ways of being in the world

Individualistic Perspective. Clients who tend to focus an *individual identity* and seek answers to problems from self as opposed to outside groups, such as the family or culture. See also *collectivist perspective.*

Individuals from Diverse Religious Backgrounds. See *diverse populations human service professionals work with.*

Individuals with Disabilities. See *diverse populations human service professionals work with.*

Individuals with Mental Illness. See *diverse populations human service professionals work with.*

Individuals Using and Abusing Substances. See *diverse populations human service professionals work with.*

Indivisible Self. One model that views wellness as the conglomeration of five factors: creative self, coping self, social self, essential self, and physical self as well as the individual's context.

Indivisible Self-Model. See *indivisible self*.

Information Gathering Questions. Questions that are intended to gather information that the helper believes will help solve the client's problems or address the client's concerns. These questions tend to be *helper-centered*. Includes *open questions*, *closed questions*, *tentative questions*, and *why questions*.

Information Giving. The process by which a helper offers the client important, "objective" information of which the client is likely unaware. Contrast with *advice giving* and *offering alternatives*.

Informed Consent. The acknowledgement of a client that he or she understands the nature and general limits of the helping relationship.

Initial Email and Phone Contact with Agency. Refers to a client's first point of contact with the agency during which it is essential for helpers to be kind and courteous to begin establishing a positive helping relationship.

Institutional Racism. When an agency or organization purposely, or out of ignorance, supports policies or behaviors that are racist.

Intake Interview. The client's initial contact with the agency which must be completed in a manner that will allow the client to be open and honest with the helper so that understanding of client issues is clear and comprehensive.

Intentional Modeling. A type of *modeling* in which the helper deliberately demonstrates a behavior for the client so he or she will view, practice, learn, and adopt the new behavior. Clients can also choose behaviors of others with the intention of viewing, practicing, learning, and adopting those behaviors.

Intermediate Beliefs. Attitudes, rules and assumptions we make based on our *core beliefs* that impact the development of our *automatic thoughts*. Based on *Aaron Beck's* theory of *Cognitive Therapy*.

International Classification of Disease. A diagnostic manual used by health care providers, now in its 10th edition (ICD-10). It identifies medical diagnoses and includes classifications from the *DSM-5*, although it does not describe them in the detail found in *DSM-5*.

Interpretation. A helper's assumptions about human behavior external to the client's understanding of reality and usually based on some external model (e.g., psychoanalysis).

Irrational Thoughts. Patterns of thought, or cognitions, that are illogical and are often related to the subsequent development of negative emotions and dysfunctional behaviors. Based on *Albert Ellis's* theory of *Rational Emotive Behavior Therapy (REBT)*

It Factor. The unique characteristics of a helper that contribute to special ways of working with and ultimately building alliances with their clients. One of the eight *characteristics of the effective helper*.

Jaffee v. Redmond. A court ruling that upheld the right of *privileged communication* for licensed social workers and likely can be applied to most licensed counselors and therapists, but not to those who are not licensed (e.g., human service professionals).

Justice. Based on *Kitchener's* moral model of *ethical decision-making*, this involves treating clients fairly and equally.

Kitchener, Karen. Developed a *moral model of ethical decision-making*.

Lack of Understanding of the Impact of Social Forces. When the helper is unaware of the social influences that have impacted the manifestation of a client's presenting concern.

Lesbian, Gay, Bisexual, and Transgender (LGBT) Individuals. See *diverse populations human service professionals work with*.

Life-Coaching. See *coaching*.

Limitations of Ethical Codes. Instances where ethical codes are limited, due to the following: some issues cannot be handled with a code, difficulties in enforcing codes, lack of public involvement in the code construction process, issues addressed by codes being handled in other ways (e.g., the courts), conflicts within a code or between related codes, and conflicts between a code and the values of the professional.

Listening. The process by which one directs his or her attention to hearing a message from another person.

Making Referrals. The process by which a helper sends a client to another provider for a variety of reasons, including: the helper is leaving the agency, because he or she feels incompetent to work with the client, or because the client has reached his or her goals and is ready to move on to another form of treatment.

McAuliffe's Definition of Culturally Competent Helping. The perspective that culturally competent helping is a consistent willingness to learn about the cultural dimensions of clients' lives and integrate cultural considerations into the helping process.

Melting Pot Myth. The misnomer that various and unique values and customs of different cultures become integrated and subsumed into the larger culture and that the cultural uniqueness is lost. See also *cultural mosaic*.

Men. See *diverse populations human service professionals work with*.

Mental Status Exam. An informal assessment where the helper assesses a client in four areas, including (1) how the client presents himself or herself (appearance and behavior), (2) the client's emotional state (affect), (3) the client's ability to think clearly (thought components), and (4) the client's memory state and orientation to the world (cognition).

Mental Status Report. A one or two paragraph written report by the helper about the findings from a *mental status exam*.

Metaphors and Analogies Using symbols, allegories, and a logical analysis to make a comparison between a client's current situation and an external event to establish empathy by responding in a manner in which the client feels heard and understood at a deep level. Considered an *advanced empathic response*.

Miracle Question. A type of *preferred goals questions* focused on quickly identifying where the client wants to be in the future, and helping the client get to his or her desired goals. Often put in a framework which asks: "If you were to wake up in the morning and find your world to be what you want it to be, what would that look like?" See *solution-focused questions*.

Modeling. The subtle or deliberate ways that the helper, or others, can demonstrate new behaviors for the client so that the client can practice, learn, and adopt those behaviors. Also called *social learning, imitation,* or *behavioral rehearsal*. See *inadvertent* and *intentional modeling*.

Monoamine Oxidase Inhibitors. A classification of medications that are used to treat depressive and anxiety disorders.

Mood-Stabilizing Drugs. A group of psychotropic medications that are used to treat bipolar disorder.

Moral Models of Ethical Decision-Making. Ethical decision-making models that emphasize the role of moral principles in making ethical decisions. One such model, by *Kitchener*, suggests examining the following moral principles: *autonomy, beneficence, nonmaleficence, justice, fidelity,* and *veracity*.

Multicultural and Social Justice Counseling Competencies. Having appropriate attitudes and beliefs, knowledge, and skills when working with nondominant clients. Areas of proficiency to assist helpers when working with diverse clients include four domains: (1) counselor [helper] self-awareness, (2) client worldview, (3) counseling relationship, and (4) counseling and advocacy intervention.

Multicultural Counseling. Having the attitudes and beliefs, knowledge, and skills to work with diverse clients.

Multiple Realities. The ability to identify multiple origins that lead to the present moment. Also speaks to varying perspectives a person or persons can have on a situation.

Narrative Therapy. A postmodern approach to helping that suggests reality is a social construction and that each person's reality is maintained through his or her narrative or language discourse.

Natural Responses. Reflecting a client's affect and content while using a natural tone and fluid response.

Neuroleptics. See *Antipsychotics*

Nonbenzodiazepines. Medications that have similar therapeutic effects as *benzodiazepines;* however, these medications have different chemical properties.

Nondogmatic. Closely related to being *nonjudgmental,* this refers to individuals who do not push their views onto others and are: open to understanding the views of others, open to feedback, and even open to changing their perception of the world after hearing other points of view. Such individuals are relatively free from biases and can accept people in their differences, regardless of dissimilar cultural heritage, values, or beliefs.

Nonjudgmental. See *nondogmatic*.

Nonmaleficence. Based on *Kitchener's* moral model of *ethical decision-making*, this involves avoiding doing harm to clients and others.

Non-Pathologizing of the Client. The process by which a helper meets with a client and treats him or her respectfully as a holistic person. Clients are perceived as "living with" mental health issues as opposed to "having" mental health issues.

Nonverbal Behaviors. Communication that is not verbal, such as one's *body posture, tone of voice, eye contact, personal space*, and *touch*.

Offering Alternatives. When the helper suggests to the client that there may be a variety of ways to address a problem and provides possible options from which the client can choose. Contrast with *advice giving* and *information giving*.

Office Atmosphere. The mood or feel of a helper's office. Providing an office space that is quiet, comfortable, and safe, and where confidentiality can be ensured.

Older Persons. See *diverse populations human service professionals work with*.

Open Questions. Questions that enable the client to have a wide range of responses and encourages more than a yes or no, forced choice response, or direct response.

Operant Conditioning. The shaping of behavior, which is brought about through the use of *positive reinforcement* and/or *negative reinforcement*.

Paradoxical Effect. The unexpected result of *stimulant* medications that calms down and focuses some people who have attention deficit disorder with hyperactivity (ADHD).

Paraphrasing. A helping skill that involves the helper reflecting back the general feelings and content of what the client has said by using similar words and phrases of the client.

Pathologizing. The process by which a helper sees a client and treats that person as if he or she has a problem. Often related to the process of giving or reinforcing a *DSM-5* diagnosis of a mental disorder to a client.

Perry, William. An adult development theorist who emphasized the learning process and cognitive development of college students. He researched college students and showed how they tend to move from dualism to relativism while in college. See *dualism* and *relativistic*.

Personal Characteristics of the Helper. See *characteristics of the effective helper*.

Personal Space. The amount of physical space between a helper and client which sends an immediate message to the client about the helping relationship and can positively or negatively affect the relationship.

Physical Self. One of the five factors of the *indivisible self model*. It includes the part of ourselves that is reflected through our biological and physical aspects of self and is related to ensuring that we have adequate physical activity in our lives (exercise) and that we eat well, have a good diet, and avoid being overweight or underweight (nutrition).

Pointing Out Conflicting Feelings or Thoughts. The process by which a helper makes a client aware of discrepancies between his or her thoughts, feelings, or behaviors.

Positive Helping. An approach to helping that is optimistic, future-oriented, strength-based, and focused on a large number of human contexts. See also *positive psychology*.

Positive Psychology. A purposeful and deliberate approach to *positive helping* which spends little time talking about problems or the past, assumes clients have strengths that can help them overcome their current situation, and focuses on positive future behaviors in the change process.

Post-Traumatic Stress Syndrome (PTSD). A client's response to trauma that involves re-living aspects of the traumatic event and experiencing distress that is significant enough to interfere with his or her ability to function.

Preferred Goals Questions. Questions that assess what the client is hoping his or future will look like. See also *miracle question*. One type of *solution-focused questions*.

Preparing for Listening. Refers to a variety of strategies that helpers can use to increase the chances that they will listen to their clients effectively, including calming oneself down, not talking and not interrupting, showing interest, not jumping to conclusions, actively listening, concentrating on feelings, concentrating on content, maintaining eye contact, having an open body posture, being sensitive to personal space, and not asking questions.

Primary Obligation: Client, Agency, or Society. The ethical code generally asserts that human service professionals' primary obligation is ensuring clients' right to: *confidentiality*, right to be respected, and right for self-determination; however, there are instances in which human service professionals also recognize, and sometimes favor, the right of other individuals and of society to be protected from harm.

Privileged Communication. The legal right of a professional to not reveal information about a client. This legal right is determined by states, and relative to mental health professionals, generally only includes licensed counselors and therapists.

Problem-Solving Models of Ethical Decision-Making. A pragmatic, hands on approach to resolving ethical dilemmas that involves following a series of eight steps.

Process Notes. Written notes that are usually brief (often one to three paragraphs long) to assist the helper in remembering salient points of a session. Clients typically do not have a right to see these as per the *Health Insurance Portability and Accountability Act (HIPAA)*.

Process Self-disclosure. Similar to the concept of *immediacy*, involves the helper sharing with the client his or her moment-to-moment experience of self in relation to the client. See also *self-disclosure*.

Professional Disclosure Statement. An informational document about the helper and helping relationship that reflects important values upheld within one's ethical codes and the helping relationship and is given to clients when first meeting them. In part, such a statement (1) supports the client's unique diversity, (2) states that the helper will keep promises made to clients, (3) acknowledges and ensures that commitments made to clients will be kept, (4) underscores that the helping relationship is confidential under all but certain circumstance (e.g., danger to self or others), and (5) encourages and supports the client's self-determination.

Protective Factors. Influences in clients' lives that guard against the likelihood of the client committing suicide or homicide.

Psychopharmacology. The scientific study and practice of using medications to treat an array of disorders. Sometimes called *psychotropic medications*.

Psychosocial and Environmental Stressors. Sources of client distress that are common concerns (e.g., job loss, marital problems, homelessness, relationship issues) and are assessed through the use of *V Codes* or *Z Codes*.

Psychotropic Medications. See *psychopharmacology*.

Purpose of Ethical Codes. Including, but not limited to: protecting consumers, furthering professionalism, denoting a body of knowledge, asserting a professional identity, reflecting a profession's underlying values and suggested behaviors, offering a framework for ethical decision-making, and offering a measure of defense in case one is sued.

Racist Attitudes and Prejudices. Having preconceived notions about the characteristics of an individual or a group that are based on generalizations about race or the characteristics of the individual or group.

Reality Therapy and Choice Theory. A theoretical framework, developed by *William Glasser*, which suggests that we are born with five needs: survival, love and belonging, power, freedom, and fun which can be satisfied only in the present. Glasser suggested that helpers, and all of us, should develop *caring habits*.

Realness. See *genuineness*.

Reflecting Deeper Feelings. The process by which a helper reflects the client's underlying feelings that he or she might not be aware of. A type of *advanced empathy*.

Reflection of Content. The process by which a helper repeats back to the client specific statements that the client has made using the same or slightly different words.

Reflection of Feeling. The process by which a helper repeats back to the client specific feelings that the client has made using either the same feeling word or a feeling word that is very similar to the one that the client used.

Reframing. A type of *confrontation* in which the helper offers the client an alternative way of viewing his or her situation followed by a discussion of this new reality.

Reinforcement Contingencies. Based on *operant conditioning*, this is the process in which a stimulus, that follows a client's actions or behaviors, increases the likelihood that the behavior will be repeated.

Relativistic. A complex form of thinking where one has the capacity to observe *multiple realities*, is sensitive to context, and understands there are many ways to view the world.

RESPECTFUL Counseling Model. An acronym that speaks to the ingredients needed by the culturally competent mental health professional. Includes understanding **r**eligion, **e**conomic class, **s**exual identity, **p**sychological development, **e**thnicity, **c**hronological/developmental challenges, **t**rauma, **f**amily history, **u**nique physical traits, and **l**anguage.

Risk Factors. Influences in a client's life that increase the likelihood of the client committing suicide or homicide.

Rogers, Carl. One of the founders of the field of humanistic counseling and education as well as the person who developed Person-Centered Counseling. Proponent of the importance of *empathy, congruence (genuineness),* and *unconditional positive regard* in the helping relationship.

Secondary Reinforcer. Based on *operant conditioning*, a type of *reinforcement contingency* that reinforces an action or behavior after it has been connected with a primary or biological reinforcer.

Selective Serotonin Reuptake Inhibitors (SSRIs). Antidepressant medications that are the most commonly used medications for treating depressive disorders.

Self-Disclosure. A helping skill by which the helper reveals a part of his or her personal life to communicate to the client an understanding about the client's experience. Self-disclosure should be done carefully and should only be conducted when a helper is trying to show the client that he or she was understood. See *content self-disclosure* and *process self-disclosure.*

Sexual Relationships with Clients. Having a sexual relationship with a client or former client. It is among the most damaging of all ethical violations and virtually all helping professions have issued prohibitions against them. See also *dual and multiple relationships.*

Silence and Pause Time. A helping skill in which a helper is intentionally quiet during a session to allow the client opportunity to reflect on what he or she has been saying, while also allowing the helper to process the session and formulate his or her next response.

SOAP Notes/Reports. One approach to writing case notes that has gained popularity over the years and which stands for Subjective, Objective, Assessment, and Plan.

Social Constructionist Models of Ethical Decision-Making. A perspective to *ethical decision-making* that involves the belief that solutions to problems occur through dialogue between clients, helpers, and others (e.g., clients, supervisors, and others in the client's world) and not necessarily the result of reading an ethics code or from some single decision-making process.

Social Justice. Impacting the broader system (e.g., agencies, cities, country) to affect positive change for clients. See *Advocacy.*

Social Learning. See *Modeling.*

Social Self. One of the five factors of the *indivisible self model.* The social self is related to how we are connected to others through our friendships, intimate relationships, and through family. It is composed of the ability to connect with others in supportive, emotional, and sometimes sexual ways (collectively called "friendship") and is also the part of us that can share deeply with others and be mutually respectful and appreciative (love).

Solution-Focused Questions. Questions that are focused on quickly identifying what behaviors have worked in a client's life, determining where the client wants to be in the future, and helping the client get to his or her desired goals. Includes *preferred goals questions, evaluative questions, coping questions, exception-seeking questions,* and *solution-oriented questions.*

Solution-Oriented Questions. Questions which broadly asks the client how the client's life would be if the problem did not exist. One type of *solution-focused questions.*

Subceive. The process by which a helper experiences a feeling beyond what the client is outwardly stating.

Sue and Torino's Definition of Culturally Competent Helping. The perspective that culturally competent helping uses both universal and culture-specific helping skills; highlights individual, group, and universal dimensions of clients; and understands individualism and collectivism when assessing clients and in the development of treatment goals.

Suicide. See *assessing for lethality: suicidality and homicidality.*

Supervision. The process by which a helper is mentored by a more experienced professional which allows the helper to examine his or her view of human nature, theoretical approach, ability at implementation of techniques, and, ultimately, effectiveness with clients.

Support. A general term that acknowledges that one role of the helper is to have the client feel as if there is someone in his or her life who the client can rely on for aid, assistance, and to promote his or her general well-being.

Tactile Cues. A helping skill in which the helper relates direct observations of the helper's own body sensations in an effort to communicate understanding to the client. These sensations are a response to what the client has said and are reflective of the client's feelings as the helper allows himself or herself to be a vessel for the client's feelings. See *duty to warn* and *foreseeable danger.*

Tactile Responses. See *tactile cues.*

Tarasoff Case. The landmark court case that set a precedent for the responsibility that mental health professionals have regarding breaking confidentiality to prevent a client from harming self or others. Suggests that professionals must act in ways to ensure that clients will not harm self or others.

Tentative Questions. Questions asked in a gentle manner that often allow for a large range of responses from the client.

Thick Descriptions. Individuals who tend to be relativistic and can identify multiple origins that led them to where they are today, see different points of view, and understand multiple perspectives to situations.

Thin Descriptions. Individuals with a tendency to think in simple, *dualistic,* and black and white ways and typically adhere to a narrow perspective of reality.

Time Management. Strategies that help mental health professionals ensure appropriate services and avoid burnout. Includes ensuring that all clients are seen within a reasonable period of time and remembering meetings, appointment times, and other obligations.

Token Economies. A behavioral technique that is based on *operant conditioning,* where a token, which is a *secondary reinforcer,* can be exchanged for a desired object.

Touch. A *nonverbal behavior* that involves physical contact between a helper and a client. Traditionally, helpers have been taught to rarely touch the client. However, some appropriate touch may be natural and enriching to the helping relationship. Research suggests that cross-cultural differences exist in the ways that clients perceive and respond to touch and other nonverbal helper behaviors.

Toxic Behaviors. Behaviors and attitudes that are debilitative to another person's well-being and are sometimes responsible for fostering low self-esteem.

Transparency. See *realness*

Unconditional Acceptance. See *acceptance.*

Unconditional Positive Regard. See *acceptance.*

Universal Identity. Along with *individual identities* and *group identities,* one of three identities that make up the person. This identity represents common or universal themes which all people share.

Unreliable Assessment and Research Instruments. When clinical and research assessments fail to produce consistent results which suggests that the assessment has poor test worthiness or consistency. This is a particular concern when assessment and research instruments are used with diverse clients.

Values in the Helping Relationship. The ethical responsibility of helpers to ensure that their values or biases are not imposed upon their clients.

Veracity. Based on *Kitchener's* moral model of *ethical decision-making*, this involves being truthful and genuine within the helping relationship.

V Codes. A classification system, being phased out for *Z codes*, that assesses for *environmental and psychosocial stressors* found in *DSM-5*.

Vicarious Traumatization. See *compassion fatigue*.

Voice Intonation and Tone. A *nonverbal behavior* related to the pitch, tone, and volume in a helper's voice.

Walking into Agency. See *agency atmosphere*.

Ward, Julea. Due on her religious beliefs, Julea Ward, a graduate student in counseling, refused to work with a client who had been in a same-sex relationship. Ward was eventually dismissed from her graduate program in counseling for incompetence and subsequently sued the program and the University. Eventually, the case was settled out of court. This case was one reason the American Counseling Association now has a stronger statement about the importance of counselors being able to counsel all clients, even when their values and beliefs vary dramatically from those of the client's.

Wellness. All aspects of the individual's life that leads to health and happiness. The *indivisible self*-model is one way to assess one's wellness. Attendance in one's own counseling, on the part of human service professionals, is one of the many important ways of working towards positive mental health. One of the eight *characteristics of the effective helper*.

Why Questions. A question that seeks a deep thoughtful response, but often results in defensiveness on the part of the client.

Women. See *diverse populations human service professionals work with*.

Working Alliance. The establishment of a trusting relationship between a helper and a client that is typically developed by a human services professional by implementing one or more the eight *characteristics of the effective helper*. A strong working alliance may be the most significant factor in positive client outcomes.

Yes/No Closed Questions. A type of *closed question* where the client is being asked to answer the question with a "yes" or with a "no" response.

Z Codes. A classification system for *environmental and psychosocial stressors*. Also see *V Codes*.

REFERENCES

Akiskal, H. S. (2008). The mental status examination. In S. H. Fatemi & P. J. Clayton (Eds.), *The medical basis of psychiatry* (pp. 3-16). Totowa, NJ: Humana. doi:10.1007/978-1-59745-252-6_1

American Counseling Association. (2011a). *Fact sheet # 6: Suicide assessment*. Retrieved from https://www.counseling.org/docs/trauma-disaster/fact-sheet-6---suicide-assessment.pdf?sfvrsn=2

American Counseling Association. (2011b). *Fact sheet # 11: Crisis counseling*. Retrieved from http://www.counseling.org/docs/trauma-disaster/fact-sheet-10---1on1-crisis-counseling.pdf?sfvrsn=2

American Counseling Association. (2014). *Code of ethics*. Retrieved from http://www.counseling.org/docs/ethics/2014-aca-code-of-ethics.pdf?sfvrsn=4

American Psychiatric Association. (2013). *Diagnostic and statistical manual of mental disorders* (5th ed.). Arlington, VA: American Psychiatric Association.

American Psychological Association. (2007). *Guidelines for psychological practice with girls and women*. Washington, DC: Author.

American Psychological Association. (2013). *HIPAA: What you need to know: The privacy rule—A primer for psychologists*. Retrieved from http://apapracticecentral.org/business/hipaa/hippa-privacy-primer.pdf

American Psychological Association. (2015). *Health and homelessness*. Retrieved from http://www.apa.org/pi/ses/resources/publications/homelessness-health.aspx

Anderson, M. L. Goodman, J., & Schlossberg, N. K. (2012). *Counseling adults in transition: Linking practice with theory* (4th ed.). New York, NY: Springer Publishing Company.

Anderson, S. K. (2012, May 10). To give or not to give advice. *Psychology Today*. Retrieved from https://www.psychologytoday.com/blog/the-ethical-therapist/201205/give-or-not-give-advice

Association for Spiritual, Ethical, and Religious Values in Counseling (2009). *Spiritual competencies*. Retrieved from http://aservic.org/?page_id=133

Baker, S. B. (2012, December 1). A new view of evidence-based practice. *Counseling Today*. Retrieved fromhttp://ct.counseling.org/2012/12/a-new-view-of-evidence-based-practice/

Ballas, C. A., Evans, D. L., & Dinges, D. F. (2009). Psychostimulants in psychiatry: Amphetamine, methylphenidate, and modafinil. In A. F. Schatzberg & C. B. Nemeroff (Eds.), *Textbook of psychopharmacology* (4th ed., pp. 843–861). Washington, DC: American Psychiatric Press.

Bannink, F. (2010). *1001 solution-focused questions: Handbook for solution-focused interviewing* (2nd ed.). New York, NY: W. W. Norton.

Barrett-Rivera, B., Lindstrom, L., & Kerewksy, S. (2013). Parenting in poverty: The experiences of fathers who are homeless. *Journal of Human Services, 33*, 73-84.

Barstow, S., & Lum, C. (2011). *Federal information resources for professional counselors*. Alexandria, VA: American Counseling Association.

Bedi, R. P. (2006). Concept mapping the client's perspective on counseling alliance formation. *Journal of Counseling Psychology, 53*(1), 26–35.

Bike, D., Norcross, J., & Schatz, D. (2009). Process and outcomes of psychotherapists' personal therapy: Replications and extensions 20 years later. *Psychotherapy: Theory, Research, Practice, Training, 46*, 19–31. doi:10.1037/a0015139

Bishop, A. (2015). Freudian psychoanalysis. In E. Neukrug (Ed.), *The Sage encyclopedia of theory in counseling and psychotherapy* (Vol. 1, pp. 436-441). Thousand Oaks, CA: Sage Publications

Bloomgarden, A., & Mennuti, R. B. (2009). Therapist self-disclosure: Beyond the taboo. In A. Bloomgarden & R. B. Mennuti (Eds.), *Psychotherapist revealed: Therapists speak about self-disclosure in psychotherapy* (pp. 3–16). New York: Taylor and Francis Group.

Bolier, L., Haverman, M., Westerhof, G. J., Riber, H., Smit, F., & Bohlmeijer, E. (2013). Positive psychology interventions: A meta-analysis of randomized controlled studies. *BMC Public Health, 13*. doi:10.1186/1471-2458-13-119. Retrieved from http://www.ncbi.nlm.nih.gov/pmc/articles/PMC3599475/

Borders, L. D., & Brown, L. L. (2005). *The new handbook of counseling supervision*. Mahwah, NJ: Erlbaum.

Brammer, L. M., & MacDonald, G. (2003). *The helping relationship: Process and skills* (8th ed.). Boston, MA: Allyn & Bacon.

227

Brown, L. C., & Bryan, T. C. (2007). Feminist therapy with people who self-inflict violence. *Journal of Clinical Psychology, 63*(11), 1121– 1133. doi:10.1002/jclp.20419

Brown, C. G., Weber, S., & Ali, S. (2008). Women's body talk: A feminist narrative approach. *Journal of Systemic Therapies, 27*(2), 92–104.

Buckley, T. R., & Franklin-Jackson, C. F. (2005). Diagnosis in racial-cultural practice. In R. T. Carter (Ed.), *Handbook of racial-cultural psychology and counseling: Theory and research* (Vol. 2, pp. 286–296). Hoboken, NJ: John Wiley.

Bussey, K. (2015). Social cognitive theory. In E. Neukrug (Ed.), *The Sage encyclopedia of theory in counseling and psychotherapy* (Vol. 2, pp. 938-942). Thousand Oaks, CA: Sage Publications.

Calmes, S. A., Piazza, N. J., & Laux, J. M. (2013). The use of touch in counseling: An ethical decision-making model. *Counseling and Values, 58*(1), 59–68. doi:10.1002/j.2161–

Carkhuff, R. R. (2009). *The art of helping in the twenty-first century* (9th ed.). Amherst, MA: Human Resource Development Press.

Center for Credentialing in Education. (2015). *Board certified coach.* Retrieved from http://www.cce-global.org/Credentialing/BCC/Requirements

Centers for Disease Control and Prevention. (2015). *Suicide: Risk and protective factors.* Retrieved from http://www.cdc.gov/violenceprevention/suicide/riskprotectivefactors.html

Chatters, S., & Zalaquett, C. (2013). Dispelling the myths of aging. *Counseling Today, 55*(12), 46-51.

Ciarrochi, J., & Mayer, J. D. (Eds.). (2007). *Applying emotional intelligence: A practitioners' guide.* New York, NY: Psychology Press.

Cole, R., Craigen, L. M., & Cowan, R. (2015). Compassion fatigue in human service practitioners. *Journal of Human Services, 34,* 117-120.

Commonwealth of Virginia Knowledge Center. (2016). *Assessing the risk of serious harm to self, module 10.* Retrieved from https://covkc.virginia.gov/Kview/CustomCodeBehind/Customization/Login/COV_Login.aspx

Constantine, M. G. & Sue, D. W. (2005). *Strategies for building multicultural competence in mental health and educational settings.* Hoboken, NJ: John Wiley & Sons.

Cooper, J. O., Heron, T. E., & Heward, W. L. (2007). *Applied behavior analysis* (2nd ed.). Columbus, OH: Merrill.

Corey, G., Corey, M. S., Corey, C., & Callanan, P. (2015). *Issues and ethics in the helping professions* (9th ed.). Belmont, CA: Cengage.

Cormier, S., Nurius, P. S., & Osborn, C. J. (2013). *Interviewing and change strategies for helpers* (7th ed.). Belmont, CA: Cengage Learning.

Corrine, S., Lawson, G., & Burge, P. L. (2012). Meaningful experiences in the counseling process. *Professional Counselor, 2,* 208-225. doi:10.15241/css.2.3.208

Cottone, R. R., & Tarvydas, V. M. (2007). *Counseling ethics and decision-making* (3rd ed.). Upper Saddle River, NH: Merrill.

Craigen, L. M., Cole, R., Paiva, I., & Levingston, K. (2014). Secondary traumatic stress and the role of the human service practitioner: Working effectively with Veterans' families. *Journal of human services, 34,* 38-51.

Crowe, A. & Averett, P. (2015). Attitudes of mental health professionals toward mental illness: A deeper understanding. *Journal of Mental Health Counseling, 37*(1), 47-62

Daniels, V. (2015). Humanistic psychoanalysis of Erich Fromm. In E. Neukrug (Ed.), *The Sage encyclopedia of theory in counseling and psychotherapy* (Vol. 1, pp. 518-524). Thousand Oaks, CA: Sage Publications.

De Jong, P., & Berg, I. K. (2013). *Interviewing for solutions* (4th ed.). Belmont, CA: Cengage Learning.

De Shazer, S. (1988). *Clues: Investigating solutions in brief therapy.* New York, NY: W. W. Norton & Company.

De Shazer, S., Dolan, Y., Korman, H., Trepper, T., McCollum, E., & Berg, I. K. (2007). *More than miracles: The state of the art of solution-focused brief therapy.* New York, NY: Routledge

Dean, L. (2015). Motivational interviewing. In E. Neukrug (Ed.), *The Sage encyclopedia of theory in counseling and psychotherapy* (Vol. 1, pp. 668-672).Thousand Oaks, CA: Sage Publications.

Dewane, C. J. (2010). Respecting boundaries: The don'ts of dual relationships. *Social Work Today, 10*(1), 18.

Dolgoff, R., Harrington, D., & Loewenberg, F. M., (2012). *Ethical decisions for social work practice* (9th ed.). Belmont, CA: Cengage Learning.

Dykeman, B. F. (2011). Intervention strategies with the homeless population. *Journal of Instructional Psychology, 38*(1), 32–39.

Egan, G., Owen, J. J., & Reese, R. J. (2014). *The skilled helper: A problem management and opportunity-development approach to helping* (10th ed.). Belmont, CA: Cengage.

Elliot, R., Bohart, A. C., Watson, J. C., & Greenberg, L. Sl. (2011). Empathy. *Psychotherapy, 48*, 43-49.

Ellis, A., & MacLaren, C. (2005). *Rational emotive behavior therapy: A therapist's* guide (2nd ed.). Atascadero, CA: Impact publishers.

Ellis, D. J. (2015). Rational emotive behavior therapy. In E. Neukrug (Ed.), *The Sage encyclopedia of theory in counseling and psychotherapy* (Vol. 1, pp. 848-853). Thousand Oaks, CA: Sage Publications.

Englar-Carlson, M., & Kiselica, M. S. (2013). Affirming the strengths in men: A positive masculinity approach to assisting male clients. *Journal of Counseling and Development, 91*, 399–409. doi:10.1002/j.1556-6676.2013.00111.x

Escobar, J. I. (2012). Taking issue: Diagnostic bias: Racial and cultural issues. *Psychiatric Services, 63*(9), 847. Retrieved from http://ps.psychiatryonline.org/doi/pdf/10.1176/appi.ps.20120p847

Evans, M. P., Duffey, T., & Englar-Carlson, M. (2013). Introduction to the special issue: Men in counseling. [Special Issue]. *Journal of Counseling and Development, 91*(4), 387-389.

Fawcett, J., & Busch, K. A. (1998). Stimulants in psychiatry. In A. F. Schatzberg & C. B. Nemeroff (Eds.), *Textbook of psychopharmacology* (2nd ed., pp. 503–522). Washington, DC: American Psychiatric Press.

Federal Emergency Management Agency. (2015). *Crisis counseling assistance and training program.* Retrieved from http://www.fema.gov/recovery-directorate/crisis-counseling-assistance-training-program#1

Fefergrad, M., & Richter, P. M. A.., (2013). *Cognitive behavioral therapy for anxiety.* New York, NY: W. W. Norton & Company.

Fisher, G. L., & Harrison, T. C. (2013). *Substance abuse: Information for school counselors, social workers, therapists and counselors* (5th ed.). Boston, MA: Pearson

Forrest, G. G. (2010). *Self-disclosure in psychotherapy and recovery.* Plymouth, United Kingdom: Jason Aronson.

Fowler, J. W. (1995). *Stages of faith: The psychology of human development and the quest for meaning.* New York, NY: Harper & Row. (Original work published 1981)

Frank, M. G., Maroulis, A., & Griffin, D. (2013). The voice. In D. Matsumoto, M. G. Frank, & H. S. Hwang (Eds.), *Nonverbal communication: Science and applications* (pp. 53-74). Thousand Oaks, CA: Sage.

Franklin, C., Trepper, T. S., Gingeric, W. J., & McCollum, E. E. (2012). *Solution-focused brief therapy: A handbook of evidence-based practice.* New York, NY: Oxford University Press.

Freeman, M. P., Wiegand, C., & Gelenberg, A. J. (2009). Lithium. In A. F. Schatzberg & C. B. Nemeroff (Eds.), *Textbook of psychopharmacology* (4th ed., pp. 697–718). Washington, DC: American Psychiatric Press.

Gallagher, B. J., & Street, J. (2012). *The sociology of mental illness* (5th ed., rev.). Cornwall-on-Hudson, NY: Sloan Educational Publishing

Garske, G. G. (2009). Psychiatric disability: A biopsychosocial challenge. In I. Marini, & M. A. Stebnicki (Eds.), *The professional counselor's desk reference* (pp. 647–654). New York, NY: Springer.

Gelso, C. (2009). The real relationship in a postmodern world: Theoretical and empirical explorations. *Psychotherapy Research, 19*, 253-264. doi:10.1080/10503300802389242

Gelso, C. J., Kelley, F. A., Fuertes, J. N., Marmarosh, C., Holmes, S. E., Costa, C., & Hancock, G. R. (2005). Measuring the real relationship in psychotherapy: Initial validation of the therapist form. *Journal of Counseling Psychology*, 52, 640–649. doi: 10.1037/0022-0167.52.4.640

Glasser, W. (2013). *Take charge of your life: How to get what you need with choice theory psychology.* Bloomington, IN: Iuniverse Inc.

Glasser, W., & Glasser, C. (2007). *Eights lessons for a happier marriage.* New York, NY: HarperCollins.

Gold, J. M. (208). Rethinking client resistance: A narrative approach to integrating resistance into the relationship building stage of counseling. *Journal of Humanistic Counseling, Education, and Development, 47*(1), 65-70. doi:0.1002/j.2161-1939.2008.tb00047.x

Goldberg, J. F., & Ernst, C. L. (2102). *Managing the side effects of psychotropic medications.* Arlington, VA: American Psychiatric Publishing.

Gompertz, K. (1960). The relation of empathy to effective communication. *Journalism Quarterly, 37*, 535–546.

Good, G. E., & Brooks, G. R. (2005). *The new handbook of psychotherapy and counseling with men: A comprehensive guide to settings, problems, and treatment approaches.* New York, NY: Wiley.

Grant, A. M., & O'Connor, S. A. (2010). The differential effects of solution-focused and problem-focused coaching questions: A pilot study with implications for practice. *Industrial and Commercial Training, 42*(2), 102-111. doi:10.1108/00197851011026090

Greer, M. (2005). Keeping them hooked in. *APA Monitor, 36*(6), 60.

Hackenberg. T. D. (2009). Token reinforcement: a review and analysis. *Journal of the Experimental Analysis of Behavior, 91,* 257-286. doi: 10.1901/jeab.2009.91-257

Hansen, J. T. (2006). Counseling theories within a postmodernist epistemology: new roles for theories in counseling practice. *Journal of Counseling and Development, 84,* 291-297

Harris, K., Edlund, M., & Larson, S. (2005). Racial and ethnic differences in the mental health problems and use of mental health care. *Medical Care, 43*(8), 775-784.

Harrison, K. (2013). Counselling psychology and power: Considering therapy and beyond. *Counseling Psychology Review, 28*(2), 107-117.

Hendrix, L. R. (2001). *Curriculum in ethnogeriatics: Core curriculum and ethnic specific modules.* Retrieved from http://web.stanford.edu/group/ethnoger/

Hersen, M., & Van Haselt, V. B. (Eds.). (2001). *Advanced abnormal psychology* (2nd ed.). New York, NY: Springer.

Hill, C. E. (2014). *Helping skills: Facilitating exploration, insight, and action* (4th ed.). Washington, DC: American Psychological Association.

History of the McKinney Act. (2015). *William and Mary School of Education Project Hope—Virginia.* Retrieved from http://education.wm.edu/centers/hope/resources/mckinneyact/

Howes, R. (2012, February 13). Eye contact in therapy, Part I: Why can't I look at my therapist? *Psychology Today.* Retrieved from https://www.psychologytoday.com/blog/in-therapy/201202/eye-contact-in-therapy-part-i

Ingraham, C. (2014, September 30). *White people are more likely to deal drugs, but black people are more likely to get arrested for it.* Washington Post, Retrieved from https://www.washingtonpost.com/news/wonk/wp/2014/09/30/white-people-are-more-likely-to-deal-drugs-but-black-people-are-more-likely-to-get-arrested-for-it/

Ivey, A. E., Ivey, M. B., & Zalaquett, C. P. (2016). *Essentials of intentional interviewing: Counseling in a multicultural world.* Boston, MA: Cengage Learning.

Jackson, C. (2012). Diagnostic disarray. *Therapy Today, 23*(3), 4–8

Jansson, B. S. (2016). *Social welfare policy and advocacy: Advancing social justice through 8 policy sectors.* Thousand Oaks, CA: Sage Publications.

Jayakar, P. (2003). *J. Krishnamurti: A biography.* New York, NY: Penguin Books. (Original work published 1986)

Juhnke, G. A., Granello, P. F., & Lebron-Striker, M. (2007). IS PATH WARM? A suicide assessment mnemonic for counselors. *Professional Counseling Digest.* Alexandria, VA.

Kahn, M. (2001). *Between therapist and client: The new relationship* (rev. ed.). New York, NY: W. H. Freeman/Owl.

Kaplan, D. M. (2014). Ethical implications of a critical legal case for the counseling profession: Ward v. Wilbanks. *Journal of Counseling and Development, 92,* 142-146. doi:10.1002/j.1556-6676.2014.00140.x

Kaplan, D. M., Kocet, M. M., Cottone, R. R., Glosoff, H. L., Miranti, J .G., Moll, E. C., …Tarvydas, V. M. (2009). New mandates and imperatives in the revised ACA Code of Ethics. *Journal of Counseling and Development, 87*(2):241-256.

Kaslow, N. J., Rubin, N. J., Forrest, L., Elman, N. S., Van Horne, B. A., Jacobs, S. C.,…Thorn, B. E. (2007). Recognizing, assessing, and intervening with problems of professional competence. *Professional Psychology: Research and Practice, 38,* 479-492. doi: 10.1037/0735-7028.38.5.47

Kelsey, D., & Smart, J. F. (2012). Social justice, disability, and rehabilitation education. *Rehabilitation Research, Policy, and Education, 26*(2–3), 229–239. doi:10.1891/216866612X664970

Kinnier, R. T., Hofsess, C., Pongratz, R., & Lambert, C. (2009). Attributions and affirmations for overcoming anxiety and depression. *Psychology and Psychotherapy: Theory, Research, and Practice, 82*(2), 153–169. DOI:10.1348/147608308X389418

Kirschenbaum, H. (2015). Values clarification. In E. Neukrug (Ed.), *The Sage encyclopedia of theory in counseling and psychotherapy* (Vol. 2, 1035-1038). Thousand Oaks, CA: Sage Publishing.

Kitchener, K. S. (1984). Intuition, critical evaluation and ethical principles: The foundation for ethical decisions in counseling psychology. *The Counseling Psychologist, 12*(3), 43–45. doi:10.1177/0011000084123005

Kitchener, K. S. (1986). Teaching applied ethics in counselor education: An integration of psychological processes and philosophical analysis. *Journal of Counseling and Development, 64*(5), 306–311. doi:10.1177/0011000084123005

Kleist, D., & Bitter, J. R. (2009). In J. Bitter (Ed.), *Theory and practice of family therapy and counseling* (pp. 43–65). Belmont,

CA: Brooks/Cole.

Kluckhohn, C., & Murray, H. A.. (1953). Personality formation: The determinants. In C. Kluckohn, H. A. Murray, and D. M. Schneider (Eds.), *Personality in Nature, Society, and Culture* (pp. 53-67). New York, NY: Alfred A. Knopf.

Knapp, M. L., Hall, J. A., & Horgan, T. G. (2014). *Nonverbal communication in human interaction* (8th ed.). Belmont, CA: Cengage.

Kotkin, J. (2010). *The changing demographics of America.* Retrieved from http://www.smithsonianmag.com/40th-anniversary/the-changing-demographics-of-america-538284/?no-ist=&page=1

Kubler-Ross, E., & Kessler, D. (2014). *On grief and grieving.* New York, NY: Scribner. (Original work published 2005)

Labardee, L., Williams, P., & Hodges, S. (2012, November 1). Counselors who coach. *Counseling Today.* Retrieved from http://ct.counseling.org/2012/11/counselors-who-coach

Lam, T., Kolomitro, K., & Alamparambil, F. C. (2011). Empathy training: Methods, evaluation practices, and validity. *Journal of Multidisciplinary Evaluation, 7,* 162–200.

Lambie, G. W., Hagedor, W. B., & Ieva, K. P. (2010). Social-cognitive development, ethical and legal knowledge, and ethical decision making of counselor education students. *Counselor Education and Supervision, 49,* 228–246. doi:10.1002/j.1556-6978.2010.tb00100.x

Laska, K. M., Gurman, A. S., & Wampold, B. E. (2014). Expanding the lens of evidence-based practice in psychotherapy: A common factors perspective. *Psychotherapy, 51,* 467-481.

Lawson, G., & Myers, J. E. (2011). Wellness, professional quality of life, and career-sustaining behaviors: What keeps us well? *Journal of Counseling and Development, 89*(2), 163–171. doi:10.1002/j.1556-6678.2011.tb00074.x

Leuzinger-Bohleber, M., & Target, M. (2002). Introductory remarks. In M. Leuzinger-Bohleber & M. Target (Eds.), *Outcomes of psychoanalytic treatment: Perspectives for therapists and researchers* (pp. 1–15). New York, NY: Brunner-Routledge.

Levitt, D. H., & Aligo, A. A. (2013). Moral orientation as a component of ethical decision making. *Counseling and Values, 58*(2), 195–204. doi:1002/j.2161-007X.2013.00033.x

Levitt, D. H., & Moorhead, J. H. (2013). Moral development. In D. H. Levitt & H. J. H. Moorhead (Eds), *Values and ethics in counseling: Real-life ethical decision making* (pp. 7-18). New York, NY: Routledge.

Levitt, H. M. (2001). Sounds of silence in psychotherapy: The categorization of client's pauses. *Psychotherapy Research, 11,* 295–309. doi:10.1080/713663985

Lewis, J. A., Dana, R. Q., & Blevins, G. A. (2015). *Substance abuse counseling.* Belmont, CA: Cengage Learning.

Lewis, J. A., Lewis, M. D., Daniels, J. A., & D'Andrea, M. J. (2011). *Community counseling: A multicultural-social justice perspective* (4th ed.). Belmont, CA: Cengage.

Ley, D. L. (2014, February 12). Life coaches and mental illness. *Psychology Today.* Retrieved from https://www.psychologytoday.com/blog/women-who-stray/201402/life-coaches-and-mental-illness

Linnell, S., Bansel, P., Ellwood, C., & Gannon, S. (2008). Precarious listening. *Qualitative Inquiry, 14,* 285–306. doi:10.1177/1077800407312041

Lo, C., Cheng, T., & Howell, R. (2013). Access to and utilization of health services as pathway to racial disparities in serious mental illness. *Community Mental Health Journal, 50*(3), 251-257. doi:10.1007/s10597-013-9593-7

Lopez, S. J., Pedrotti, J. T., & Snyder, C. R. (2015). *Positive psychology: The scientific and practical explorations of human strength* (3rd ed.). Thousand Oaks, CA: Sage Publications.

Martin, E. D. (Ed.) (2007). *Principles and practices of case management in rehabilitation counseling.* Springfield, IL: Charles C. Thomas.

Martin, G., & Pear, J. (2015). *Behavior modification: What it is and how to do it* (1

Matson, J. L., & Boisjoli, J. A. (2009). The token economy for children with intellectual disability and/or autism: a review. *Research in Developmental Disabilities, 30,* 240-248. doi:10.1016/j.ridd.2008.04.001

Matsumoto, D., & Hwang, H. S. (2013a). Facial expressions. In D. Matsumoto, M. G. Frank, & H. S. Hwang (Eds.), *Nonverbal communication: Science and applications* (pp. 15-52). Thousand Oaks, CA: Sage.

Matsumoto, D., & Hwang, H. S. (2013b). Cultural influences of nonverbal behavior. In D. Matsumoto, M. G. Frank, & H. S. Hwang (Eds.), *Nonverbal communication: Science and applications* (pp. 97-120). Thousand Oaks, CA: Sage.

Matsumoto, D., Frank, M. G., & Hwang, H. S. (Eds.). (2013). *Nonverbal communication: Science and applications.* Thousand Oaks, CA: Sage.

McAuliffe, G. (2013a). Culture and diversity defined. In G. McAuliffe (Ed.), *Culturally alert counseling: A comprehensive introduction* (2nd ed., pp. 3–23). Los Angeles, CA: Sage Publications.

McAuliffe, G. (2013b). *Culturally alert counseling: A comprehensive introduction* (2nd ed.). Thousand Oaks, CA: Sage Publishing.

McAuliffe, G. (Ed.). (2018). *Positive counseling: A guide to promoting clients' strengths and growth.* San Diego: Cognella Academic Publishers.

McAuliffe, G., Gomez, E., & Grothaus, T. (2013). Conceptualizing race and racism. In G. McAuliffe (Ed.), *Culturally alert counseling: A comprehensive introduction* (2nd ed., pp. 89–124). Thousand Oaks, CA: Sage Publications.

McBride, R. G. (2012). Survival on the streets: Experiences of the homeless population and constructive suggestions for assistance. *Journal of Multicultural Counseling and Development, 40*(1), 49–61. doi:10.1111/j.2161-1912.2012.00005

McElroy, S. L., & Keck, P. E. (2009). Topirmate. In A. F. Schatzberg & C. B. Nemeroff (Eds.), *Textbook of psychopharmacology* (4th ed., pp. 795–810). Washington, DC: American Psychiatric Press.

Miller, G. (2012). Criticism continues to dog psychiatric manual as deadline approaches. *Science, 336,* 1088–1089. doi:10.1177/0004867413518825

Milliken, T., & Neukrug, E. (2009). Perceptions of ethical behaviors of human service professionals. *Human Service Education, 29,* 35-48.

Myers, J. E., & Sweeney, T. J. (2008). Wellness counseling: The evidence base for practice. *Journal of Counseling and Development, 86,* 482–493. doi:10.1002/j.1556-6678.2008.tb00536.x

Nassar, J. L., & Devlin, A. (2011). Impressions of psychotherapists' offices. *Journal of Counseling Psychology, 58,* 310–320. doi:10.1037/a0023887

National Alliance of Direct Support Professionals. (2011). *Making a world of difference in people's lives: Community support skill standards (CSSS).* Retrieved from https://www.nadsp.org/library/csss.html

National Alliance of Mental Illness. (2016a). *African American mental health.* Retrieved from https://www.nami.org/Find-Support/Diverse-Communities/African-Americans

National Alliance on Mental Illness. (2016b). *Mental health by the numbers.* Retrieved fromhttps://www.nami.org/Learn-More/Mental-Health-By-the-Numbers

National Association of Social Workers (NASW). (2008). *Code of ethics.* Retrieved from http://www.socialworkers.org/pubs/code/code.asp

National Organization of Human Services. (1996). Ethical standards of human service professionals. *Human Service Education, 16,* 11-17.

National Organization for Human Services. (2015). *Ethical standards for human service professionals.* Retrieved from http://www.nationalhumanservices.org/ethical-standards-for-hs-professionals

Neukrug, E. (2011). *Counseling theory and practice.* Belmont, CA: Brooks/Cole.

Neukrug, E. (2015). *The Sage encyclopedia of theory in counseling and psychotherapy* (Vols. 1-2). Thousand Oaks, CA: Sage Publications

Neukrug, E. (2016). *The world of the counselor* (5th ed.). Boston, MA: Cengage Learning.

Neukrug, E. (2017). *Theory, practice, and trends in human services: An introduction* (6th ed.). Boston, MA: Cengage Learning.

Neukrug, E., & Ellis, D. (2015). Albert Ellis. In E. Neukrug (Ed.), *The Sage encyclopedia of theory in counseling and psychotherapy* (Vol. 1, pp. 333-336). Thousand Oaks, CA: Sage Publications.

Neukrug, E., & Fawcett, R. (2015). *Essentials of testing and assessment: A practical guide for counselors, social workers, and psychologists* (3rd ed.). Belmont, CA: Cengage Learning.

Neukrug, E., & Milliken, T. (2011). Counselors' perceptions of ethical behaviors. *Journal of Counseling and Development. 89,* 206–216.

Neukrug, E., & Schwitzer, A. M. (2006). *Skills and tools for today's counselors and psychotherapists: From natural helping to professional counseling.* Pacific Grove, CA: Brooks/Cole.

Neukrug, E., Bayne, H., Dean-Nganga, L., & Pusateri, C. (2012). Creative and novel approaches to empathy: A neo-Rogerian perspective. *Journal of Mental Health Counseling, 35*(1), 29–42.

Neukrug, E., Britton, B., & Crews, C. (2013). Common health-related concerns of men and their implications for counselors. *Journal of Counseling and Development, 91,* 390-397.

Neukrug, E., Kalkbrenner, M. T., & Griffith, S. A. (2017*).* Barriers to counseling among human service professionals: The development and validation of the fit, stigma, & value (FSV) scale. *Journal of Human Services, 37,* 27-40.

Neukrug, E., Milliken, T., & Walden, S. (2001). Ethical practices of credentialed counselors: An updated survey of state licensing boards. *Counselor Education and Supervision, 41*(1), 57–70.

Newport, F. (2011, December 23). *Gallup: Christianity remains dominant religion in the United States: Majority still says religion is very important in their lives.* Retrieved from http://www.gallup.com/poll/151760/Christianity-Remains-Dominant-Religion-United-States.aspx

Nishino, S., Mishima, K., Mignot, E., & Dement, W. C. (2009). Sedative-hypnotics. In A. F. Schatzberg & C. B. Nemeroff (Eds.), *Textbook of psychopharmacology* (4th ed., pp. 821–842). Washington, DC: American Psychiatric Press.

Norcross, J. C. (2010). The therapeutic relationship. In B. L. Duncan, S. D. Miller, B. E. Wampold, & M. A. Hubble (Eds.), *The heart and soul of change* (2nd ed., pp. 113–142). Washington, DC: American Psychological Association.

Norcross, J. C. (Ed.). (2011). *Psychotherapy relationships that work: Evidence-based responsiveness.* New York, NY: Oxford University Press.

Olson T. R., Christopher, P. J., Janzen, J. I., Petraglia, J., & Presniak, M. D. (2011). Addressing and Interpreting defense mechanisms in psychotherapy: General considerations. *Psychiatry: Interpersonal and Biological Processes, 74*(2), 142-165.

Orlinsky, D. E., Schofield, M. J., Schroder, T., & Kazantzis, N. (2011). Utilization of personal therapy by psychotherapists: A practice-friendly review and a new study. *Journal Of Clinical Psychology, 67,* 828-842. doi: org/10.1002/jclp.208

Pagliery, J. (2014, August 18). CNN Money: Hospital network hacked, 4.5 million records stolen. Retrieved from http://money.cnn.com/2014/08/18/technology/security/hospital-chs-hack/index.html

Patterson, J., Albala, A. A., McCahill, M. E., & Edwards, T. M. (2010). *The therapist's guide to psychopharmacology: Working with patients, families, and physicians to optimize care* (rev. ed.). New York, NY: Guilford Press.

Perry, W. G. (1970). *Forms of intellectual and ethical development in the college years: A scheme.* New York, NY: Holt, Rinehart, & Winston.

Pew Research Center. (2014). *U. S. Hispanic and Asian populations growing, but for different reasons.* Retrieved from http://www.pewresearch.org/fact-tank/2014/06/26/u-s-hispanic-and-asian-populations-growing-but-for-different-reasons/

Pickersgill, M. D. (2013). Debating DSM-5: Diagnosis and the sociology of critique. *Journal of Medical Ethics, 0,* 1-5. doi:10.1136/medethics-2013-101762

Pisani, A. R., Murrie, D. C., & Silverman, M. M. (2015, December 14). Reformulating suicide risk formulation: From prediction to prevention. *Academic Psychiatry,* 1-7. Retrieved from http://link.springer.com/article/10.1007%2Fs40596-015-0434-6

Polanski, P. J., & Hinkle, J. S. (2000). The mental status examination: Its use by professional counselors. *Journal of Counseling and Development, 78,* 357-364. doi.org/10.1002/j.1556-6676.2000.tb01918.x

Pope, M. (2008). Culturally appropriate counseling considerations for lesbian and gay clients. In P. B. Pedersen, J. G. Draguns, W. J. Lonner, & J. E. Trimble (Eds.), *Counseling across cultures* (6th ed., pp. 201–222). Thousand Oaks, CA: Sage.

Preston, J. D., O'Neal, J. H., & Talaga, M. C. (2013). *Handbook of clinical psychopharmacology for therapists* (7th ed.). Oakland, CA: New Harbinger Publications.

Puig, A., Baggs, A., Mixon, K., Park, Y. M. Kim, B. Y., & Lee, S. M. (2012). Relationship between job burnout and personal wellness in mental health professionals. *Journal of Employment Counseling, 49,* 98-109. doi:10.1002/j.2161-1920.2012.00010.

Pusateri, C. G., & Headley, J. A. (2015). Feminist therapy. In E. Neukrug (Ed.), *The Sage encyclopedia of theory in counseling and psychotherapy* (Vol. 1, pp. 414-418). Thousand Oaks, CA: Sage Publishing.

Qaseem, A., Barry, M. J., & Kansagara, D. (2016). Nonpharmacologic versus pharmacologic treatment of adult patients with major depressive disorder: A clinical practice guideline from the American college of physicians. *Annals of Internal Medicine Intern Medicine.* Retrieved from http://annals.org/article.aspx?articleid=2490527. doi:10.7326/M15-2570

Rankin, L. (2013). *Mind over medicine: Scientific proof that you can heal yourself.* Carlsbad, CA: Hay House.

Ratts, M. J., Singh, A. A., Nassar-McMillan, S., Butler, S. K., & McCullough, J. (2014). *Multicultural and social justice counseling competencies.* Retrieved from https://www.counseling.org/docs/default-source/competencies/multicultural-and-social-justice-counseling-competencies.pdf?sfvrsn=20

Remley, T. P., & Herlihy, B. (2014). *Ethical, legal, and professional issues in counseling* (4th ed.). Upper Saddle River, NJ: Prentice Hall.

Remley, T. P., Herlihy, B., & Herlihy, S. B. (1997). The U.S. Supreme Court decision in *Jaffe v. Redmond:* Implications for counselors. *Journal of Counseling and Development, 75,* 213–218.

Resnick, P. (2011, March 20). Suicide risk assessment. *Psychiatric Times.* Retrieved from http://www.psychiatrictimes.com/suicide/suicide-risk-assessment

Resnick, R. (2015). Gestalt therapy In E. Neukrug (Ed.), *The Sage encyclopedia of theory in counseling and psychotherapy* (Vol. 1, pp. 456-461). Thousand Oaks, CA: Sage Publications.

Rice, R. (2015). Cognitive-behavioral therapy. In E. Neukrug (Ed.), *The Sage encyclopedia of theory in counseling and psychotherapy* (Vol. 1, pp. 194-199). Thousand Oaks, CA: Sage Publications.

Rice, R. (2015). Narrative therapy. In E. Neukrug (Ed.), *The Sage encyclopedia of theory in counseling and psychotherapy* (Vol. 1, pp. 691-700), Thousand Oaks, CA: Sage publications.

Ridley, C. R., Mollen, D., & Kelly, S. M. (2011). Beyond microskills: Toward a model of counseling competence *The Counseling Psychologist, 39,* 825–864. doi:10.1177/0011000010378440

Ritter, K. (2015). Sexual minority affirmative therapy. In E. Neukrug (Ed.), *The Sage encyclopedia of theory in counseling and psychotherapy* (Vol. 2, pp. 828-931). Thousand Oaks, CA: Sage Publishing.

Robinson, D. S., Rickels, K., & Yocca, F. D. (2009). Buspirone and gepirone. In A. F. Schatzberg & C. B. Nemeroff (Eds.), *Textbook of psychopharmacology* (4th ed., pp. 487–502). Washington, DC: American Psychiatric Press.

Rogers, C. R. (1942). *Counseling and psychotherapy: New concepts in practice.* Boston, MA: Houghton-Mifflin.

Rogers, C. R. (1957). The necessary and sufficient conditions of therapeutic personality change. *Journal of Consulting Psychology, 21,* 95–103. doi:10.1037/h0045357

Rogers, C. R. (1959). A theory of therapy, personality and interpersonal relationships as developed in the client-centered framework. In S. Koch (Ed.), *Psychology: A study of science, Vol. 3, Formulations of the person and the social context* (pp. 184–256). New York, NY: McGraw-Hill.

Rogers, C. R. (1961). Ellen West and loneliness. In H. Kirschenbaum & V. L. Henderson (Eds.), *The Carl Rogers reader* (pp. 157–167). Boston, MA: Houghton Mifflin.

Rogers, C. R. (1980). *A way of being.* Boston, MA: Houghton Mifflin.

Rudow, H. (2013, January 9). Resolution of EMU case confirms ACA code of ethics, counseling profession's stance against client discrimination. *Counseling Today.* Retrieved from http://ct.counseling.org/2013/01/resolution-of-emu-case-confirms-aca-code-of-ethics-counseling-professions-stance-against-client-discrimination/

Schwitzer, A. M., & Rubin, L. C. (2015). *Diagnosis and treatment planning skills: A popular culture casebook approach* (2nd ed.). Thousand Oaks, CA: Sage Publications.

Scott, A. T. (2014). The after effects of hurricane Katrina on children. *Journal of Human Services, 34,* 174-178.

Scott, C. L., & Resnick, P. J. (2005). Violence risk assessment in persons with mental illness. *Aggression and Violent Behavior, 11*(6), 598-611. doi:10.1016/j.avb.2005.12.003

Segal, J., Johnson, W., Miller-Knight, W., Prince, S., Anderson, K., Sonnenberg, J., …Dale, H. (2011). Dilemmas: A dress code for counselors. *Therapy Today, 22*(9), 28-31.

Selfridge, M. A. (2014). Post-traumatic stress disorder. *Journal of Human services, 34,* 179-183.

Sewell, H. (2009). *Working with ethnicity, race and culture in mental health.* Philadelphia, PA: Jessica Kingsley Publishers.

Shallcross, L. (2011). Breaking away from the pack. *Counseling Today, 53*(9), 28–36.

Smart, J. (2012). *Disability across the development life span: For the rehabilitation counselor.* New York, NY: Springer Publishing Company.

Sommer, R. (2007). *Personal space: The behavioral basis of design.* Bristol, England: Bosko Books.

Sommers-Flanagan, J. & Sommers-Flanagan, R. (2015). *Clinical interviewing* (5th ed.). Hoboken, NJ: John Wiley & Sons.

Strong, T., & Zeman, D. (2010). Dialogic Considerations of confrontation as a counseling activity: An examination of Allen Ivey's Use of confronting as a microskill. *Journal of Counseling and Development, 88*(3), 332-339.

Substance Abuse and Mental Health Services Administration. (2016). *Home page.* Retrieved from http://www.samhsa.gov/

Sue, D. W. (1992). The challenge of multiculturalism: The road less traveled. *American Counselor, 1*(1), 6–15.

Sue, D. W., & Sue, D. (2013). *Counseling the culturally diverse* (6th ed.). Hoboken, NJ: John Wiley and Sons.

Sue, D. W., & Torino, G. C. (2005). Racial-cultural competences: Awareness, knowledge, and skills. In Carter, R. T. (Ed.), *Handbook of racial-cultural psychology and counseling: Theory and research* (pp. 3–18). Hoboken, NJ: Wiley.

Summers, N. (2016). *Fundamentals of case management: Skills for the human services.* Boston, MA: Cengage Learning.

Sun, A. (2012). Helping homeless individuals with co-occurring disorders: The four components. *Social Work, 57*(1), 23–37. doi:10.1093/sw/swr008

Sung, K., & Dunkle, R. (2009). How social workers demonstrate respect for elderly clients. *Journal of Gerontological Social*

Work, 53, 250-260. doi:10.1080/01634370802609247.

Suzuki, L. A., Kugler, J. F., & Aguiar, L. J. (2005). Assessment practices in racial-cultural psychology. In R. T. Carter (Ed.), *Handbook of racial-cultural psychology and counseling: Theory and research* (Vol. 2, pp. 297–315). Hoboken, NJ: John Wiley.

Szymanski, D. (2013). Counseling lesbian, gay, bisexual, and transgendered clients. In G. J. McAuliffe (Ed.), *Culturally alert counseling: A comprehensive introduction* (2nd ed., pp. 415–554). Thousand Oaks, CA: Sage Publications.

Tarasoff et al. v. Regents of University of California, 529 P.2d 553 (Calif. 1974), vacated, reheard en banc, and affirmed 551 P.2d 334 (1976).

Taylor, M., Bradley, V., & Warren, R. (Eds.). (1996). *The community support skill standards: Tools for managing change and achieving outcomes: Skill standards for direct service workers in the human services.* Cambridge, MA: Human Services Research Institute.

Terni, P. (2015). Solution-focus: Bringing positive psychology into the conversation. *International Journal of Solution Focused Practices, 3*(1), 8-16. doi:10.14335/ijsfp.v3i1.25

Thompson, J. T. (1973). *Beyond words: Nonverbal communication in the classroom:* New York, NY: Citation press.

Thompson, R. A. (2016). *Counseling techniques: Improving relationships with others, ourselves, our families, and our environment* (3rd ed.). New York, NY: Routledge.

Toporek, R. L., & Lewis, J. A., & Crethar, H. C. (2009). Promoting systemic change through the ACA advocacy competencies. *Journal of Counseling and Development, 87*, 260–268. doi:10.1002/j.1556-6678.2009.tb00105.x

Trepal, H. C. (2013). Counseling men and women: Considering gender and sex. In G. McAuliffe (Ed.), *Culturally alert counseling: A comprehensive introduction* (2nd ed., pp. 383-425). Thousand Oaks, CA: Sage publications.

Trepper, T. S., McCollum, E. E., De Jonhg, P., Korman, H., Gingerich, W., & Franklin, C. (2014). Solution-focused therapy treatment manual for working with individuals. In J. S. Kim (Ed.), *Solution-focused brief therapy: A multicultural approach* (pp. 14-31). Thousand Oaks, CA: Sage Publications.

Trice-Black, S., & Foster, V. (2001). Sexuality of women with young children: A feminist model of mental health counseling. *Journal of Mental Health Counseling, 22*(2), 95-11. doi:10.17744/mehc.33.2.p1ht7pt2533n3g2r

U.S. Census Bureau. (2014). *2012 National population projections: Summary tables.* Retrieved from http://www.census.gov/population/projections/data/national/2012/summarytables.html

U.S. Census Bureau (2016). *U.S. census bureau projections show a slower growing, older, more diverse nation a half century from now.* Retrieved from http://www.census.gov/newsroom/releases/archives/population/cb12-243.html

U.S. Department of Health and Human Services (2001). *Mental health: Culture, race, and ethnicity: A supplement to mental health: A report to the Surgeon General.* Retrieved from http://download.ncadi.samhsa.gov/ken/pdf/SMA-01-3613/sma-01-3613.pdf

U.S. Department of Health and Human Services. (n.d.). *Understanding health information privacy.* Retrieved from http://www.hhs.gov/ocr/privacy/hipaa/understanding/index.html

U.S. Department of Housing and Urban Development (2014). *The 2013 annual homeless assessment report (AHAR) to Congress.* Retrieved from https://www.hudexchange.info/resources/documents/2014-AHAR-Part1.pdf

U.S. Department of Justice. (2014a). *Freedom of information act guide: 2004 Edition.* Retrieved from http://www.usdoj.gov/oip/introduc.htm

U.S. Department of Veterans Affairs. (n.d.) *Suicide prevention mini-clinic.* Retrieved from http://www.mentalhealth.va.gov/communityproviders/clinic_suicideprevention.asp#sthash.rGObS941.dpbs

Urofsky, R. I., Engels, D. W., & Engebretson, K. (2008). Kitchener's principle ethics: Implications for counseling practice and research. *Counseling and Values, 53*, 67–78. doi:10.1037/h0069608

Van Nuys, D. (1995-2015). *An interview with William Glasser, MD and Carleen Glasser on happier marriages.* Retrieved from http://www.behavioralconnections.org/poc/view_doc.php?type=doc&id=28730&cn=289

Van Rooyen, H., Durrheim, K., & Lindegger, G. (2011). Advice-giving difficulties in voluntary counselling and testing: A distinctly moral activity. *AIDS Care, 23*, 281–286. doi:10.1080/09540121.2010.507755

Videbeck, S. L. (2014). *Psychiatric mental health nursing* (6th ed.). New York/Washington, DC: Lippincott, Williams, & Wilkins/American Psychiatric Press

Vogel, D. L., Wester, S. R., Larson, L. M. (2007). Avoidance of counseling: Psychological factors that inhibit seeking help. *Journal of Counseling and Development, 85*, 410-422.

Wampold, B. E. (2010). The research evidence for common factors models: A historically situated perspective. In B. L. Duncan, S. D. Miller, B. E. Wampold, & M. A. Hubble (Eds.), *The heart and soul of change* (2nd ed., pp. 49–82).

Washington, DC: American Psychological Association.

Wampold, B. E., & Budge, S. L. (2012). The relationship—and its relationship to the common and specific factors in psychotherapy. The *Counseling Psychologist, 40*, 601-623. doi:10.1177/0011000011432709

Watzlawick, P., Beavin, J. H., & Jackson, D. D. (1967). *Pragmatics of human communication: A study of interactional patterns, pathologies, and paradoxes.* New York, NY: Norton

Weishaar, M. E. (2015). Aaron T. Beck. In E. Neukrug (Ed.), *The Sage encyclopedia of theory in counseling and psychotherapy* (Vol. 1, pp. 87-89). Thousand Oaks, CA: Sage Publications.

Welfel, E. R. (2013). *Ethics in counseling and psychotherapy: Standards, research, and emerging issues* (5th ed.). Pacific Grove, CA: Brooks/Cole.

Wexler, D. B. (2009). *Men in therapy: New approaches for effective treatment.* New York: W. W. Norton.

Williams, S. (2013). *Mental health service utilization among African American emerging adults* (Unpublished doctoral dissertation). Washington University, St. Louis, MO.

Wong, D. F. K. (2006). *Clinical case management for people with mental illness: A biopsychosocial vulnerability-stress model.* New York, NY: Routledge.

Woodside, M. R., & McClam, T. (2013). *Generalist case management: A method of human service delivery* (4th ed.). Belmont, CA: Cengage Learning.

Wubbolding, R. E. (2015). Reality therapy. In E. Neukrug (Ed.), *The Sage encyclopedia of theory in counseling and psychotherapy* (Vol. 2, pp. 856-860). Thousand Oaks, CA: Sage Publishing.

Zur, O. (2007). *Boundaries in psychotherapy: Ethical and clinical explorations.* Washington, DC: American Psychological Association.

Zuroff, D. C., Kelly, A. C., Leybman, M. J., Blatt, S. J., & Wampold, B. E. (2010). Between-therapist and within-therapist differences in the quality of the therapeutic relationship: effects on maladjustment and self-critical perfectionism. *Journal of Clinical Psychology, 66*, 681-697. doi:10.1002/jclp.20683

AUTHOR INDEX

SUBJECT INDEX

CPSIA information can be obtained
at www.ICGtesting.com
Printed in the USA
FSHW021802301120
76449FS